Bathroom
Remodeling

Bathroom Remodeling

Leon A. Frechette

TAB Books
Division of McGraw-Hill, Inc.
Blue Ridge Summit, PA 17294-0850

Unless otherwise noted, illustrations and photos are the author's own work.

FIRST EDITION
FIRST PRINTING

© 1994 by **Leon A. Frechette.**
Published by TAB Books.
TAB Books is a division of McGraw-Hill, Inc.

Library of Congress Cataloging-in-Publication Data
Frechette, Leon A., 1954–
    Bathroom remodeling / by Leon A. Frechette.
      p. cm.
    Includes index.
    ISBN 0-8306-4479-2 (pbk.)
    1. Bathrooms—Remodeling. I. Title.
TH4816.3.B37F74 1993
643'.52—dc20   93-30750
                                          CIP

Acquisitions editor: Kimberly Tabor
Editorial team: Joanne Slike, Executive Editor
                  Lori Flaherty, Managing Editor
                  Susan J. Bonthron, Editor
Production team: Katherine G. Brown, Director
                  Susan E. Hansford, Typesetting
                  Joanne Woy, Indexer
Design team: Jaclyn J. Boone, Designer
                Brian Allison, Associate Designer
Cover design: Sandra Blair Design, Harrisburg, Pa.   HT1
Cover photo: Kraftmaid Advertising, Cleveland, Oh.   4441

To all who plan to remodel their bathrooms!

Acknowledgments

I would like to thank the many people who helped turn this book into a reality for their hard work and dedication in creating a worthwhile tool that can benefit consumers and professionals alike.

Thanks to Calvin Lea, Chromastat, for the special attention he gave to converting my color photos to black and white; to Karl D. Houser, Gypsum Association, for taking the time to review the wallboard chapter for accuracy; to Armand D. Raponi, United States Gypsum Company, for all the wonderful detailed illustrations and photos used throughout this book; to Wilbur L. Unrue, NIBCO INC., for supplying the how-to artwork and information on working with plumbing fittings used throughout the plumbing chapter; to Holly Carlson and Barry Myers, Holly's Plumbing, for taking the time to make sure the plumbing chapter stayed on track; to Terry J. Gibbons, The Swan Corporation, for providing valuable information and photographs for the chapter on bathtub and shower enclosures; to Rob Marzulli, Eastern Paralyzed Veterans Association, for his time in directing me to the correct people for assistance on barrier-free requirements and for the use of their diagrams throughout the book; to Lisa Strosser, Armstrong World Industries, Inc., for the photo and the information about vinyl flooring products used in the book; and to Robert J. Kleinhans, Tile Council of America, Inc., for answering my many questions over the phone and for the information supplied and used throughout the book.

I would like to offer special thanks to Tom Craig, Certified Plan Examiner, City of Spokane, Washington, for the hours he spent reading the text and reviewing diagrams to make sure they agreed with the codes required for a successful bathroom remodeling project, and to Karen Craig for her hard and dedicated work in organizing and editing our second book together. We have a lot more coming down the pike!

Thanks also to Kimberly Tabor, Tab Books, for publishing this long-overdue book. Even though this project is over, we've only just begun to scratch the surface of getting useful and needed information to the readers.

If I missed anyone, it wasn't intentional. There just isn't enough paper—and you know who you are! Again, many thanks to all . . .

Notices   xii

Introduction   xiii

1 Analyzing the job   1
Water damage   1
Outdated & worn out   2
Updating & meeting codes   3
Other considerations   4
Final notes   4

2 Floor plans   6
Enlargement   6
Barrier-free design   9
Design & layout   16

3 Hire professionals or do it yourself   21
Do you have what it takes?   23
Professionals   24
General Conditions   27
Contracts   29

4 Tools & materials   31
Safety equipment   31
Power tools   31
Cleanup tools   34
Materials commonly used   37

5 Costs   40
Contractor classifications   41
Specialty contractors   41
Itemizing is the key   42

6 Demolition   44
Installing new tile in tub/shower area   44
Installing new floor covering   47
Asbestos   47
Removing floor covering /underlayment   47
Installing a new tub   49
Gutting the room completely   49

7 Framing   52
Windows & doors   53
New doors & windows   55

CONTENTS

Dryer vent ductwork   59
Subflooring   62
Ceilings   65
Skylights   67
Corners & partitions   71
Hot tub or whirlpool bath   72
Miscellaneous   76

8   Plumbing   78

Other products   78
Rough-in layout   81
ABS & PVC definitions   88
Venting   101
Copper water supply lines   103
Tool tips   111

9   The electrical system   114

New products   114
Electrical symbols & parts   118
Wire size & capacity   121
Wire specifications   123
Panel box & new circuits   124
GFCI, outlets, & switches   124
Tips to remember   128
Fishing for an outlet   131
Wiring diagrams   131

10   Wallboard techniques & finishing   141

Wallboard products   141
Preventive measures   145
Installing wallboard   146
Taping products   153
Smooth walls   162
Textured walls   162
Wallpaper   166
Paint   167

11   Flooring   168

Resilient flooring   168
Nonresilient flooring   171
Hardwood & carpeting   171

Warranties   171
Underlayment   172
Installing sheet goods   178
Nonresilient installation   182
Special applications   184

12   Cabinets & countertops   185

Required tools   188
Helpful hints   189
Preparation   189
Installing cabinets   190
Installing countertops   194
Installing tile   202

13   Tub & shower enclosures   204

Fiberglass panels   205
Tile   208
Shower rods   222
Shower doors   222

14   Doors, windows, & base moldings   226

Doors   226
Windows   233
Wooden base molding   239
Rubber base molding   240

15   Electrical & plumbing fixtures & trims   243

Electrical fixtures   243
Plumbing fixtures   246

16   Caulking, trimming, & touch-up   256

Door hardware   256
Doorstop   258
Accessories   259
Grab bars   259
Caulking   260

Appendix   Contributing organizations & companies   264

Index   268

About the author   274

Notices

Bosch®	Robert Bosch Power Tool Corporation
CLOSET MAID®	Clairson International Corporation
Crescent®	CooperTools
Dow Corning®	Dow Corning Corporation., U.S.A.
DUROCK™ **DUR-A-BEAD**™ **SHEETROCK**™	United States Gypsum Company
E-Z Ancor® **Rock-On**™ **Hi-Lo**™	ITW Buildex and Illinois Tool Works, Inc.
FANTECH™	Fantech, Inc.
Helping Hands™	C.R.S., Inc.
Hole Hawg®	Milwaukee Electrical Tool Corporation
Homax®	Homax Corporation
Hyde®	The Hyde Group
Infloor®	Gyp-Crete Corporation
IRON-AWAY®	IRON-AWAY Inc.
Kwikset®	Kwikset Corporation
Malco™	Malco Products, Inc.
Milwaukee®	Milwaukee Tool Corporation
MR. STEAM®	Sussman-Automatic Corporation
National Electrical Code®	National Fire Protection Association
NIBCO®	NIBCO Inc.
Powerbore® **Screw-Mate**®	Stanley Tools
RE-BATH®	RE-BATH Corporation
Romex®	General Cable Company
Skil®	Skil Corporation
SHOWER TOWER™ **SwanTile**™ **SWANSTONE**® **Tubwal**®	The Swan Corporation
Teflon®	DuPont Fluorocarbon Resins
The Broadway Collection®	The Broadway Collection, a Division of Broadway Industries, Inc.
The Soft Bathtub®	International Cushioned Products Inc.
Therma-Floor™	Gyp-Crete Corporation
Uniform Building Code™ **VELUX**®	International Conference of Building Officials (ICBO) VELUX-AMERICA Inc.

IF YOU NEED A STEP-BY-STEP ACCOUNT of bathroom remodeling and repair from the approach of a professional contractor, *Bathroom Remodeling* is your key. The purpose of this book is to help you understand the proper way to start and the details required to finish the job. It will also provide some insight into what it takes to remodel a bathroom so you can make intelligent decisions about whether to do some or all of the work yourself or hire a remodeling professional. If you choose to hire a contractor, you will be able to follow the work in progress knowledgeably. For homeowners who don't know where to begin, the book also details the tear-out of existing structures.

For contractors new to the business who do not yet have the practical experience of bidding and remodeling bathrooms, this book will become a reference tool you can use in your business. You will learn how to itemize a job for the customer, a process which can help to eliminate costly misunderstandings between the two of you. It can also serve as a good sales tool when dealing with potential customers who have a hard time visualizing or understanding the process. It can be used to help answer questions for a customer while bidding the job. This book will also help you to perform the work in the proper sequence for a smooth and efficient job.

Whether you do the work yourself or hire a professional, your work schedule needs to comply with the codes established and enforced by the local building department. This includes building, electrical, and plumbing codes. Be aware that electrical permits and inspections sometimes fall under state jurisdiction depending on your state and whether you live in the city or county.

Your local building department might follow one of the three widely accepted codes—Uniform Building Code (UBC), Building Official and Code Administrator (BOCA), and Southern Building Code Official (SBCO)—or it might follow its own adopted codes. All new work should meet the codes in force in your area, but allowances might be made depending upon your structure. The staff at the building department is aware that sometimes situations arise, particularly on remodeling projects, when it is difficult to meet the building codes. However, they do have some latitude and can help you solve a problem in a way that will comply with the codes and still satisfy you. It would be in your best interests to keep an open mind, work with the department, and be willing to compromise. It is much easier to get along with an inspector if he knows what is going to happen prior to its happening than if he discovers a problem afterwards. That's something to think about!

One final caution: The information contained in this book is intended to be an aid or a resource to you and is not the final word on any given topic. Neither the author, the publisher, nor the contributors assume any liability for your use of these materials. You are specifically cautioned (as mentioned before) that each state and municipality has its own laws and practices which should be consulted, and the information herein is of a general nature only as it relates to legal concepts.

Bathroom Remodeling is laid out in the same way a contractor would look at the job to bid it. Photos are used in analytical order, showing both the materials and the tools to be used. The simplicity of this book will make it a valuable asset to homeowners and professionals alike.

Analyzing the job

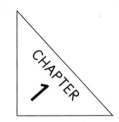

THE MOST IMPORTANT QUESTION you can ask yourself is "How much of the bathroom should I remodel?" This key chapter will help you to analyze your project realistically, and possibly save you thousands of dollars. Take a moment now to walk into your bathroom—and don't forget to bring this book. Pause for a minute or two, and think about where you're going to start, and the order in which you should proceed. It can be confusing, but *Bathroom Remodeling* will guide you through the different phases of your remodeling project.

Over the course of twenty years in the remodeling field, I developed a system that I applied successfully to every bathroom job I surveyed with a prospective customer. Follow my method in the order listed below, and take a realistic look at your bathroom.

Check for water damage on the floor around the toilet. Signs to look for are:

Water damage

- Discoloration of the adjacent floor covering.
- Spongy floor around the toilet.
- Water coming up through the tiles.

If you have vinyl flooring, the water could be traveling under the floor covering from another fixture. However, the water is probably seeping through the wax bowl ring, or the toilet flange is broken.

Look for water damage on the floor where it meets the front of the tub or shower. Signs to look for are:

- Loose tiles.
- Discoloration of wood and vinyl floors.
- Vinyl flooring curled up in front of the tub or shower.

Water might be leaking around and under the shower curtain, under the shower door track, or at the ends of the inside of the

1-1 *Unattended water damage.*

shower track where the track meets the walls (1-1). Water damage in this area is also an indication that the bead of caulk on top of the flooring up against the tub is either gone or starting to separate, which allows water to siphon between the tub and floor covering.

Check for water damage to the plumbing wall. The plumbing wall contains the fixtures (faucets, spout, and shower head, if any). Signs to look for are:

- Loose tiles about 2 feet up from the tub or shower pan.
- Loose tiles around the outside of the tub down to the floor.
- Blistered paint, loose wallboard, and mildew on the wall in the same area.

There might be a leak in the fixtures themselves, or water might be leaking behind the finish trim.

If you have a window in the tub/shower area, you will want to check for water damage to the interior shower wall and for water stains on the exterior siding under the bathroom window. Look for loose tiles below the window, and check for a spongy feel to the wall, both indications that water is leaking down through the ledge or sill of the window. Also, if you have a wooden window, it might not be properly sealed and might absorb water as you shower.

Look for water damage to the soap dish wall. Check for loose tiles below the soap dish all the way down to the top of the tub or shower pan. This is an indication, especially if you have a metal soap dish mounted in a tile wall, that water is leaking behind the soap dish every time you take a shower.

Outdated & worn out

You might want to replace your fixtures if any of the following apply:

- Tub, toilet, and wash basin are out of style.
- Fixtures are worn out, water stained, or chipped.
- Porcelain is missing or there are rust marks.
- You need to install barrier-free fixtures.
- You want to change the color of your fixtures.

How are your faucets, in the shower area as well as the wash basin? If they are out of style, leaking, hard to use, or just plain worn out, you might want to replace them. There are many stylish choices on the market today. You might also consider water-saving faucets.

Do you have a wooden or a metal window in the shower area? You might consider either installing a metal window or removing the window completely.

What about the bathroom cabinet? Perhaps you don't have one, or the one you have is too big or too small, or the wrong color or style. Is it time to change the countertop to tile, plastic laminate, or something completely new? How are the mirror and medicine cabinet? Are there any? Is it time for something new?

Check the condition of your floor covering. Is it damaged? What kind of floor covering is it—tile, carpet, or vinyl? What would you like to have? If your floor covering is out of style, now is the time to consider a change.

Look for lead drainpipes. In some areas, plumbing codes require the replacement of such pipes in order to install new bathroom fixtures. If you have lead pipes, check with your local building department to see what is required for you to meet the codes. It can be costly, but it is well worth doing.

Does your bathroom have a fan? If not, it should! If you do have a fan, does it have enough CFMs (cubic feet per minute) to carry the moisture out of the bathroom? I'll discuss CFMs in chapter 9.

How's the heat? Does your bathroom have enough, or are you looking for a system that provides more? Maybe you just want something different.

What about lighting? Can you see yourself clearly in the mirror when the lights are on? Are the lights in the right locations? Maybe it's time for new fixtures, and you might want to consider energy-saving units.

Do the electrical outlets meet local electrical codes? Do you even have outlets? If so, are they correctly sited and comfortable to use? Should one or all of the outlets be ground-fault circuit interrupter (GFCI) outlets (1-2) required by today's codes?

Updating & meeting codes

1-2 *Ground-fault circuit interruptor (GFCI) outlet.*

Other considerations

Would you like to make the bathroom bigger? Should you add a new bathroom somewhere else? Could you improve the layout of the bathroom? I'll discuss bathroom layout in chapter 2.

What type of interior walls do you have? Are they lath and plaster, rock plaster, or wallboard? Should you remove the old wall covering and install new, or install wallboard over existing walls?

How should the interior walls be finished? Should they be painted or should you hang wallpaper? Maybe you'd like to combine the two. What role does moisture play?

Final notes

Are you planning to replace the floor covering? You'll have to remove the toilet, replace the wax bowl ring, and possibly replace the toilet flange. Depending on the size of your bathroom, you might have to remove the wash basin and cabinet. Most likely, you'll need to remove and install new underlayment. All rubber or wooden base molding will have to be removed before the flooring and underlayment can be removed.

Do you plan to install a new tub? Be prepared to open up three walls just to remove the existing tub. If the room is small, the toilet, wash basin, and cabinet might also have to be removed as well. Before you can install a new tub, you will also need to remove the base moldings, floor covering, and underlayment.

Do you plan to replace lead drainpipes, change plumbing pipes, or rewire? The areas where the plumbing and wiring are located in the walls and ceiling will need to be opened up for access. Also, depending on your situation, you might have to remove the toilet, wash basin, cabinet, and tile in the shower area. If you have a basement under the bathroom and it has a finished ceiling, consider that you might have to open up that ceiling in order to reach the plumbing or wiring.

Please do not try to do any of the work until you have read the *entire* book. The last three items were just advance warnings that if you plan to change one item in your bathroom, you might have to remove three others. My intention is to help you analyze your needs, realistically identify your priorities, and understand the construction of your bathroom. Planning ahead is key whether you do the work yourself or hire a professional. Happy remodeling!

CHAPTER
2

Floor plans

HAVE YOU TAKEN THE TIME to analyze and evaluate your bathroom by looking for water damage or for outdated or worn-out fixtures, tile, or floor covering? Is it time for the plumbing and wiring to be updated to meet building codes? Have you established your priorities? During this evaluation process, you might have discovered that it is not necessary to remodel the entire bathroom but only certain areas. If so, then specific information contained in the relevant chapters will help to guide you through those individual projects.

Enlargement

If you plan to remodel the entire bathroom, begin by considering its overall size. Over the years, I have found that the question most often asked by customers is "Can I make my bathroom bigger?" Experience has taught me that it is usually not an option, but don't be discouraged by what I say. Many factors determine whether enlargement is a possibility. These are questions you'll need to ask yourself:

- Is the bathroom you hope to enlarge on the main floor?

- What kinds of rooms surround the bathroom?

- Do you have living space above or below the bathroom?

- How many people live in your home?

- How many bedrooms do you have?

- If you were to use space from a nearby room to enlarge the bathroom, would it detract from the resale value of your home?

- Would it cost too much to enlarge the existing bathroom?

- Would it be better to invest in a new bathroom above or below the existing bathroom?

- Are you planning to build an addition in the future?

- Can you plan a bathroom in the new addition?

- How large is your laundry room?

- Would it be possible to add bathroom facilities to the laundry room?

- If you have more than one bathroom, would it be easier to remodel or enlarge one of them?

- Does the master bedroom have a bathroom?

- Is there room in the master bedroom for a new bathroom?

- Do you know where your main sewer line is?

- Are you on a septic tank or a sewer system?

By now you are probably wondering if you can make any alterations! To help you decide, the "before" and "after" plans shown in 2-1 and 2-2 might lend themselves to your situation. These plans are actual jobs that I have done in the past, and you can see the changes that were made. There are still a few more facts you need to consider before you can draw up your new plans:

- Have you scheduled a new bathtub, shower, whirlpool bath, or hot tub into your bathroom plans? If so, what is the size of the unit you have chosen?

- Are you going to use a shower stall? What size shower pan are you going to use? The code requires a shower pan that is a minimum of 1,024 square inches (32"×32") in size and able to contain a 30-inch circle within the pan. This is especially important to know if you are going to custom-make a shower pan. If you are replacing an existing shower pan, in most cases (depending on the inspector), you can replace it with the same size.

- What is the size of the bathroom cabinet you're going to use?

- Is there enough room for the shower door to swing out?

- Is there enough room for the main bathroom door to swing in?

- Can all the plumbing fixtures be kept on the same wall?

- If there is a room above the new bathroom, will it be possible to conceal the plumbing in a closet or in another wall?

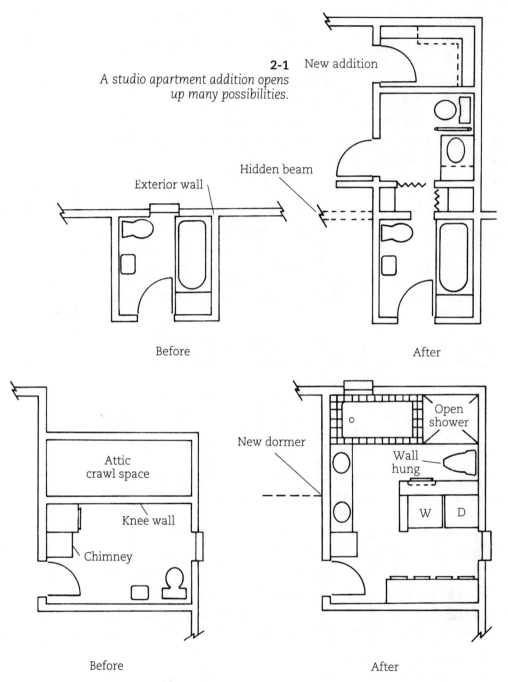

2-1 A studio apartment addition opens up many possibilities.

New addition

Hidden beam

Exterior wall

Before

After

Attic crawl space

Knee wall

Chimney

New dormer

Open shower

Wall hung

W   D

Before

After

2-2 Unused attic crawl space can generate space for an enlarged bathroom.

8   Bathroom Remodeling

Sometimes there are situations with the plumbing that are very difficult to figure out. When that happens, I always tell the customer that I want to bring in a plumber to evaluate the situation, and I rely on his professional opinion in order to finish the bathroom plans. If you find yourself facing this situation, don't worry. You might need a plumber on this job anyway, so call him (but before you do, please read chapter 3). One final note: Continue with your ideas on paper, so if you do decide to call a plumber, you'll have plans to show him. It's a good way to communicate with a professional.

Barrier-free design

One last important factor to consider in your new bathroom plans is whether you should use a barrier-free design. If you (or a family member) are restricted to a wheelchair or walker, a barrier-free design is one way to make life a little easier and more convenient.

Basically, *barrier-free design* means "an architecture which does not inhibit access or use by all people, disabled or nondisabled." In other words, no obstacles to restrict freedom of movement.

Barrier-free bathrooms for individuals who are disabled, as well as for older adults who have reduced mobility, pose a challenge in design. I recommend you contact the following organizations for more information concerning the Americans with Disabilities Act and barrier-free bathroom (or new home) design:

National Easter Seal Society
70 East Lake Street
Chicago, IL 60601

Ask for *The Americans With Disabilities Act Resource Catalog.*

U.S. Department of Justice
Office on the Americans with Disabilities Act
Washington, DC 20530
1-202-514-0301

Ask for *Federal Register, Title III of the Americans with Disabilities Act.*

Eastern Paralyzed Veterans Association
75-20 Astoria Boulevard
Jackson Heights, NY 11370-1177

Ask for any of the following documents:

- *Accessible Building Design.*

- *Barrier-Free Design: Selected Federal Laws and ADA Accessibility Guidelines.*

- Resource sheet containing other related information.

The information and diagrams contained in this chapter and throughout this book are not the final word but are intended to be used as a guide as you design your barrier-free bathroom. The measurements recommended in the following diagrams are only the minimum requirements. Consult with your local building department to ensure that your plans comply with the building codes in your area.

When designing your barrier-free bathroom, put yourself in the position of the wheelchair user. Begin your barrier-free design with the overall floor area. Be sure to provide a full 25 square feet (a 5' circle) of floor space to allow wheelchair users to make a complete 360° turn (2-3). You should have at least 30" by 48" of clear floor space in front of a wash basin to allow a forward approach (2-4). On barrier-free sinks, the faucet should be mounted toward the front and should have large lever handles. For toilet fixtures, please review 2-5A and 2-5B. Notice the height and placement of the handrails and toilet paper dispenser. W.C. stands for *water closet* (toilet).

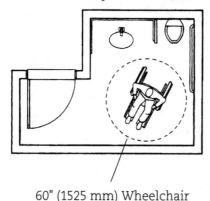

60" (1525 mm) Wheelchair
turning diameter

2-3 *Required space for a wheelchair to make a 360° turn.*
Eastern Paralyzed Veterans Association

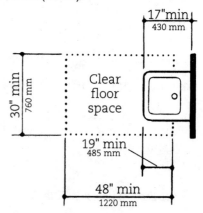

2-4 *Required floor space for a barrier-free wash basin.*
Americans with Disabilities Act Accessibility Guidelines (ADAAG), 7/26/91, as published in the Federal Register

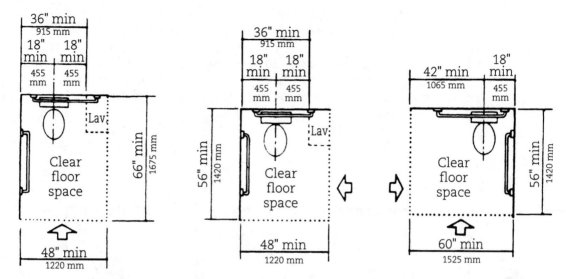

2-5A *Clear floor space at toilets can allow a left-handed or right-handed approach; arrows show the direction of access.* ADAAG, 7/26/91, as published in the Federal Register

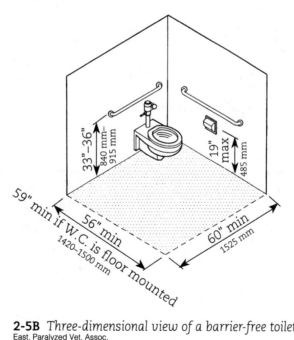

2-5B *Three-dimensional view of a barrier-free toilet.*
East. Paralyzed Vet. Assoc.

Figure 2-6 shows two common wheelchair transfers to toilets: diagonal and side approaches. It is important to keep in mind that placement of a wash basin immediately to the side of the toilet precludes the side approach transfer. To accommodate a side transfer, the space adjacent to the toilet must remain clear of obstructions for 42" from the centerline of the toilet (2-5A, third diagram) and a wash basin must not be located within this clear space.

18"–30" | 18"
455 mm–760 mm | 455 mm

1
Takes transfer position, swings footrest out of the way, sets brakes.

2
Removes armrest, transfers.

3
Moves wheelchair out of the way, changes position (some people fold chair or pivot it 90° to the toilet).

4
Positions on toilet, releases brake.

Diagonal approach

42" | 18"
1065 mm | 455 mm

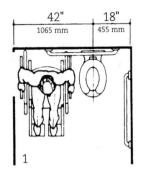 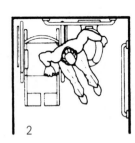 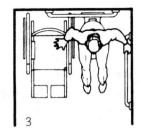

1
Takes transfer position, removes armrest, sets brakes.

2
Transfers.

3
Positions on toilet.

2-6 *Two wheelchair transfers.* ADAAG, 7/26/91, as published in the Federal Register

A transfer shower stall should be at least 36" square with a seat and have a minimum of 36" by 48" of clear floor space in front of the stall (2-7A). Figure 2-7B shows the proper seat design and maximum measurements. Figure 2-8 shows a roll-in shower stall that fits in the same space as a standard tub (minimum 30" by 60" without a seat). The minimum clear floor space is 36" by 48". A handrail has been installed all around the shower stall.

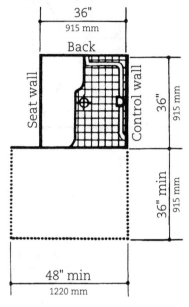

2-7A *Shower size and clearances.* ADAAG, 7/26/91, as published in the Federal Register

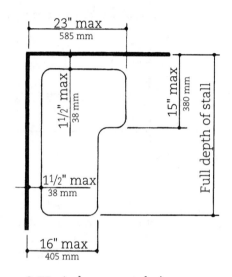

2-7B *A shower seat design.* ADAAG, 7/26/91, as published in the Federal Register

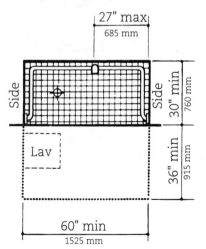

2-8
This barrier-free shower can be incorporated into most homes with an existing 60" bathtub space. ADAAG, 7/26/91, as published in the Federal Register

Floor plans   13

Figure 2-9 shows two roll-in showers with folding seats. Notice the clear floor space, seat size, and size of the shower stall. Also note the placement of the handrail in relation to the seat.

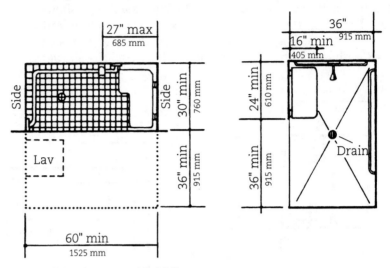

2-9 *Roll-in showers with folding seats.* ADAAG, 7/26/91, as published in the Federal Register

Figure 2-10 shows two easy-to-access bathtubs: one with a removable seat (standard 60" tub), the other with a permanent seat unit (60" long plus a 15" allowance for the seat). The arrows indicate the direction of access.

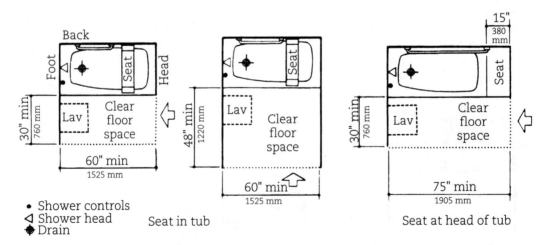

- Shower controls
◁ Shower head
◆ Drain

2-10 *Clear floor space at bathtubs.* ADAAG, 7/26/91, as published in the Federal Register

14   Bathroom Remodeling

Entry doors should have a net opening of 32" measured from the doorstop to the door face when the door is in a 90° open position (2-11). The force required to push or pull interior doors open cannot exceed five pounds.

The diagrams in 2-12A and B show two possible configurations of a bathroom with a roll-in shower. This particular shower fits exactly within the dimensions of a standard bathtub. Because the shower does not have a lip, the floor space can be considered part of the required wheelchair maneuvering space. The bathroom therefore provides enough floor space to be considered barrier-free. This design provides accessibility in an area where space is limited. The alternate roll-in shower (2-12B) also provides sufficient room for the "T-turn."

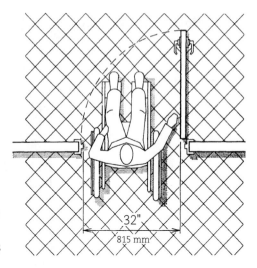

2-11 *Wheelchairs require a 32" opening.*
East. Paralyzed Vet. Assoc.

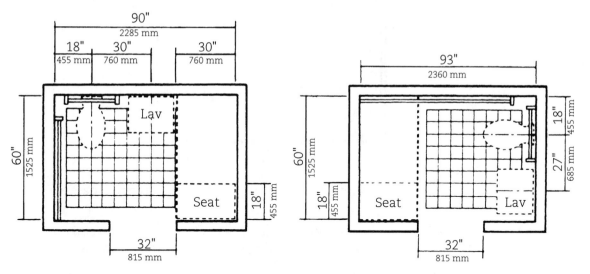

2-12A and B *Two barrier-free designs.* ADAAG, 7/26/91, as published in the Federal Register

Other items related to a barrier-free bathroom installation such as lever-type door handles, low mirrors, nonskid floors, accessible toilets, faucets with loop or lever handles, and grab bars might be required. Some of these items are discussed and/or illustrated in their related chapters.

Design & layout

Before you start to draw your bathroom design on paper, you need to know a few basic facts:

- A standard bathtub is 60" long and 30" wide.

- A toilet requires 30" of space and a minimum of 24" of space in front of the bowl (2-13).

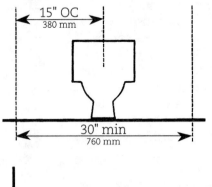

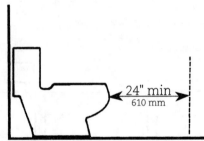

2-13
Space required for standard toilet installation.

- A vanity requires a space 24" wide to accommodate a wash basin.

- Doors should be a minimum of 30" wide. Be careful not to design a door opening with an inconvenient swing.

To get you started, I've included a few samples of bathroom designs to show you what bathrooms drawn to scale look like on paper (2-14 through 2-20), which might also provide helpful ideas. The upper and lower bathrooms in 2-21 show how the plumbing was laid out with one bathroom on top of the other.

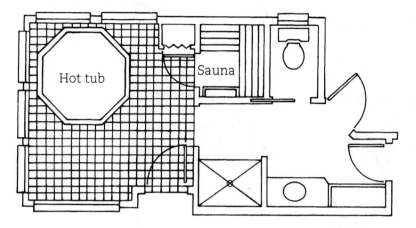

2-14
"Recreational" bathroom with sauna and hot tub.

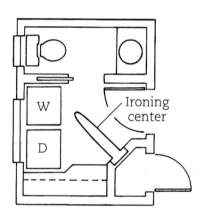

2-15 *This laundry room incorporates a half bath and built-in ironing board.*

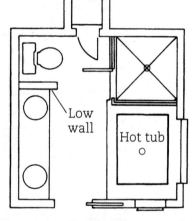

2-16 *Excellent master bathroom design.*

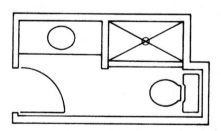

2-17 *Simple three-piece layout with a shower stall. Note toilet recessed into wall to provide full shower access.*

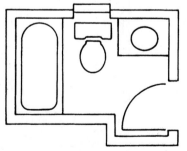

2-18
Common three-piece layout with a bathtub; window over toilet gives room an open feeling.

Floor plans   17

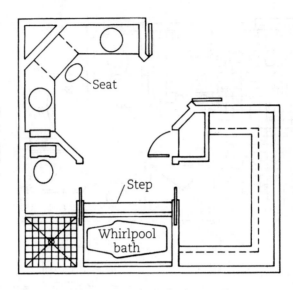

2-19
A dream bathroom: walk-in closet, sit-down vanity, and whirlpool bath.

Seat

Step

Whirlpool bath

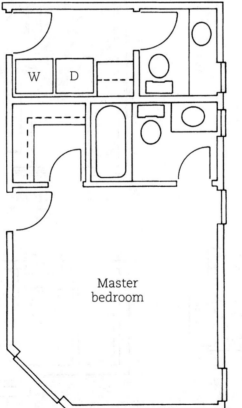

2-20
Simple bathroom layout off a master bedroom; note back-to-back plumbing and convenient location of laundry facilities.
Ken Duncan

W D

Master bedroom

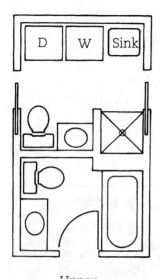

Upper

2-21
Added space above an existing bathroom provides many possibilities.

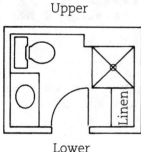

Lower

Most architects and draftsmen use a scale of ⅛" or ¼" to 1" when drawing such plans. They also use an architect's triangular (or a standard flat) scale which reads from ³⁄₃₂" through 3" to 1". Since bathrooms are usually small, I recommend a ½" scale when drawing your plans. Personally, I find this larger size easy to work with, and it still allows the entire drawing to fit on one sheet of planning paper. You don't need to purchase one of the scales mentioned above—you can use a standard 12" ruler, but the scales are easier to use than a ruler.

I recommend you read the rest of this book to get other ideas that could affect your bathroom design. Once you have all your basic information outlined, use graph paper to make a scale drawing of your bathroom. For reference, review 2-14 through

2-21 while you draw yours to scale. You will need to make two drawings: your bathroom exactly as it now exists, with every measurement marked down, and your new design.

Once you have "before" and tentative "after" plans, you can speed up the planning process if you go to your local copy shop and make a few copies of your plans. Now you can cut out the fixtures, cabinets, etc., and arrange (and rearrange) them until you reach a plan that works for you. Another time-saving tool is a template designed with house plan fixtures: door swings, cabinets, bathroom fixtures, and many other symbols (2-22). These templates, scaled from ⅛" to ½", are inexpensive and can be purchased at most art supply stores.

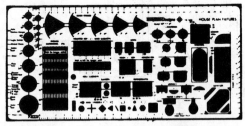

2-22 *House plan fixture template.*

With all the suggestions contained in this chapter and throughout this book, you have a lot to consider in your new design. Good luck with your new plans!

Hire professionals or do it yourself

ONLY YOU KNOW HOW MUCH of the remodeling work you are capable of doing, but you might want to consider the following questions. Keep in mind that I'm not trying to discourage you from doing the work yourself—that's how I got into this business. My intention is to help you understand what it really takes to start and finish this project (3-1 through 3-6).

3-1 and 3-2 *Bathroom remodelling job after bathroom is stripped.*

3-3 to 3-6 *Photo metamorphose from the ground up.*

Understanding and know-how Ask yourself whether you are capable of doing the following:

- Understand the proper way to dismantle your bathroom from start to finish.
- Disconnect the plumbing, do the rough-in, and install the fixtures, cabinets, countertops, and tile.
- Remove the underlayment and install a new floor covering.
- Disconnect the electrical fixtures, rough in the wiring, and install a fan or relocate the lights.

The proper tools Each individual job requires specific tools and skillful handling of those tools. How many tools will you need to purchase or rent? Does your remodeling budget cover tool expenses?

Professionalism You might convince yourself that you are capable of doing the work, but the issue I am addressing now is the quality of that work. I have found that quality comes with years of experience, patience, and the understanding of each individual phase involved in the project. I recommend that you visit two or three bathrooms at your local home show. This is a good way to see top quality in a finished bathroom, and it's a great source of ideas.

Financing In most cases, lack of money is a big factor in deciding how much of the job you're going to do. Are you prepared to call in—and pay for—a professional if you should get in over your head? If you do decide to use a professional, ask your contractor what part of the job you can do in order to save money. Most contractors will work with you.

Time This is an important consideration, especially if this is the only bathroom in your house. You need to assess realistically both how much time it will take to do the job and how much time *you* can spend to get the job completed. What is your time worth to you? You might find that you will need a full remodeling contractor who can handle the job in a reasonable time frame. If you do choose to hire a contractor, please read the rest of this chapter before you make your first

Do you have what it takes?

call. However, if you have the time, if remodeling the bathroom will not inconvenience the family, and if you feel comfortable about taking on the task after reading the rest of this book, go ahead. I have confidence you'll do a great job!

Professionals

If, after you read this book, you choose to tackle the job yourself, I recommend that you consider hiring the following subcontractors. With all the bathrooms I've remodeled or built new over the years, I have gained a real respect for these professionals. They are experts in their fields, and I found that my jobs went a lot faster and easier with their help.

Plumbers   First, they know what it takes to meet the local plumbing codes. Second, they have the proper tools to do the job as well as experience in handling unusual situations. Read chapter 8 for more on plumbing.

Electricians   You must comply with electrical codes. Since many of us are not familiar with wiring, I find this area best left to an expert. Read chapter 9 for more on electrical work.

Drywall tapers   These professionals are worth their weight in gold! Taping is a slow and messy job, but these contractors are fast, good, and know the real art of achieving a quality finished product. Read chapter 10 for more on taping.

To assist you in selecting and working with a contractor, I would like to include some questions and answers that many customers over the years have asked.

"What should I do before I start looking for a contractor?"
There are three important areas that should be considered: project analysis, background work, and costs. First, pinpoint your project. For example, if you are considering remodeling your entire bathroom or installing a new tub, ceramic tile, floor covering, or maybe even building a new bathroom, take it one step at a time. If your main priority is to install a new bathtub with a ceramic tile surround, then start with this project first. A contractor can do the whole job for you, but it will be easier for you to discuss it with him one step at a time.

Next is the background work. When you have narrowed your job down, draw a plan or sketch of the project. In addition to reading this book, it might be helpful to go to the library and consult other books in conjunction with your proposed project. Your local stores carry a variety of home remodeling and do-it-yourself magazines. Pick up a few and clip pictures. All this background work also ensures that nothing in your conversations with contractors is lost in the translation.

Finally, there is cost. At this point you might or might not have a rough idea as to what your proposed project will cost, but you should have clearly defined the project you want to undertake. Your next step is to get estimates and/or itemized bids (see chapter 5). Keep in mind that the prices you'll be quoted are based on current costs and that most contractors will only guarantee their prices for approximately 30 days.

"Where do I start looking for a contractor?" To find a contractor, start with the yellow pages in your phone book. Ask neighbors and friends who recently had remodeling work done for their recommendations on a contractor. Your local newspaper and community papers available at the grocery store also carry ads from contractors.

"How do I qualify a contractor?" You'll need to know if the contractors are licensed (not required in some states), bonded, and insured. For verification, contact your state's department of labor and industries or the contractors state license board. I would also call the local Better Business Bureau and ask about the contractor's performance record.

"How many appointments should I make?" I recommend that you make appointments to discuss your plans with three different contractors. Each contractor will probably have different ideas on how your project should be approached, which can help you reach intelligent decisions. You will also have an opportunity to see firsthand how courteous the contractors are and how well they represent their businesses, which can indicate how well you might be able to work together. When explaining your project, you don't have to be perfect in your details because a professional contractor will be able to interpret what you're saying, but this is certainly the time to show him your written ideas and clippings.

Listen to the contractor carefully to see if he offers good advice on how to improve your job. During this time, you'll be able to judge what type of contractor he is by how well he listens and whether he helps you through your description. Depending on the size of your project, I would recommend that this initial meeting take at least an hour. This should give you enough time to share ideas, go over details, and communicate with the contractor in a comfortable fashion.

"Should money be the deciding factor in choosing a contractor?" Price should not be the deciding factor in choosing a contractor. A good rule of thumb is to not choose the lowest bid, especially if that bid is significantly lower than the others. The majority of legal claims against contractors are against those who underestimated their jobs. However, you won't want to rule out the low-bid contractor if all the bids are quite close.

"Why should I ask for references and how many should I get?" Ask the contractor for three references: one that is similar to your project and two others. Do not hesitate to call those references, for they were once in the same situation and they understand how you feel. When you visit their homes, you'll be able to see the differences in styles and quality for each of the contractors. Ask the contractor's reference customers the following questions and, of course, include any others that apply to your circumstances.

- Did the contractor start and finish the project as stated in his contract?

- Was the contractor organized, and did he keep the area around the project clean?

- Was the contractor polite and professional at all times while on and off the project site?

- Was this the first project the contractor had done for them? If not, what were the other projects?

- How well did the contractor deal with extra work and change orders?

- Did the contractor suggest up-to-date materials and methods?

- Did they experience any difficulties during the course of the project? How well did the contractor handle these situations?

- Was the job completed to their complete satisfaction? Did the contractor have to return to perform warranty work?

After you have gone through this entire procedure, you should be comfortable enough to make your decision and select a remodeling contractor.

General Conditions

Before signing a contract, you should know about General Conditions (3-7). General Conditions list your legal rights, and they also cover the warranties, rules, and regulations concerning the job. The General Conditions should benefit both you and your contractor. They are normally found on the backs of contracts and/or proposals. If the contract does not already have General Conditions, have them written in before you sign it. A contract can have as many as 17 or more General Conditions, but here are the four that I consider most important:

1. The contractor shall provide and pay for all materials, labor, tools, and other items as necessary to complete the project. All materials shall be of top quality, and all workers and subcontractors shall be skilled at their trades.

2. All permits and licenses necessary for the completion of the project shall be secured, and their cost shall be part of the total contract sum. Contractor will comply with all laws and regulations bearing on the conduct of the work.

3. The owner may order changes in the work, the contract sum being adjusted accordingly. All such orders and adjustments shall be in writing. Claims by the contractor for extra costs not shown on the estimate/bid must be made in writing on Extra Work or Change Order Forms and given to the owner before execution of the involved work.

4. The contractor shall re-execute any work that fails to conform to the requirements of the contract due to faulty material or workmanship which appears within a period of

GENERAL CONDITIONS

Article 1. The Contract includes The Agreement and its General Conditions, together with the Drawings and/or Specifications. Two or more copies of each, as required, shall be signed by the parties and one signed copy of each retained by each party.

The intent of these documents is to provide for all labor, materials, appliances and services of every kind necessary for the proper execution of the project, and the terms and conditions of payment therefor.

The documents are to be considered as one, and whatever is called for by any one of the documents shall be as binding as if called for by all.

Article 2. Except as otherwise noted, Contractor shall provide and pay for all materials, labor, tools, and other items necessary to complete the project.

Unless otherwise specified, all materials shall be new and of top commercial quality. All workmanship shall be of commercial quality.

All workmen and subcontractors shall be skilled in their trades.

Article 3. Permits and licenses necessary for the completion of the project shall be secured and their costs advanced by the Contractor, appearing in the Specifications as additional costs to be paid by Owner as part of the total contract sum. Contractor shall comply with all laws and regulations bearing on the conduct of work, and shall notify Owner if the Drawings and/or Specifications are a variance therewith.

Article 4. Contractor shall adequately protect the work, adjacent property of Owner, and the public, but shall be responsible only for damage or injury due to his act or neglect.

Article 5. Contractor shall permit and facilitate observation of the work by public authorities at all times and by the Owner and/or his agents **at such times as will not interfere unduly with completion of the work, nor subject Contractor to undue risks of injury to Owner.**

Article 6. Owner may order changes in the work, **the Contract Sum being adjusted accordingly.** All such orders and adjustments shall be in writing. Claims by Contractor for extra cost not shown in the Estimate/Bid must be made in writing to Owner before execution of the involved work.

Article 7. Contractor shall re-execute any work that fails to conform to the requirements of the contract and that appears during the course of the work, and shall remedy material defects due to faulty materials or workmanship which appear within a period of **ONE YEAR** from the date of completion of the contract. The provisions of this article apply to work done by direct employees of Contractor and to work done by subcontractors. In reference to concrete work, warranty shall cover faulty materials, or workmanship. Cracks in concrete should be reviewed as most are caused by weather conditons. Damages due to any imporper use or failure to properly maintain by Owner after completion of the work by Contractor are expressly exempted from this limited warranty of Contractor. **Correction and repair of such defects will be subject to additional charges by Contractor.**

Article 8. Should the Contractor neglect to execute the work properly or fail to perform any provisons of the contract, Owner after 3 days notice to Contractor, and Contractor's security, if any, may terminate this Agreement.

Article 9. Should the work be stopped by any public authority for a period of thirty days or more, through no fault of Contractor, or should the work be stopped through act or neglect of Owner for a period of 3 days, or should Owner fail to pay Contractor any payment within 3 days after it is due, then Contractor may, upon 3 days written notice to Owner, stop work or terminate the contract and recover from Owner payment for all work executed and any loss sustained plus reasonable profit and damages.

Article 10. Payments shall be made as provided in the Agreement. The making and acceptance by Contractor of the final payment shall constitute a waiver of all claims by Owner against Contractor, other than those arising from unsettled liens or from faulty work appearing within **ONE YEAR,** as contained in Article 7 for the General Conditions, and of all claims by Contractor except for any previously made and remaining unsettled. **Payments otherwise due may be withheld on account of defective work not remedied or liens of Contractor's labor or suppliers filed against Owner's property.**

Article 11. The final payment shall not be due until the Contractor has delivered to Owner a release of any liens arising out of this contract, or receipts in full covering all labor and materials for which a lien could be filed, or a bond satisfactory to the Owner indemnifying Owner against any such lien.

Article 12. Owner has the right to have other contracts in connection with the work, if Contractor has not provided subcontracts for affected phases of the project, then Contractor shall properly cooperate with any such additional contractor.

Article 13. Time shall be of the essence in this Agreement.

Article 14. If Contractor is delayed at any time in the progress of the work by changes ordered in the work by the Owner, by labor disputes, fire, unusual delays in transportation, unavoidable casualty, or other causes beyond Contractor's control, then the time for Contractor performance shall be extended for such reasonable time as Owner's and Contractor' Attorney's may together agree.

Article 15. Areas of Owner's premises in which Contractor is to work must be cleared by Owner of Owner's personal property in order to avoid possible damage. Owner may hire Contractors to remove such personal property, but Owner expressly agrees that Contractor will not be liable for any damage to such personal property during any such clearing. Contractor becoming an agent of Owner during such phase of operation. Owner shall have the right to direct such clearing operation. Owner agrees that this right to direct Contractor's work shall end upon completion of clearing operation.

Article 16. Contractor agrees that only top grade materials are to be used in performing this Agreement. The parties agree that all salvage resulting from work under this contract is to be retained by Contractor unless other agreements are contained in the written specifications.

Article 17. Owner and Contractor agree that the Specifications prepared in conjunction with this contract reflects necessary labor and materials based on preliminary inspection of Owner's premises. **The Specifications do not cover additional labor or materials as may be required to perform this Agreement after previously concealed portions of the premises have been opened to inspection by the demolition operation. Such additional labor and material shall be included in a change order excuted by the parties prior to commencement of the extra work involved.**

We recognize the laws are constantly changing. It is important that you check the laws in your state.

Contractor's License # _____

Bond # _____

Expiration Date _____

3-7

An example of General Conditions.

one year from the date of completion of the contract. This shall include all work performed by the contractor, employees of the contractor, and subcontractors. Damages due to improper use or failure by the customer to properly maintain said item after completion of the work by the contractor are expressly exempted from the limited warranty. Correction and repair of such defects under these circumstances are subject to additional charges by contractor.

In addition to studying the General Conditions, there are five other steps you should take before you sign a contract:

Contracts

1. Date, name, and address: When you receive your contract, make sure the date is correct. Check the spelling of your name. If you are married, the names of both spouses should be listed. If the address where the project is to be done differs from the billing address, it also should be noted on the contract.

2. Contents of the project: The project should be explained completely in writing. The contractor will list the material, permit, and labor costs involved. Never make assumptions— make sure nothing is omitted! If you don't understand something in this section, be sure to ask the contractor and, if necessary, have the contractor rewrite it for you.

3. Dates of work: Be sure there are start and finish dates concerning your project and that the allotted amount of time seems reasonable.

4. Payment schedule: The contract must show the amount agreed upon by you and your contractor. I would recommend that a payment schedule be written into your contract. Agree on a deposit up front and then divide the remaining balance into three equal payments: the first payment due at the project's halfway point, the second payment due at the two-thirds mark, and the final payment held until three days after completion of the project, final inspections (if required) have been made, and the approvals have been received. This suggested payment schedule is merely a rule of thumb and might not apply in your state. Be sure that the payment

schedule you and your contractor agree upon complies with local and state laws.

5. Signature and date: Sign the contract only after you and the contractor have gone through the General Conditions and the contents of the project. The contractor's license number (if required in your state) should be on the contract, and make sure that both you and your contractor sign and date two identical contracts. Retain one copy for your records.

Many books are available to help you hire and work with the right contractor. Books can be found in your local library and bookstores, or you can write to me for a copy of my book for consumers, *The Helping Hands™ Guide to Hiring a Remodeling Contractor*. The back of this book contains an order form to help you obtain your copy.

Generic business forms can be purchased at stationery stores. Even if you plan to perform the work on your remodeling project yourself, you will want to know in advance how much the project will cost and exactly where those dollars will be spent. It can be difficult to remember all the different materials that can go into a job. Itemized Bid Sheets clearly spell out the many materials and products that might be required by your remodeling project. These sheets will help you to organize your thoughts as you itemize the requirements of the job and calculate expenses.

Many contractors use their own contract/agreement forms to spell out the terms and conditions of their work. These documents should protect your rights as a customer as well as the rights of the contractor. If the contractor you wish to hire does not use a written contract, you might want to detail the terms of your job and the agreed upon payment schedule on the Contract/Agreement forms and the Extra Work and/or Change Order forms contained in the Helping Hands™ packet.

Unscrupulous contractors cannot be stopped entirely, but following the procedures detailed in this chapter can help to keep you from becoming a victim. Time spent in carefully selecting a contractor is time well spent!

Tools & materials

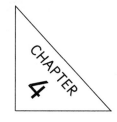

PROPER TOOLS ARE ESSENTIAL to achieving a professional-looking job. The tools recommended in this chapter are necessary to complete an entire bathroom remodeling project. This doesn't mean you have to go out and buy all these tools, however. To determine which tools you need, first you have to decide how much of the job you plan to do. Some of the tools listed can be rented from a local rental center; check the yellow pages of your phone book under *Tools—Renting* or *Rental Service Stores.*

Some of the tools described in this chapter and throughout the book are for consumer use, and some are considered to be "professional." Some of the professional tools can be purchased from a local retailer, while others are only available at a contractor's supply house. Some suppliers sell miscellaneous tools and items to the public—you only need to ask.

To decide what tools you will need, study the uses itemized for each tool. **Be sure to read and follow all tool instructions carefully, especially when working with power tools.**

Safety equipment

The following safety equipment is considered essential to protect your health during both the demolition phase of the project and during construction as you work with power and hand tools:

• Earplugs or other hearing protection.
• Safety goggles.
• Respirator.
• Proper work clothes.

Power tools

10" Electric miter saw   The miter saw is used for cutting wooden base moldings, casings around a door, and the hardwood edge for a countertop.

10" Table saw The table saw is used to rip hardwood (countertop edges), filler pieces for cabinets to be butted against a wall, finish panels for upper or lower cabinets, and countertops.

7¼" Electric circular saw The circular saw is used as the main tool for cutting plywood, underlayment, countertops, 2×4s, 2×6s, joists, etc., for framing and finish work.

Reciprocating saw A valuable tool, this saw is used to open walls and floors and to cut floor joists for plumbing, roofing material for skylights or roof vents, siding for dry vents, etc. (4-1).

Milwaukee Electric Tool Corporation

4-1 *Model 6527 Reciprocating Saw.*

Laminate trimmer This is used to trim plastic laminate on countertops and the wash basin cutout area (4-2). A standard router can accomplish the same thing.

Plunge router A handy tool when working with solid surface countertop material, the plunge router is used to rout bevels, apply a design to the edges of countertops, and make the wash basin cutout. It's also used when installing the shower surround and back splash.

Jigsaw A jigsaw is used to make wash basin cutouts and notches in countertops, and to cut underlayment, cabinet finish panels, the bathroom tissue cutout in the cabinet, a hole in the underlayment for the soil pipe (toilet), and shower or tub surrounds.

½" Heavy-duty drill The spade-handle drill is primarily used for stirring premixed drywall compound or for any other heavy-duty uses (4-3).

Ryobi America Corp.

4-2 *Model R-70 Tile Base Laminate Trimmer.*

4-3
*Model DW130 ½"
Heavy Duty Spade
Handle Drill.*

DeWalt Industrial Tool Co.

½" Drill This drill is used to drill holes in cabinet stiles, studs for plumbing and electrical work, shower and tub surrounds, and ceramic tiles.

Screwdriver A high-torque screwdriver with rpms at 0 to 2500 (4-4) is good for attaching underlayment to subflooring, cabinets and shower frames to walls, and hinges to frames. For wallboard framing members, consider using a screwdriver with rpms at 0 to 4000.

4-4
*Model 6907
Hi Torque
Screwdriver.*

Skil Power Tools

½" Heavy-duty hammer drill The hammer drill is handy to use when working in concrete; for example, when you are remodeling or installing a bathroom in the basement. When working around concrete, you might also need a stud gun to attach treated plates (bottom 2×4 or 2×6 of a wall) to the floor, a jackhammer, concrete and tile saws, and a grinder. These tools can be very expensive—you might want to consider renting them.

4"×24" Belt sander The belt sander is used to sand seams in solid surface countertop materials and underlayment and to sand other miscellaneous items (4-5).

4-5
Model 1273DVS 4"×24" Dustless Belt Sander.

Robert Bosch Power Tool Corporation

Finish (orbital) sander This sander is normally used after a belt sander.

Palm sander A palm sander can be used in areas where a finish sander is too large (4-6). It also follows the finish sander, and is good for smoothing rough areas on moldings and edges on countertops.

Cleanup tools

The following tools are just as important as the power and hand tools you'll select to do the job. The basic tools used to keep the job site clean will, in turn, make your work environment safer. Be sure to include the following: wet and dry shop vacuum, broom, dustpan, clean white rags, mop and bucket, shovel, and possibly a wheelbarrow. You might want to consider renting a large refuse container to store waste materials temporarily during demolition.

4-6 *Model SV 12SA Palm Sander.*

Hitachi Power Tools U.S.A. Ltd.

Now that you have an idea of the safety equipment and power and cleanup tools you might need, here is a list of some of the basic hand tools required.

Rough work Framing hammer, 3-pound hand hammer, 10-pound sledge hammer, ripping and flat pry bars, nail puller, metal handsaw or hacksaw, crosscut handsaw, cold and flooring chisels, staple gun, sawhorses, 12" combination square (4-7), chalk line, heavy-duty extension cord, stepladder, and extension ladder.

Finish work Finish hammer, rubber mallet, 25-foot tape measure, nail set, block plane, utility knife, razor blade scraper, 2' and 4' levels, ¾" and 1" wood chisels, spring clamps, adjustable clamps, carpenter square, 2"×8' straightedge, caulking gun, bevel finder, scratch awl, file, butt (door hinge) marker, rubber sanding block, and knee pads.

Boring Drill bit extension; auger, wood, metal, spade, masonry, and countersink bits (4-8); hole saw; and flat or Forstner-style wood-boring bits (4-9).

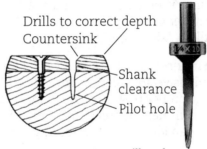

4-8 *Screw-Mate Drill and Countersink.* Stanley Tools

Vents/ducts Dryer duct vents, heat supply ducts, and exhaust fan duct vents; five-blade crimper; and aviation snips.

Plumbing Ratchet pipe cutter for cutting cast iron pipe (available at rental centers); propane torch; two-in-one fitting/tube brush (for cleaning insides and outsides of copper pipes); pipe wrenches; slip-joint pliers; adjustable open-end monkey wrench; fixed spud wrench; adjustable basin, chain, and strap wrenches; mini and regular tube cutters; pipe cutter (for cutting inside-out on ABS and PVC pipe); pipe saw (4-10); and folding hex keys.

4-10
Model 10-2312
14-Point Pull Saw.

Hand tools

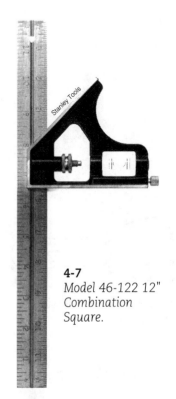

4-7
Model 46-122 12"
Combination
Square.

4-9 *Powerbore (Forstner-style) Wood Boring Bit.*

Electrical Slip-joint, long-nose, diagonal, and linesman pliers; Phillips head, slotted-tip, and Robertson-style screwdrivers; voltage tester; receptacle circuit tester; cable rippers; wire strippers and crimping tool; and fish tape (with reel and winder).

Wallboard Keyhole wallboard saw; rolling wallboard lifting tool; wallboard hammer (4-11); 4", 6", 10", and 12" joint knives; hand sander; pole sander; power-driven compound mixer; plastic joint compound pan; 4' T-square; and hopper.

4-11
*Model SR-15
Wallboard Hammer.*

Hart Tool Co.

Tile Tile hole saw; stationary tile cutter; nipping tool; ceramic tile cutter; carbide-bit rod saw blade (used with hacksaw); rubber grouting float; sponges; V-notched trowel for ceramic tile (¾₆"×⁵⁄₃₂" deep); and square-notch trowel for quarry tile.

Flooring Square-notch trowel for vinyl (¼₆"×¼₆"×¼₆" deep); adhesive spreader for cove base (¾₆"×⁵⁄₃₂" deep—4-12); and roller. For proper trowel usage, follow the manufacturer's recommendations found on the back of the adhesive container. For an idea of point sizes and their proper uses, see 4-13.

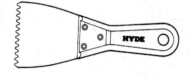

4-12 *Cove Base Adhesive Spreader.* HYDE GROUP

For wallboard, metal, and ceramic tile.
3/16" × 5/32" deep.
Uncarded 4" × 9" base.

Double notched. For vinyl materials. 1/16" × 1/16", 1/16" deep
1/32" × 1/16", 1/32" deep.
Uncarded 4" × 9" base.

Double notched. For linoleum and asphalt materials. 1/8" × 3/32", 3/32" deep,
1/32" × 1/16", 1/32" deep.
Uncarded 4" × 9" base.

For quarry tile.
1/4" × 1/4", 3/8" deep.
Uncarded 4" × 9" base.

For parquet flooring
3/16" × 1/4" deep.
Uncarded 4" × 9" base.

4-13
Recommended trowel specifications. HYDE GROUP

Wallpaper Shaver; 4½" scraper; plumb bob; hardwood roller; tapered plastic roller; flat foam roller; vinyl trimmer; stainless steel shears; folding trestle; clear plastic and triangle trim guide; smoothing tool; smoothing brushes; paste brush; water tray; and adhesive roller.

Paint & clear finishes Paintbrushes, both nylon and natural bristles of various sizes; roller tray, roller, and long handle; masking tape; drop cloths; rags; paint can lid opener; and stirring sticks.

Laminate Laminate (extension) roller; carbide scoring tool; straightedge; old Venetian blind slats.

Some of these tools can be used in different phases of the job. There are a few more tools that could be added, but this gives you a good idea of the many different types of tools required to remodel a bathroom.

If you want your project to last, it is important to use quality materials. Many of these products, such as floor coverings, also provide warranty protections. I understand that you might have budgetary considerations, but less expensive substitutions should not be made for certain materials. Some of these must-use materials and their functions are listed below.

Materials commonly used

Plywood I do not recommend the use of particle board as an underlayment for vinyl or other resilient-finish floorings because it swells when it comes in contact with water and might void the warranty on your finish flooring material. Instead, use APA-rated (American Plywood Association), exterior marked *sanded face* plywood. This plywood has a solid sanded surface for the direct application of resilient flooring and special inner-ply construction (with exterior glue) for superior performance under a concentrated load. It also provides excellent dimensional stability and eliminates excessive swelling (and the resulting buckling or humps) around nails if it is applied as recommended.

Felt paper This product is recommended for use between the subfloor and the underlayment. It provides a good barrier against the cold and moisture of a crawl space or an unfinished basement, and it helps to eliminate squeaking floors. Felt paper can also be used to help match up new underlayment with existing underlayment, a common problem on remodeling projects. If this situation occurs, you can lay either 15- or 30-pound felt between the subfloor and underlayment to raise the underlayment to a level which matches existing underlayment or adjoining finish flooring.

Cementitious backer units (cement board) This product is highly recommended for floors, countertops, and tub and shower enclosures for use under ceramic, quarry, and mosaic tiles as well as thin-cut stone. It serves as a substitute for underlayment, particleboard countertops, and water-resistant wallboard. This product is lightweight, strong, and highly resistant to water damage. Keep in mind that these products come in different thicknesses for different applications.

Water-resistant wallboard Commonly known as *green board*, this material is used behind tub and shower enclosures. It is chemically treated to combat moisture penetration and is water-resistant all the way through. It is designed for the adhesive application of ceramic or plastic tiles as well as tub and shower fiberglass surround kits. This product cannot be applied to an exterior wall over insulation with a vapor barrier (see chapter 10).

Wallboard Installed over framing members (2×4 or 2×6) or over existing walls and ceilings, standard gypsum wallboard is not recommended for use in areas where there is direct contact with water. Normally, ½" wallboard is used on 16"-center applications, and ⅝" is used if the framing is on 24" centers. On 24" centers, ⅝" wallboard eliminates the "sags" in ceilings and the "waves" in walls frequently created when ½" wallboard is used.

Countertop Use plywood with exterior glue (sanded on one side) or particleboard countertop as well as high-density board. Plywood and particleboard are recommended for plastic laminate, but particleboard is not recommended for use under ceramic, quarry, or mosaic tiles.

Tile It is not recommended that ceramic tile be used on floors or countertops as it is soft and might crack if a heavy object is dropped on it. Ceramic tile is good for walls and ceilings, however. Quarry or mosaic tiles work well for floors and countertops.

Wood floors If the proper steps have been taken to ensure a waterproof surface, wood floors work well; however, I do not recommend their use directly in front of a bathtub or shower or in any place where there will be direct contact with water.

Carpet Use of carpet in the bathroom is not recommended because of the moisture and the risk of mildew.

One important point that you should keep in mind when working with building products is that many of them absorb moisture during cold and damp weather. I highly recommend that during these weather conditions you bring your materials indoors and allow them to be at room temperature for about a week. That way, all moisture has an opportunity to evaporate, thus lessening the possibility of shrinking and warping, especially in the wood products. Nothing is more discouraging than installing moldings only to see them shrink, exposing the joints. Unfortunately, this is a lesson I have learned the hard way. A little extra care for your building materials can save you time and unnecessary grief!

CHAPTER 5

Costs

IT IS VERY IMPORTANT to know what the costs will be before you actually start your remodeling project. The best thing to do is to visit hardware and lumber stores to check out all the different tools, materials, and products and their costs. Be sure to keep a list of the items, their costs, and the stores where you found them. I recommend that you not try to do this task in just one weekend. Instead, take your time and spend several weekends on your research.

You might also want to pick up a few do-it-yourself magazines on bathrooms. Get different ideas of products you might like to use so you know what to look for when pricing. Reading the rest of this book will also help you to decide how much of the job you really want to do or if you would prefer to hire out, which will also determine your costs. There is no guarantee that doing any of the work yourself will save any money, especially if you have to buy tools. It also depends on what your time is worth to you.

After reading chapter 4, you should have an idea as to the variety of tools required to finish each phase of a job. By now you should also have a pretty good idea of some of the different types of materials and products it will take to complete this project. I have developed itemized bid sheets which are included in the Helping Hands™ packet mentioned in chapter 3. These bid sheets can help to outline all the materials used and the labor involved in doing a bathroom project, including the use of subcontractors.

You will also need to include in your calculations the costs of any permits (building, electrical, plumbing, etc.) that may be required. Each municipality has its own requirements for permits and inspections; you can call your local building department for information on permit requirements and costs.

Another expense to consider is the cost of properly disposing of construction debris, including the safe handling of hazardous materials. Depending on your project, you may be able to salvage some materials which could be sold to a used building materials dealer. This is certainly an option worth considering, and it might cover your debris costs!

If you should decide to hire a general contractor, subcontractor, or specialty contractor, keep in mind that the prices quoted by individual contractors will vary. In order to understand their fees, you need to know what each contractor can do for you.

Contractor classifications

General contractors bid the job, order materials, hire subcontractors and/or specialty contractors, and supervise the overall job. They rely heavily on lead carpenters, working supervisors who oversee the rest of the crew and subcontractors, keep track of materials, and (most importantly) handle customer relations which includes extra work and change orders, maintaining schedules, and dealing with any problems that should arise. A general contractor could handle an entire bathroom project himself, depending on your state's licensing requirements.

Subcontractors are like general contractors, and the term normally applies to plumbers, electricians, and excavators. Most states require them to be licensed as such, and their bond is lower than that of general contractors (with the exception of excavators who carry more than one bond). Subcontractors are in business for themselves, have their own customers, and rely on general contractors for the majority of their business. A subcontractor generally has two or three general contractors as customers, but in reality, the general contractor hires the subcontractor.

Specialty contractors are licensed like subcontractors, but they generally specialize in up to two specific—but related—trades; for example, a cabinet installer might also install floor coverings, a tile contractor might also install laminate countertops, and so on. For smaller and/or cosmetic jobs, a specialty contractor could handle the entire project.

Subcontractors and specialty contractors are essentially the same. Don't assume, however, that all specialty contractors can handle your bathroom project. Some prefer to do new construction only, and it is up to you to ask which area they prefer.

To help you understand the many types of specialty contractors that could be involved in your project, I have listed them below:

Specialty contractors

- Cabinetmaker.
- Carpet installer.
- Concrete (flatwork) contractor.

- Concrete cutter.
- Concrete sealing and waterproofing contractor.
- Deck builder.
- Electrician.
- Excavator.
- Finish carpenter.
- Fireplace installer.
- Flooring contractor.
- Footing installer.
- Foundation contractor.
- Framer.
- Gas piping and venting contractor (may be a plumber or an HVAC contractor).
- Gutter contractor.
- Hazardous materials (e.g., asbestos) removal expert.
- Heating, ventilating, and air conditioning (HVAC) contractor.
- Insulation contractor.
- Mason.
- Painter.
- Paving contractor.
- Plumber.
- Pumping contractor.
- Roofer.
- Siding contractor.
- Taper.
- Tile installer.
- Wallboard installer.
- Wallpaper installer.
- Window installer.

Itemizing is the key

The majority of contractors will bid your job by estimating. Keep in mind that an estimate is only an educated guess. The total price you will pay could be hundreds of dollars more! What I strongly recommend is that you get an *itemized bid*. This will show you the actual finished cost before you enter into a contractual agreement with the contractor.

Another advantage of an itemized bid is that if the total cost is too high, you can review the itemized sheets with your contractor's help and make adjustments. Finally, banks and credit unions prefer to get itemized bids because they put everything into perspective for their loan packages.

From experience, I know there are customers who will add work or make changes while the job is in progress. To those readers who think this might describe themselves, I would also recommend that you add, to your figures or to the contractor's bid, a 15 percent (or higher) contingency factor to cover any changes or overruns.

If you have selected a bid, remember that contractors generally guarantee their prices for only 30 days.

Some contractors like to bid the job cost plus a percentage while others like to work by the hour or bid by square footage. Try to avoid these. The only truly reliable way to bid a job is to break it down into separate phases, itemize the material and labor costs for each phase, total them up, and add a 15 percent contingency factor to the total. Oh yes, don't forget the sales tax! It takes longer for the contractor to produce an itemized bid, but I believe the end result is well worth it.

Whether you are doing the work yourself or hiring a contractor, you will still want to know where and how your funds will be spent. If you hire a professional but want to purchase your own products, remember that you will be responsible if that product is defective. For example, if you buy a toilet and two days after the plumber installs it a leak develops because of a crack, you will have to pay the plumber to take the toilet out so you can exchange it for a new one, and then you will have to pay the plumber to install your new toilet. I know of one case where three toilets were installed over a two-week period, but because the plumber supplied the toilet and manufacturing defects were to blame, the customer was never involved in the transaction.

Generic estimate forms, contracts, and change order forms can be purchased at a stationery store. However, if you would like to purchase copies of the business forms referred to in chapters 3 and 5, an order form for the Helping Hands™ packet can be found at the back of the book.

If you're like me and you want to know where your dollars and cents are being spent, you'll want to use the itemized method. Estimates can lead to expensive surprises!

CHAPTER 6

Demolition

BEFORE YOU CAN START ANY REMODELING PROJECT, you will have to do some demolition. How ambitious your plans are determines how much demolition is required. One way to save on expenses when doing any remodeling project is to remove as little as possible during this phase of the project.

Safety is important! As you perform demolition work, be sure to wear the appropriate protective clothing, gloves, boots, goggles, and hearing protection. **It is also extremely important when working on projects where plumbing and electrical fixtures are involved that you turn off both the water supply and the electrical breakers feeding the fixtures.**

The following paragraphs describe the demolition involved for typical bathroom remodeling projects.

Installing new tile in tub/shower area

If you plan to reuse the existing bathtub, be sure to cover it with some sort of protection before you begin any work. Falling tiles or dropped tools can permanently mar the surface of your tub, so you will want the protection to remain in place throughout your remodeling project. New on the market is a disposable plastic molded tub protector which will completely cover and protect the surface of your bathtub.

If you have decided to keep the tub because you prefer not to open the walls but the finish of the tub is marred, that's OK. You have a couple of options to consider, but both procedures need to be performed by a professional or a factory-authorized installer. One option is to have your tub refinished. If you choose this option, be sure to check out the quality of the work and look at reference jobs. Depending on the company, this might only be a temporary solution.

The second option is to have a liner installed. Re-Bath markets a product manufactured from a converted high-impact ABS with a nonporous surface that is custom molded to fit over your existing tub. This is one way to keep the cost down as well as to minimize down-time, especially if you only have one bathroom.

Whether you currently have tile or a shower kit of some kind, the first thing you need to remove is the base molding from the wall on both sides of the tub/shower area. To remove rubber or vinyl base molding, insert a stiff putty knife between the base molding and the wall at one end of the molding and pry it away from the wall. Once a small section is loose, grab that end and pull. It is important that you pull the molding down toward the floor. If you try to pull the molding straight out or up, the adhesive might tear the wallboard surface up the wall as you pull. Rubber or vinyl base molding is generally not salvageable; you will need to purchase and install new moldings.

To remove wooden base moldings, use a stiff putty knife as described above for rubber base moldings. Always start with the smallest piece. Be careful not to damage the top edge of the moldings when prying with the putty knife. Once you get it started, use a flat bar or a small crowbar to remove the remaining base moldings.

The nails that hold the moldings to the wall will either remain in the wall or still be in the base moldings. If the nails remain in the moldings, cut them off from the backside. If you try to pound them out through the front, you will damage the face of the moldings.

To cut the nails off, use end-cutting nippers (6-1). Grab the nail close to the wood and pull on it a little bit (about $\frac{1}{16}$" to $\frac{1}{8}$"). Then go back and cut the nail close to the surface. Later, after the molding has been reinstalled, you can conceal the nail hole on the face with matching putty.

6-1 *Crescent 72-7 End-Cutting Nippers.*

Another technique that works well is to pull the nail out completely through the backside of the base molding. When it comes time to reinstall the molding, select a finish nail with a larger head than the nail you removed, and nail again in the existing hole.

Once the base molding has been removed from around the tub or shower area, remove the plumbing trim pieces, the casing around the window (if you have one in the shower area), and the shower rod or door. With a keyhole wallboard saw, cut through the wall surface, and along the edge of the tile or

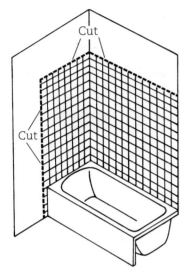

6-2 *A few choice cuts can save a big mess!*

shower enclosure all around the shower area (6-2). When you reach a stud, either tip the saw blade so you skim the surface of the stud as you cut the wallboard, or pull the blade out of the wall and reinsert it about 2" farther along, bypassing the stud completely. You can then go back and cut those areas with a wallboard saw. Remove the wallboard material and the attached shower wall surface (tile or shower kit) as one unit and discard.

You might discover after you open the wall in the tub area that there is not a stud near the outside corners of the tub to allow nailing for the new wallboard. If this is the case, cut the wall horizontally (starting at the top of the previously cut area) to expose the nearest stud on both sides of the tub. Then cut vertically to the floor. At this point, install a new 2×4 against this stud to serve as a nailer for new wallboard material. If there is no stud from the edge of the tub to about 2" in, now is the time to install a 2×4 or 2×6 to serve as a backer to which you can later attach a shower door (6-3).

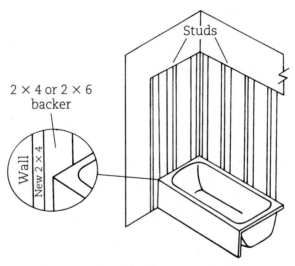

6-3 *Including a backer makes it easier to install a shower door later.*

46   Bathroom Remodeling

You have a couple of choices here, but regardless of which way you choose, the first things you'll have to remove are the toilet, the base moldings, and any metal molding where the flooring meets the carpeting in the threshold of the doorway.

To remove the toilet, turn off the water supply to the toilet tank first, and then flush the toilet. Use a sponge to soak up any water remaining in the bottom of the tank and bowl, then disconnect the water supply to the tank. Pry off the finish caps that cover the nuts fastened to the bolts that secure the toilet bowl to the floor. Unscrew the nuts and rock the bowl from side to side. Then twist the bowl and lift straight up.

Installing new floor covering

At this point you'll have to determine if the existing flooring, backing, lining felt, or asphaltic "cutback" adhesives contain asbestos fibers. You might need to send a sample of the flooring to a testing laboratory for analysis. Until you know for sure, it is important not to cut into the floor covering with any power tools that could create dust. Various government agencies have regulations governing the removal of in-place asbestos and its safe disposal; check with them to make sure you are in compliance. An asbestos-removal expert might be required.

The Resilient Floor Covering Institute has published a booklet called *Recommended Work Practices for the Removal of Resilient Floor Coverings*, which outlines safe procedures for working with floor materials containing asbestos fibers. For a free copy of this booklet, write to:

Resilient Floor Covering Institute
966 Hungerford Drive, Suite 12-B
Rockville, MD 20850

Asbestos

If asbestos is not a factor in your project, consider whether or not you want to remove only the floor covering, leaving the existing underlayment in place. It can be done, but it's hard work and a lot of prep work has to be done to the underlayment before a new floor covering can be installed over it. To remove resilient floor covering, grab it by a corner and pull up. The floor covering will separate from its backing. Then you must scrape off both the backing material and the adhesive from the underlayment.

Removing floor covering/ underlayment

Your other option is to remove the flooring and underlayment totally, which, in my opinion, is much easier. If your bathroom is small, remove the vanity (cabinet) so you won't have to cut around it. There is a trick to removing underlayment. First, use either the reciprocating or the circular saw (I personally prefer the reciprocating saw) and cut around the toilet flange by about 2" (6-4). Be careful not to cut through the subfloor. If you use a circular saw, set your blade to match the thickness of the underlayment, normally ⅜" to ¾". Be sure to use a saw blade that will cut through nails.

Next, make cuts in the center of the doorway and around all door casings as well (6-5). These cuts allow you to remove the underlayment from under the door jambs and casings without damaging either of them.

If you have a tile floor, such as quarry or mosaic, you need to find out what type of underlayment you have in order to choose your next step. You must remove some of the tiles (a 12" by 12" area) to look at your underlayment. The best way to start this is to smash one tile with a hammer. However, before you even pick

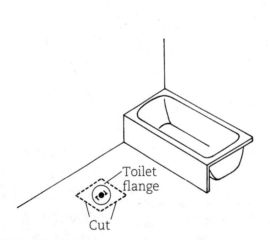

6-4 *This little procedure can save a lot on your plumbing bill!*

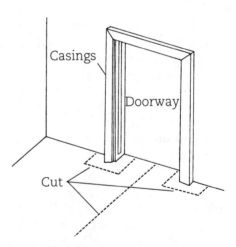

6-5 *These cuts in the underlayment help protect door jambs and casings during demolition.*

up that hammer, **put on your safety goggles!** This is an absolute must because small tile shards will fly everywhere! Once this first tile has been removed, you can use a chisel and hammer to pry up adjoining tiles. If you have a wood underlayment, you will need to remove tiles wherever you need to make the cuts shown in 6-4 and 6-5. If you find concrete under the tiles, you will need to remove all the rest of the tiles. When all the tiles you need to remove are gone, scrape off the remaining adhesive from the underlayment. Sometimes heating the adhesive with a small heat gun makes it easier to remove.

Installing a new tub

If you have removed the wall material in the tub area and the underlayment as described above, then I would seriously consider installing a new tub and plumbing at this time because you have to go through these steps anyway in order to get the old tub out. If you decide to install a new tub, there is only one other step you might have to take if you have a basement with a finished ceiling, or if the plumbing wall is on the back of a finished exposed wall or is in a closet. You will need to open that ceiling or wall in order to get to the necessary plumbing to remove and install a new bathtub. This is not a big problem because an access panel can be mounted on the wall to neatly cover the hole. This panel will provide permanent access to your plumbing should repairs be necessary in the future.

Gutting the room completely

If you have very ambitious remodeling plans, the best way to approach the job might be to gut the room completely. This also provides opportunities to repair or replace structural members, wiring, ductwork, or plumbing pipes.

Complete plumbing redesign

When space is limited because there is a low crawl space, take out everything in the bathroom that is mounted on the floor. Once the floor is clear, remove the underlayment and the subfloor (6-6). This is a good time to replace or fix sagging floor joists or to provide additional support beneath them (6-7).

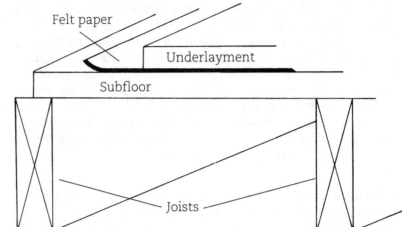

Felt paper

Underlayment

Subfloor

6-6
Anatomy of a floor.

Joists

6-7
Preventive measures at this stage create a safe and solid floor.

Fully gutting a bathroom

As you can see in 6-8 and 6-9, gutting the bathroom involves opening up the walls, removing the door and window frames, removing the plumbing fixtures, and removing the underlayment and subfloor. Go slow, take your time, and cut as little as possible. It is easier to make another cut than it is to repair or replace. Also, your bathroom is put together like a puzzle, so it comes apart the same way.

6-8 *Removing the wall covering gives you full access to your plumbing.*

6-9 *Removing the underlayment to access plumbing also lets you look for and repair structural damage.*

Before you do anything, read this book thoroughly and study your bathroom as well. Have a carefully thought-out plan before you pick up that hammer or saw, and have a clear picture in your mind and on paper of the steps you plan to take. Being careful and cautious holds down your expenses!

Framing

BY NOW YOU SHOULD HAVE A CLEAR DIRECTION to follow and a set of plans from which to work. Figures 7-1A and B illustrate "before" and "after" drawings of the same job. As you can see from the "after" drawing, a lot of preplanning was involved. Careful attention to detail in the early stages will pay off in the end.

7-1A

Main bathroom had access only through the master bedroom.

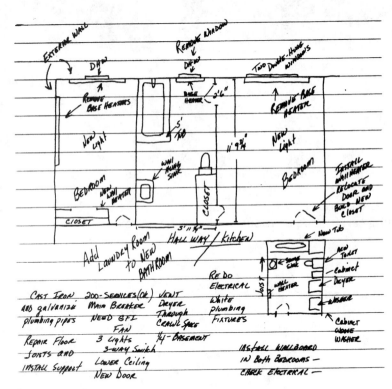

Before

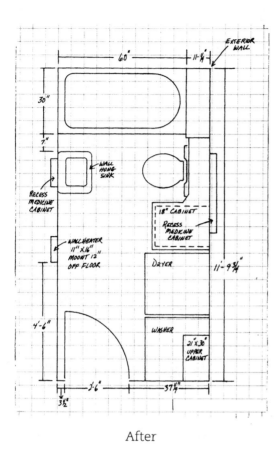

7-1B
By rearranging the fixtures, I was able to relocate the door and add laundry facilities.

After

Begin with the windows. From experience, I have found that any window—metal or wooden—installed in the tub or shower area causes nothing but trouble. The problem is always water. I recommend that you eliminate this window if at all possible. Before doing so, however, check with your local building department. You might be required to install an exhaust fan to meet building codes.

Figure 7-2 will familiarize you with the framing parts of a window opening. If you have a wooden window, start by removing all the interior and exterior trim pieces. Then look for nails in the vertical parts of the frame and the sill of the window. By inserting a hacksaw blade or a metal handsaw between the trimmers (wall framing) and the frames of the windows, and between the sill of the window (in older homes) and the sill of the framing, you can cut the nails and pull the window into the room (7-3).

Windows & doors

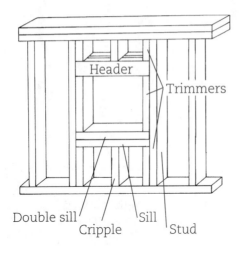

Header

Trimmers

Double sill

Cripple

Sill

Stud

7-2 *Anatomy of a window.*

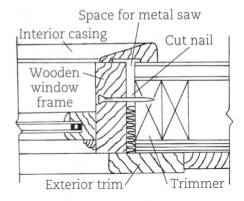

Space for metal saw

Interior casing

Cut nail

Wooden window frame

Exterior trim

Trimmer

7-3 *Horizontal cross section.*

For metal windows, remove the exterior trim to reveal the nailing fin that encircles the frame of the window. Once you have taken out the nails with a nail puller, you'll be able to remove the window from the exterior side of the house (7-4).

7-4

Remove the exterior trim to reach the nailing fin.

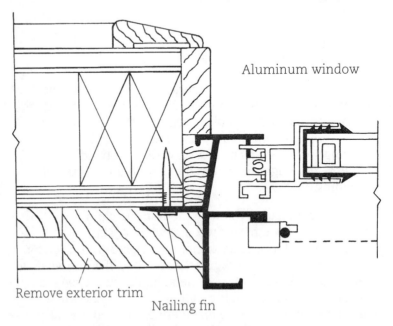

Aluminum window

Remove exterior trim

Nailing fin

Now you are ready to frame in the window, and the best way to do this is to nail in the top plate and the bottom plate. At this point you can measure for the inside trimmers and center stud(s) if necessary, cut them, and nail them in place (7-5). Now you can install an exterior piece of plywood, the felt, and your siding to match (7-6). This same method works for closing in existing doors. Remember to insulate this space after the electrical and plumbing are in but before the wallboard is installed.

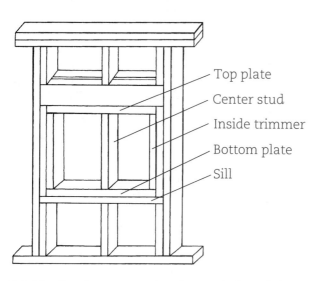

Top plate

Center stud

Inside trimmer

Bottom plate

Sill

7-5 *The framing parts to close in an existing window.*

7-6 *To install siding over existing framed-in window, adjust seams in siding to camouflage perimeter of window.*

Before you can install a new door, you'll have to cut a rough opening. If the door size is 30" by 6'8", you will have to frame a rough opening that measures 35" by 6'10½" (7-7). Make sure your rough opening frame has a 3" allowance for the two 1½" trimmers. This will also give you about ¼" of space between the trimmer and the doorframe on both sides, where you'll be able to use the wooden shims that are necessary to install a door. The actual installation of the door is described in chapter 14.

New doors & windows

Once you have cut your opening, completely removing the studs, you will be able to fit your completed rough opening doorframe into place. A complete rough opening frame consists of two studs, the header, and the bottom plate all nailed together as shown in 7-7. Once the rough opening is in place, the bottom plate inside the rough opening must be removed in order to install the trimmers. How much of the plate should be cut off depends on the length of the bottom plate. For example, if it extends beyond the rough framing stud more than 12", then cut the plate out (7-8) and install the trimmers. If the plate extends less than 12" from the stud, then go ahead and install the trimmers on top of the bottom plate (7-9).

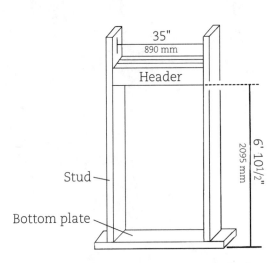

7-7 *Specifications for a rough opening of a door.*

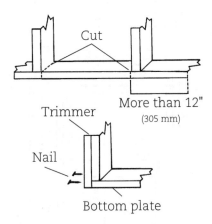

7-8 *Here, there is more than enough plate beyond rough opening framing members to allow bottom plate to be cut out before installing trimmers.*

Once the trimmers are in place, cut out the plate with a handsaw or a reciprocating saw. You will find it easier to use the reciprocating saw in this situation if you insert the blade upside down. This allows you to bring the entire tool closer to the plane of the underlayment. When using a power tool to cut out the bottom plate, be careful not to cut into the subfloor, which can weaken the area.

The main reason why the plate is cut after the trimmers are installed is because nailing a trimmer into a short plate could

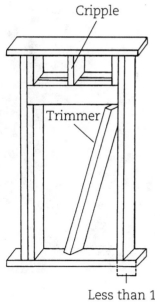

Cripple

Trimmer

7-9
Installing a trimmer on a short plate.

Less than 12"
(305 mm)

cause the plate to split. The most common situations in which this rule of thumb applies are when doors are located close to corners, or an existing plate joint is located within 12" of the rough opening. Once the trimmers are installed, you can install the upper trimmers and center cripple as shown in 7-9 and 7-10. The cripple shown above the new door in 7-10 provides support for load bearing (second floor) as well as backing to which to the ledger for a new lower ceiling can be fastened.

It is very important that you build the rough opening doorframe as one unit and keep the bottom plate in place until it is completely installed into the area allowed. This helps to keep the frame straight and aligned. If either of the studs gets out of alignment (7-11), your door will not close properly.

If you choose to install a window, follow the same steps as in framing a door opening, with one exception: a sill is required between the studs at the rough opening measurement of the height of the window. Once this is done, you can finish the framing by adding in the upper and lower trimmers and the upper and lower center cripples. You might want to review 7-2 for proper cripple, sill, and trimmer placement.

7-10
Center cripple above new door.

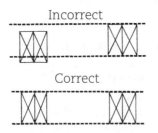

Incorrect

Correct

7-11
Correct alignment of rough door opening ensures that your door will operate properly.

When installing a new window on a remodeling project, it is not necessary to open up the interior walls until the very end. You can do all the work from the exterior side. Remove the siding and sheathing in the general area. If you encounter plumbing pipes or electrical wires, you might or might not be able to relocate them. You will have to face that situation when it occurs. In order to protect the interior walls from damage, use a handsaw to cut the studs, and an electric drill and screw gun when installing the framing pieces.

Install the rough opening in pieces—first the upper trimmers (cripples if needed), then the header. Next, install the lower trimmers (cripples if needed) and then the sill. Finally, install the two side trimmers. Now you can cut around the finished rough opening with a keyhole wallboard saw, remove the wallboard, and install the window. Complete the exterior siding and trim, and finish by trimming the interior of the window. This method is the least expensive and creates the least amount of disruption.

If you have decided to incorporate a laundry room into your bathroom, then you are required to install a dryer vent. Take advantage of the opportunity, if the floor joists are exposed, to conceal the vent piping parallel to and between them. Secure the ductwork to a framing member with a plumbing strap to keep the pipe as straight as possible. The same holds true when installing any type of ductwork.

Use a 4" galvanized or aluminum pipe (not vinyl), adjustable elbows, metal duct tape, a five-blade crimper (7-12), and aviation snips. With these tools, you can accomplish some of the toughest jobs. A 2×4 nailed to the underside between two joists prevents the weight of the pipe from causing it to sag, and possibly separate at the seams, especially if it is installed over a long run.

Dryer vent ductwork

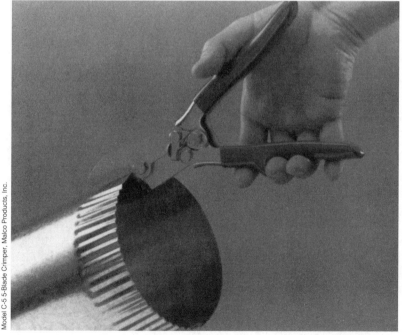

7-12
Even precrimped pipe might need a crimper tool for a good fit.

Dryer vent ductwork should be seamed with metal duct tape which will actually fuse the pipe together. You do not want to use cloth tape which can dry out and fall off, and you must not fasten the duct sections together with screws—it will create a fire hazard.

The damper system requires a 4¼" hole (¼" larger than the 4" standard pipe) through the rim joist to the exterior of the building. The best way to cut this hole is to use either a hole saw or a reciprocating saw. I prefer to use a 4¼" hole saw. If possible, begin by drilling a pilot hole through the center of the backside of the rim joist. Drill all the way through the siding (7-13) and be sure to use a ³⁄₁₆" or smaller bit. If you encounter any obstacles outside, it will not be difficult to repair this very small hole and relocate your venting. In addition, if your hole is larger than the pilot drill bit on the hole saw, you will not be able to use the hole saw effectively.

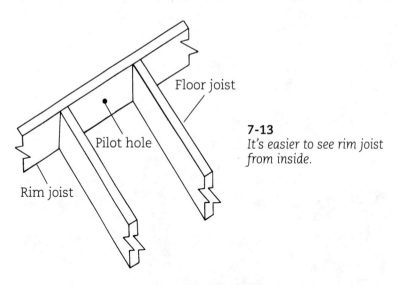

Floor joist

7-13
It's easier to see rim joist from inside.

Pilot hole

Rim joist

With the pilot hole drilled, you can now go to the exterior siding, place the pilot drill from the hole saw in the previously drilled pilot hole, and drill your hole (7-14). Be sure your drill is large enough to handle a hole saw. As a precaution, your power drill should have a side handle so you can use both hands to prevent the drill from twisting out of your hands. Sometimes the dryer vent lands squarely on top of the overlap between two

Model HSW68, Malco Products, Inc.

courses of siding, as shown in 7-14. If this happens, you will need to use small wooden filler pieces on the backside of the damper and up against the upper siding lap to ensure a secure vertical installation and proper damper operation.

With the hole cut, you can now make that all-important trial fit of your damper installation. Once you feel comfortable with the fit, remove the damper, apply latex caulk to the backside of the damper hood, and install the unit. Some damper hoods come with two or four pre-drilled holes. If you find yours only has two holes, then drill the other two holes in the outside corners. Install the damper (7-15) using galvanized or stainless steel screws, not nails. Recheck to make sure the damper door opens and closes.

7-15 *Notice the location of the fasteners.*

Once you install the damper and before the pipe is connected, it is a good idea to install the plastic flange plate that comes with the damper kit. First apply latex caulk on the inside of the flange plate and around the damper pipe to prevent moisture and cold air from entering the home. Then mount the flange plate, pushing the flange into the caulk up against the backside of the rim joist.

Subflooring

Until all the plumbing is completed and the main wires have been pulled, you will not be able to install the entire subfloor. While the area is open, take the opportunity to cover the ground with 4- or 6-mil black polyethylene as a moisture barrier, and install insulation with the fiberglass facing the barrier (7-16). To help hold the insulation in place while you staple the tabs to the joists, use insulation hangers between the joists.

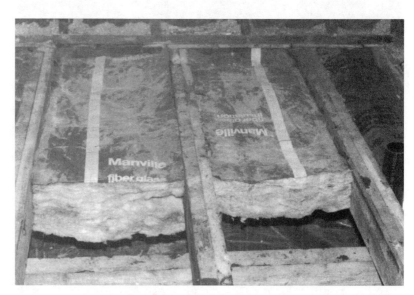

7-16
Insulating the floor.

Now you are ready to lay part of the subfloor so you can frame for the tub (7-17). In some cases you might have to install a double subfloor, especially if you decide to apply underlayment over existing floors in adjoining rooms. The second subfloor is mainly a filler to match up to existing flooring before the underlayment is installed. This is a common practice in older homes.

Figure 7-18 shows the subfloor opened up to accept the bathtub waste and overflow; the floor joist was trimmed to make room for the drainpipe and P-trap. During the planning stages, you

7-18
Tight situations like this require you to trim the floor joist.

might discover a floor joist right where the drainpipe needs to be located, so you'll need to plan for an opening (pocket) for that plumbing (7-19). If you have to cut a floor joist in order to create the pocket, then it would be a good idea to add extra support to the existing joists on either side of the cut joist so as not to weaken this important framing member. This will help

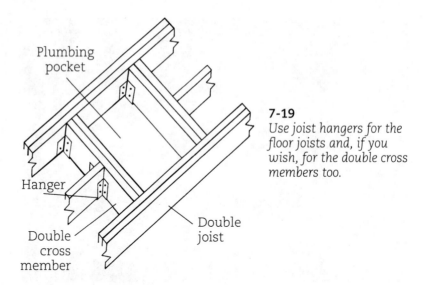

Plumbing pocket

Hanger

Double cross member

Double joist

7-19
Use joist hangers for the floor joists and, if you wish, for the double cross members too.

support the load of a tub, or perhaps a whirlpool bath. For safety's sake, use joist hangers for the floor joist you have to cut off. It will help support the joist and will make nailing easier.

Now you are ready to install the bathtub. If you have a steel tub, you will need to provide adequate support (cast iron tubs do not require additional support). In order to do this, you need to determine the height (back of the tub) from the underside of the tub's flange to the floor, and then transfer that measurement to the back wall against which the tub will be installed. Then nail a 1×4 or 2×4 horizontally (7-20) on that

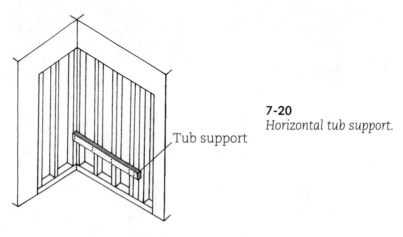

Tub support

7-20
Horizontal tub support.

measurement (making sure it's level), and a 2×4 vertically in each corner where the tub will meet the wall. An additional 2×4 might be required next to the plate to properly support the 2×4 under the corner of the bathtub (7-21). Read the instructions supplied with the tub to make sure you are meeting that manufacturer's requirements for support.

Once you get the rough-in plumbing and electrical completed (see chapters 8 and 9), you can finish the subfloor and the framing (7-22).

7-22 *Ledger screwed onto the framing members.*

7-21 *Additional 2×4 next to plate properly supports 2×4 under corner of tub.*

Ceilings

What should you do if you have high ceilings? You could leave them as they are, or you could lower the ceiling. From experience, I have found that if a bathroom is less than 6' wide, you can use 2×4s for ceiling rafters. If it is over 6', then use 2×6s. However, before installing either 2×4s or 2×6s, contact your building department for the proper code requirements. Also, check to see what grade (quality) of lumber should be used. For example, should the lumber be stamped 2 or better? There is one last requirement to check on and that is the minimum ceiling height. Normally, that would be 7'6", but be sure to check. If you plan to install wallboard in a tub or shower ceiling, wallboard manufacturers recommend that the framing members (ceiling rafters) in that area not exceed 12" on center. I've found 16" on center to be just fine, but again, check your building department for code requirements. With that in mind, install a 2×4 ledger around the perimeter of the room as shown in 7-22. If the walls on the other sides of the bathroom walls are finished and you want to preserve them in their existing condition (without cracks), then screw (don't nail) the ledger onto the framing members.

Install the joist hangers using hanger nails 16" on center (12" on center over tub or shower areas). Then drop in the ceiling rafters. Make sure you put nails into both sides of the joist hangers and on into the rafters to secure the entire unit. One benefit to installing a lower ceiling is that the extra space between the original ceiling and the new ceiling can conceal the plumbing if you decide at some future date to install a bathroom above this existing bathroom (7-23). It is cost-effective for you to plan now while the ceiling is exposed.

7-23 *Plumbing parts can be neatly packaged in the new ceiling space.*

If you are looking for a little more light, consider installing a skylight (7-24). The framing is the same as installing a window. You can install skylights in composition, shake, or tile roofs (7-25 and 7-26). Skylights are available to fit standard rafter spacing—either 16" or 24" on center—which makes for easy installation. They are also manufactured in larger widths that require more extensive framing on your part. If you decide to put in a skylight that exceeds your 16" or 24" on center truss spacing, consult either the manufacturer of your truss system or a structural engineer for guidance (an "engineered fix") on how to proceed.

Skylights

VELUX-AMERICA INC.

7-24
Skylight above a whirlpool bath.

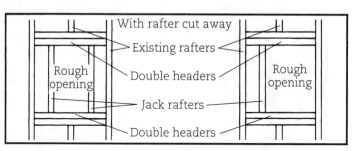

7-25
Skylights bring in fresh air as well as additional light.

7-26 *Don't be intimidated by your roofing material; leaded flashing conforms to roof tiles.* VELUX-AMERICA INC.

If you need to cut a roof rafter, be sure to install a header at the top (peak-side) and a cross-member at the bottom (ground-side). The header will help support the rafter and take the roof load (7-27). Double headers are highly recommended. The cross-member will tie in and support the lower half of the cut rafter. If the skylight is smaller than the total width of the space between the two rafters, then you need to frame within the new opening with jack rafters.

7-27
These diagrams show proper header and jack rafter placement. VELUX-AMERICA INC.

With rafter cut away
Existing rafters
Rough opening
Double headers
Rough opening
Jack rafters
Double headers

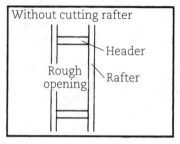

Without cutting rafter
Header
Rough opening
Rafter

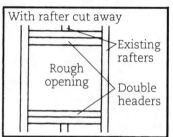

With rafter cut away
Existing rafters
Rough opening
Double headers

This type of framing also applies when you cut across the ceiling joist (7-28). There is one more thing to consider when framing between the ceiling joists. The area between the skylight and the finish ceiling has to be framed to create a shaft (7-29). How you frame the shaft determines how much natural light will enter the bathroom and where the light will be directed. Figure 7-30 illustrates two types of shafts. A good rule of thumb when building a beveled shaft is to take the length of the skylight, divide that measurement in half, and use that measurement to build the bevel on the backside (toward the center of the house) of the shaft. This method lets in plenty of light, and provides enough room to remove the insect screen. The flared shaft provides optimum light distribution and a more attractive appearance. Flaring the light shaft is an economical way to make a small window seem larger. Keep in mind how you would like the finished area to appear. If necessary, review 7-24 to get an idea of the finished installation.

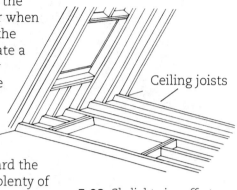

Ceiling joists

7-28 *Skylight size affects location of ceiling opening.* VELUX AMERICA INC.

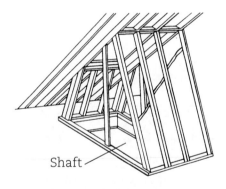

Shaft

7-29 *Shaft framing is not as complicated as it looks.* VELUX-AMERICA INC.

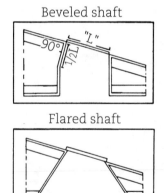

Beveled shaft

Flared shaft

7-30 *Two types of shaft.* VELUX-AMERICA INC.

More expensive skylights come with a pre-built curb and flashing system. Each manufacturer has recommendations when it comes to the size of the curb, proper flashing application, and securing the skylight to the curb. Follow the directions supplied with the unit. However, if you choose to install a single- or double-insulated acrylic skylight, commonly known as a *bubble*, you will be required to create your own flashing system (7-31 and 7-32). I recommend extending the curb 3" to 5" above the finished roof, depending on the slope of the roof, the weather conditions in your area, and the applicable codes.

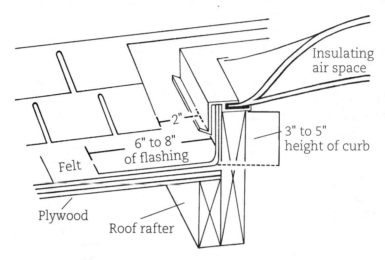

7-31
Flashing and curb installation.

Insulating air space

2"

6" to 8" of flashing

Felt

3" to 5" height of curb

Plywood

Roof rafter

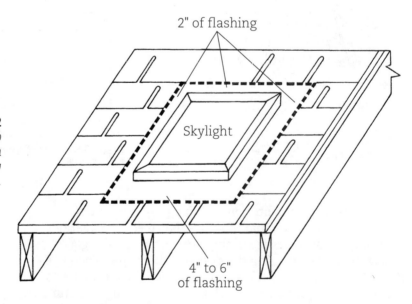

7-32
2" of flashing on sides and top of skylight help drain rainwater and prevent snow buildup.

2" of flashing

Skylight

4" to 6" of flashing

70   Bathroom Remodeling

Now you are ready to finish framing, but there are still a couple of tips you should know on how to frame a corner or a partition (an interior dividing wall). A 2×4 corner consists of two studs with three 2×4 spacer blocks about 12" long placed flat between the studs (one at each end and one in the center) all nailed together. When it is complete, it should measure 4½" (7-33).

Corners & partitions

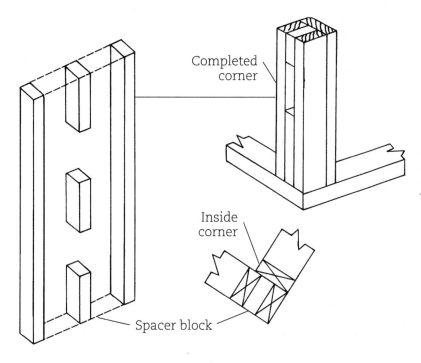

Completed corner

Inside corner

Spacer block

7-33
This corner provides solid fastening surfaces for two walls and wallboard.

The same is true for a partition, with the exception that the inside blocks (or a full 2×4 to creat a "solid partition") are turned sideways (the 3½" way), for a total width of 6½" when constructed. The turned 2×4 can accept a new wall being nailed into it (7-34).

If you use a solid partition as a corner, make sure the wall enclosing the tub extends at least 1½" out from the edge of the tub to allow room for wallboard corner bead and installation of base molding. This solid partition can also provide secure backing for a shower door.

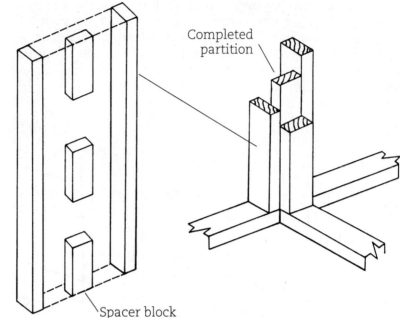

7-34
Small scraps of wood can come in handy.

Completed partition

Spacer block

Hot tub or whirlpool bath

Hot tubs and whirlpool baths really require you to do your homework before you can attempt to do the framing. The best way to start is to read the literature supplied by the manufacturer of the product. Specifically, what you are looking for is the weight when the unit is completely filled, including body capacity. Finding the total weight is important because it will help determine how to structurally frame for the unit. Consult your building department for the code requirements in your area.

Keep in mind when purchasing a whirlpool bath that they come in different sizes, shapes, and configurations that can radically affect your plans. Before you start, study the unit you want to purchase carefully and notice where the pump is located. You must decide how to access this pump once the tub has been placed in position. Some units have an access panel in the tub's skirt.

Figure 7-35 shows standard framing for a unit that sits on the level floor and extends into a bay area centered on the middle window. Now take a look at 7-36, and notice the cutout for the

7-35
Imagine how the tub for this bathroom in progress will be.

7-36
Note location of hot and cold water supply lines.

drainpipe. Here's a case where a floor joist was located in the opening of the cutout. Since the joist met—and possibly even exceeded—the code, it was large enough to allow the plumber to drill for the drainage pipe. Also note where the hot and cold water supply lines are located. The tub has been positioned so the pump and water connections are easily accessible from the room side.

Figures 7-37A through D show the framing for a tub that will be set into the floor so that it is partly above and partly below the floor, frequently called a *sunken* installation. Notice in 7-37B that joist hangers are used for both floor joists and cross members. Cut back the wallboard on the ceiling below far enough so you can tie into existing floor joists.

7-37A
For safety, cover hole with strong plywood adequately secured to floor so no one can fall through!

7-37B
Note use of joist hangers.

Whenever you set a hot tub unit into a floor, you must consider the space below, especially if it is a living space such as a basement. The walls built under this hot tub became a closet with a door—a great way to provide support and usable space at the same time (7-37C). If your hot tub unit requires a step or steps (7-37D), be sure to consult your building department, because a handrail might be required. In addition, use a nonskid surface on the treads.

7-37C
The space under this hot tub became a closet.

7-37D
This hot tub unit requires a step.

One last suggestion here—you might want to incorporate a steam room in your plans. They work well with hot tubs or whirlpool baths (7-38).

7-38
Imagine the luxury and convenience of a private steambath.

As you can see, a lot of planning must be made if you decide to include any of these products into your bathroom remodeling project.

Miscellaneous

Don't forget to frame for your medicine cabinet. Basically, just like framing for a window, you will need to know the measurements of your rough opening. If you plan to install your medicine cabinet on a bearing wall, the structure of your roof might require the installation of a header. This situation does not occur very often, but you should be aware that a header might be required.

There are other areas you should consider when framing. For example, if you are using a built-in heater, be sure to trial fit your heater to make sure that the framing is large enough to accept both the fixture and the wiring. You must also allow for backing (nailer) support for a wall-hung wash basin or toilet, shower head, rafter corners (where the ceiling meets the wall as shown in 7-39), grab bars, mirrors, and a shower/tub door. Also, an extra 2×4 to support the light box might help to get the proper distance from your light fixture to the top of the medicine cabinet.

You might discover, once it is installed, that the soil pipe extends beyond your stud wall, which will interfere with your wallboard installation. If this should occur, you will need to nail furring strips cut the same width as the framing members to the studs to bring the wall into the room beyond the soil pipe.

Remember that city, county, or state inspectors for electrical, plumbing, and building will have to inspect and approve different phases of the job. In fact, the first inspection will probably be *prior to any concealment of the work*. If you have hired a professional, he will request inspections at appropriate times. If you are doing the work yourself, be sure to ask in advance the different phases the inspectors will need to see. Remember the Nigerian proverb: "Not to know is bad; not to wish to know is worse."

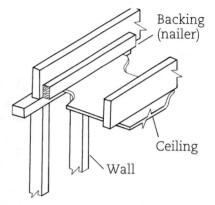

7-39 *Notice the backing attached to the joist—it is important to not float your wallboard. This situation is frequently encountered in basements.*

CHAPTER 8

Plumbing

YOU HAVE JUST FINISHED THE ROUGH-IN FRAMING, but it is still possible—especially after reading this chapter—that you might have to alter some of that framing. That's OK. Before starting the plumbing, you need to decide if you are going to do the work yourself or if you plan to hire a plumbing contractor. To me, plumbers are well worth the money because they have all the proper tools as well as experience and knowledge of the plumbing codes.

If you decide to do this phase of the job yourself, take the time to consult with the plumbing inspector at your building department. The inspector can answer any questions you might have (if you know what to ask!) and can give you other information that will help you to meet code requirements.

Other products

Are you bored with your plain, functional bathroom? If so, then this is the perfect time to consider new fixtures, some with jazzy new features. If you heat your home with hot water, then consider using a radiator equipped with an integral chromium-plated towel rail which is constantly heated by the radiator water. Or how about a corner whirlpool bath? With a contemporary skirt to match the bath, you'll have style as well as easy access to the pump and drain. This could be a great addition to a bedroom suite.

How about a trip back in time? If this idea appeals to you, look at the elegant Victorian bath shown in 8-1, which includes a china pedestal sink and a cast iron claw foot tub with a rim covered in oak. This would make an excellent guest bath.

Do you prefer a contemporary look? You can't go wrong with the sleek and fluid lines of this faucet's gold metal loop handle and chrome body (8-2). It also features a hot limit safety stop to prevent accidental scalding.

How about a classic style from the past? Figure 8-3 depicts a solid brass faucet—just the look for a claw foot tub. Keep in mind

8-1 *Victorian bath.*
Sunrise Specialty

American Standard

8-2
*Chrome and gold
contemporary faucet.*

The Broadway Collection

8-3
Classic solid brass faucet.

that your plumbing pipes will be exposed, so you might want to install chrome or brass plumbing parts to match the faucet.

What about fixtures for a barrier-free design? Figure 8-4 features a bathtub with a unique entrance, eliminating the difficulty of stepping over a sidewall. The convenient walk-in bathtub is

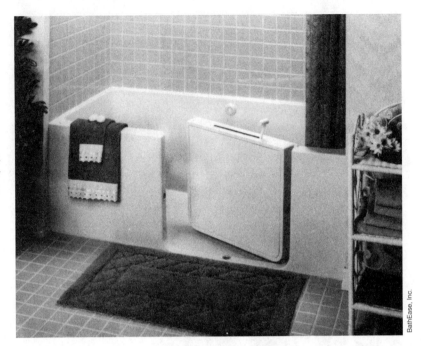

8-4
Tub designed for walk-in entry.

combined with a shower, and can also be customized with a whirlpool jet system. It is not, however, wheelchair accessible.

A standard toilet installation is not tall enough to be considered barrier-free. If you are planning a barrier-free bathroom, the toilet should be 17¼" high (18" with a seat) to make it wheelchair accessible.

For those in wheelchairs, a wash basin at a comfortable height is a must. The faucet should be mounted toward the front, with large lever handles.

Figure 8-5 shows a unique bathtub that comfortably conforms to the body once hot water is added. This bathtub is also available as a whirlpool bath. The nonslip surface of this tub minimizes the risk of a fall and greatly reduces the chance of injury should a fall occur.

When designing your shower area, you might want to consider installing two shower heads or a complete shower system (with

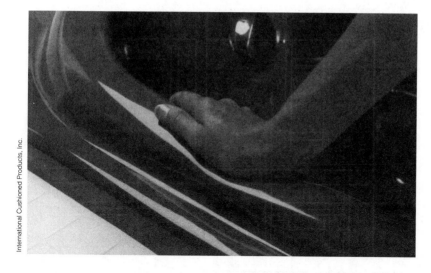

8-5
The Soft Bathtub.

more than two heads). If you are adding a whirlpool bath, a secondary hot water tank might come in handy. What about a bidet or a wall-hung toilet where the soil pipe (drain) comes through the wall? Now is the time to consider other types of fixtures—while the walls are still open.

Rough-in layout

Once you have reached some decisions about the fixtures you plan to install, it is time to carefully plan your rough-in plumbing, because its correct placement is essential at this stage of the project. Before you can begin, however, there are a few basic measurements that you need to know. Keep in mind that these measurements are only suggestions and personal preference could dictate some changes, such as the height of the wash basin or shower head. Some measurements cannot be changed, such as the location of the toilet flange from the finish wall.

The recommendations throughout this chapter are not the final word. Be sure to follow local building and plumbing codes. If you have any doubts—ask!

Figure 8-6 shows a rough-in layout for a basic three-fixture bathroom. The recommended measurements are keyed to numbers in the figure which are explained in the following paragraphs. It is important to know that the measurements are

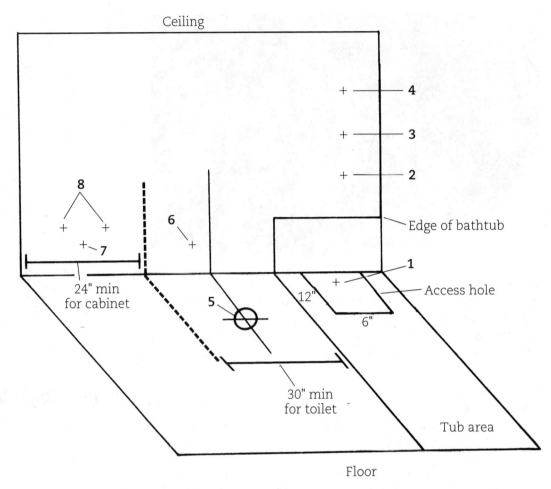

Ceiling

4

3

2

Edge of bathtub

8

7

6

1

24" min
for cabinet

Access hole

5

12"

6"

30" min
for toilet

Tub area

Floor

8-6 *Standard rough plumbing layout for a three-fixture bathroom setting.*

always given as "dead center." Remember, also, that there is a big difference between rough framing and a finished wall. This can have quite an impact, especially when a toilet is involved, because a half-inch difference (the thickness of wallboard) between rough and finish can determine whether or not you can set the toilet.

Bathtub measurements

1 The bathtub drain in the floor is 3" below the finish floor level and out 1½" from the rough wall. The tub drain is also centered in 30" of space, the width of the bathtub. You will need to cut a 6" by 12" access hole in the subfloor, 11" in from the sidewall, for the waste and overflow drains. If you are installing a shower, make sure you have your shower pan in hand so you can correctly locate the drain.

2 The tub spout is located 5" above the top edge of the bathtub.

3 The tub faucet is 10" to 12" above the top edge of the bathtub. In a shower stall, the shower faucet should be 48" from the finish floor.

4 The shower head should be 48" to 54" from the tub faucet.

Toilet measurements

5 The toilet drain from the center of the drain to the rough framing is 12½" and is centered in 30" minimum of finished space. This applies to a standard toilet installation. There are specialized toilets on the market that require different rough plumbing dimensions. Be sure to check the installation instructions included with your toilet.

6 The water supply is located 6" up from the finish floor and is 6" to the left of the center of the toilet drain as you face the wall. Bring the water supply line out 5" to 6" from the rough framing. It will be cut off later when it is time to install the shutoff valve.

Wash basin measurements

Once you have established the height and width of the cabinet you plan to install, you can determine where and how high to locate the drain. For the measurements shown in 8-6, the drain is centered in the minimum 24" space required for a wash basin. Smaller cabinets and wash basins are available if your bathroom does not have this much space for a vanity and wash basin.

7 The wash basin drain is 18" to 20"above the finish floor, depending upon the height of the cabinet, and is centered in a minimum of 24" of cabinet space.

8 The water supply lines are 4" to the left and right of the drain. Bring the lines out 5" to 6" from the rough framing (they will be cut off later when it is time to install the shutoff valves) and 22" to 24" off the finish floor, depending upon the height of the cabinet.

If you are installing a wall-hung sink for a barrier-free design, be aware that there are specific measurements regarding the overall sink height and the P-trap location that will affect the drain's location. Figure 8-7 provides a cross section of a barrier-free wash basin with all the required measurements.

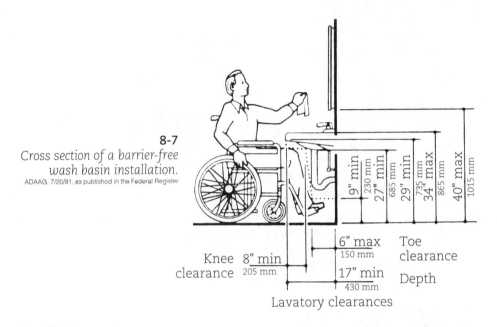

8-7
Cross section of a barrier-free wash basin installation.
ADAAG, 7/26/91, as published in the Federal Register

9" min / 230 mm
27" min / 685 mm
29" min
34" max / 735 mm
865 mm
40" max / 1015 mm

Knee clearance 8" min / 205 mm

6" max / 150 mm   Toe clearance
17" min / 430 mm   Depth

Lavatory clearances

Washing machine outlet box

If you plan to install a laundry in your bathroom, it would be a good idea to install a washing machine outlet (standpipe and water supply) box. A location just above the washing machine provides easy access to the shutoff. Install the trap to code, between 6" minimum and 18" maximum above the floor, and then locate the standpipe (also to code) 18" minimum to 30" maximum above the trap. These measurements should put the washing machine outlet box at a convenient height.

Venting requirements

Figure 8-8 shows the maximum run from the vent pipe to the trap arm (that's from the center of the P-trap back to the vent pipe). This illustration is known as *wet venting* and is typically used for half baths in older homes. The numbers in 8-8 correspond to the measurements discussed in the following paragraphs.

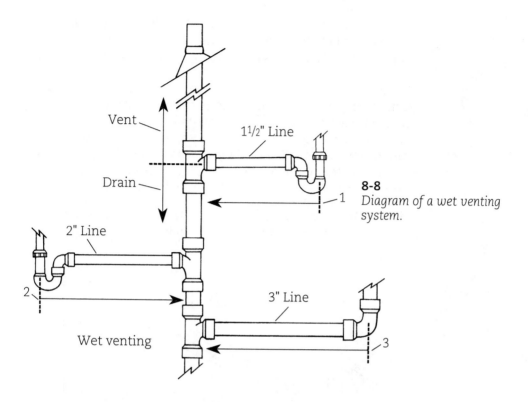

Vent

1½" Line

Drain

8-8
Diagram of a wet venting system.

2" Line

1

2" Line

2

3" Line

3

Wet venting

1. For a 1½" drainpipe, typically used for wash basins, bathtubs, and whirlpool baths, the maximum run is 42" to the vent pipe. Thereafter, the drain needs to be 2" for both bathtubs and whirlpool baths (8-9).

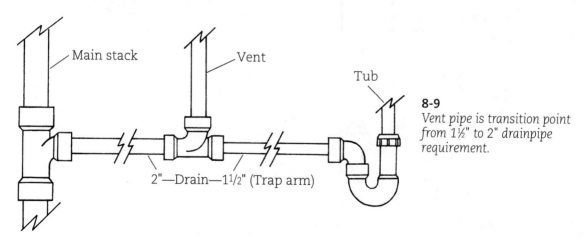

Main stack

Vent

Tub

8-9
Vent pipe is transition point from 1½" to 2" drainpipe requirement.

2"—Drain—1½" (Trap arm)

2. For a 2" drainpipe, typically used for a shower, dual wash basins, and laundry facilities, the maximum run is 60".

3. For a 3" drainpipe, the toilet, the maximum run is 72".

In your area, you might be required to install a dry venting system. This means that each fixture, except the toilet, has a 1½" vent that runs vertically and then runs horizontally with a ¼" to 1' slope upward to connect back into the 3" main vent. The minimum venting for a toilet is 2". Plumbing codes prohibit changing the direction of the vent pipe from vertical to horizontal at any point lower than 6" above the highest fixture served by that vent.

Figure 8-10 shows the horizontal vent at 42" off the finish floor. This exceeds the 36" minimum required for the wash basin.

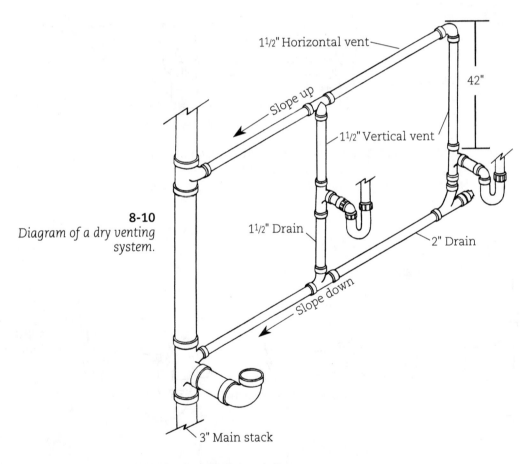

8-10
Diagram of a dry venting system.

Plumbers are so used to working with a 42" maximum for the trap arm distance that they automatically raise the horizontal vent to the same measurement. They also find it more comfortable to work at that height. Keep in mind that you cannot exceed the maximum measurement for the trap arm distance on a wet venting system as described earlier and shown in 8-8.

As you work with your plumbing configurations to meet codes, remember to allow enough framing space for your medicine cabinet or window. If you are planning for a recessed medicine cabinet, you might discover that the vent pipe is in the way. If you cut the vent piping above and below the medicine cabinet (allow enough room for framing and vent fittings), you can redirect the vent piping to one side or the other of the medicine cabinet. The flood line (i.e., the flood rim of a fixture) determines what fittings to use. If you are below the 6" flood line, in most cases you will be able to use a 45° elbow (8-11A). In the situation illustrated by the figure, a drainage fitting rather than a venting fitting is used to meet plumbing codes. You will need to comply with the codes in force in your area. If you are above the 6" flood line, then you can use a 90° elbow (8-11B). A 45° elbow is considered "vertical" while a 90° elbow is considered "horizontal." If your existing vent pipe is ABS or PVC, then use the same type of material to complete the redirection. However, if your existing vent pipe is galvanized, proceed by

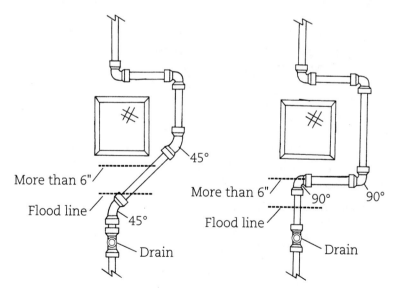

8-11A and B
Redirecting vent pipe below and above 6" flood line.

cutting the pipe with a metal saw, then construct the rerouting pipe in ABS or PVC and reconnect it to the galvanized end using a no-hub coupling (as shown later in this chapter).

ABS & PVC definitions

Before you can actually begin work on the drains, waste, and vents, you need to know what materials you are going to use and the different fittings involved. This part of the chapter will outline that information so you can get started. As mentioned earlier, you might already have galvanized pipes installed. But what if you have plastic pipes? What kind are they?

ABS (acrylonitrile-butadiene-styrene) DWV (drain, waste, vent) is black and is very resistant to a wide variety of materials ranging from sewage to commercial household chemicals. It is easy to work with, is joined by solvent cementing, and can easily be connected to steel, copper, or cast iron through the use of transition fittings.

PVC (polyvinyl chloride) DWV is white and is characterized by its high physical properties and resistance to corrosion and chemical attack by acids, alkalis, salt solutions, and many other chemicals. Like ABS, it is easy to work with and is also joined by solvent cementing.

CPVC (chlorinated polyvinyl chloride) is normally gray and has the same chemical characteristics as PVC but is used for water supply lines, both hot and cold. It is joined by solvent cementing. While it might be a quick and easy solution for plumbing projects, be sure to check with your building or plumbing department to ensure that it meets code.

There are a few basic facts you need to know about ABS and PVC solvent cement:

- Be sure to read and follow the manufacturer's directions when working with ABS or PVC solvent cement. Use only in a well-ventilated area.
- ABS solvent cement should be used *only* for joining ABS pipe and fittings.
- PVC solvent cement should be used *only* for joining PVC pipe and fittings.

- The solvent cement containers should always be covered when not in use to prevent excessive evaporation. *Do not use thinner.* Cement that shows signs of thickening or is lumpy should be discarded.

- A good joint is stronger than the pipe as the solvent chemically welds the fitting to the pipe. If you make a mistake, you will have to cut it out and put in a new fitting.

Figure 8-12 outlines in detail how to read the basic size of DWV reducing fittings. Take, for example, the DWV 45° double **Y** (lower right of 8-12) if you were working on a 3" drain line. Of the four

Drain, waste, & vent parts

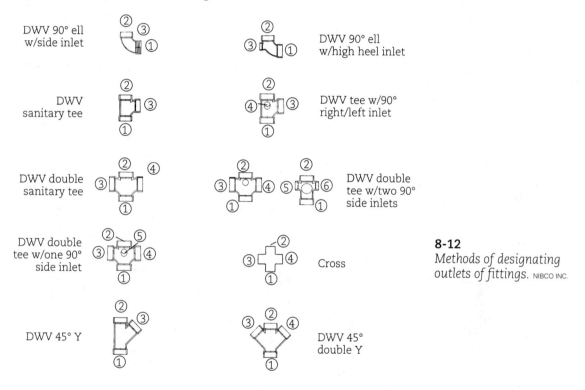

DWV 90° ell w/side inlet

DWV 90° ell w/high heel inlet

DWV sanitary tee

DWV tee w/90° right/left inlet

DWV double sanitary tee

DWV double tee w/two 90° side inlets

DWV double tee w/one 90° side inlet

Cross

8-12
Methods of designating outlets of fittings. NIBCO INC.

DWV 45° Y

DWV 45° double Y

Note: The largest opening establishes the basic size of a reducing fitting. The largest opening is named first, except for double branch elbows where both branches are reducing; the outlet is the largest opening and named last in both cases. In designating the openings of reducing fittings, they should be read in the order indicated by the sequence of the numbers 1, 2, 3, 4, 5 and 6. In designating the outlets of side outlet reducing fittings, the side outlet is named last.

openings, (1) could be used for the drain line going to the basement, (2) would continue the line through the roof to be used as the vent, (3) might pick up a 1½" drain line from the wash basin, and (4) might pick up a 2" drain line from the shower. The part you would need to order is a 45° double Y 3"×3"×2"×2". The manufacturers of the fittings do not produce a 45° double Y at 3"×3"×1½"×2". Instead, you need to reduce the 2" hole to a 1½" size using a flush bushing 2"×1½" in the (3) opening.

Fittings are commonly listed and sold two different ways: by descriptive name, and by number. The number serves essentially as a code for a very specific item description. Figure 8-13 is the key to understanding the item numbers. For example, if a fitting is listed as 5807-2, 8-13 shows the type of fitting to which these numbers correspond. The first two digits (58) refer to the type of material—in this case, ABS. The second two digits

DWV fittings

1 2 3 4-5

1 2 Type of materials	3 4 Type of fitting & description		5 Types of connections		
48 = PVC	01 = Coupling	48 = Offset Closet Flange	Numerical Suffix	Letter Suffix	LT = Long Turn
58 = ABS	03 = Female Adapter	51 = Closet Flange	2 = Fitting Connection	A = Adjustable Closet	N = No Hub
	04 = Male Adapter	53 = Closet Flange-Flush	3 = Female Connection	Flange	NS = No Stop
	05 = Soil Pipe Adapter	55 = Closet Flange	4 = Male Connection	B = Double Fixture Tee	P = Fits Pipe I.D.
	06 = 45˚ Ell	W/Knockout Test Plug	7 = Slip Joint Connection	CL = Water Closet Ell	R = Right
	07 = 90˚ Ell	60 = 60˚ Ell	9 = Side Inlet	CLAY = Clay	RP = Repair
	08 = 22 1/2˚ Ell	61 = 90˚ Ell W/Heel Inlet	13 = Female Connection	CO = Cleanout	S = Stack Upturn
	10 = Wye	63-73 = Various Stack	Indicating Hub x Fipt x Hub	DC = Dust Cap	SD = Sewer Drain
	11 = Tee	Fittings	14 = Female Connection	DP = Dust Plug	ASTM-D2852
	12 = Long Turn TY	76 = Return Bend	Indicating Hub x Hub x Fipt	EH = Extra Heavy	SW = Swivel
	14 = Test Tee	W/CO Hub x SJ	16 = Female Connection	EL = Extra Long	TE = Trap Ell
	16 = Cleanout	77 = Return Bend Hub x SJ	Indicating Hub x C.O. x Hub	F = Flush	TPA = Tray Plug
	17 = Cap	78 = Return Bend	17 = Female Connection	FX = Fixture Tee	Adapter
	18 = Plug	W/CO Hub x Hub	Indicating Fipt x Hub x Hub	KO = Knockout	TY = TY-Seal
	19 = Blind Flange	79 = Return Bend W/CO Hub x Hub	18 = Female Connection	L = Lead & Left	V = Vent
	26 = Plug (SPIG)	80 = P-Trap W/CO Hub x SJ	Indicating Fipt x Fipt x Hub	LH = Low Heel	
	27 = Cap (FIPT)	81 = P-Trap Hub x SJ	19 = Baffle Tee Hub x Hub x Hub	LR = Long Radius	
	28 = Cross	84 = P-Trap W/CO Hub x Hub			
	29 = Nipple	85 = P-Trap Hub x Hub			
	30 = True Y	91 = Drum Trap	Fitting terms and abbreviations		
	34 = Double Y	92 = P-Trap w/Union Hub x SJ			
	35 = Double Tee	95 = P-Trap W/Union	FIPT – Female NPT Thread		
	36 = Double Long	Hub x Hub	SPIG – Male End (Spigot)		
	Turn TY		MIPT – Male NPT Thread		
	37 = Double Ell		NPSM – Straight Thread for Mechanical Joint		
			SJ – Slip Joint		
			HUB – Plastic Socket		

8-13 *Key to NIBCO DWV fittings.* NIBCO INC.

(07) refer to the type of fitting and its description. According to 8-13, 07 is a 90° ell. The final digit (2) indicates the type of connection, and the example number is a fitting connection.

Many basic fittings and their corresponding key numbers are illustrated in 8-14. The actual use of many of these fittings is shown in 8-15. You will need to use many of these fittings in order to assemble correctly the plumbing required for your bathroom.

Adapters

    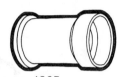

4801-7
5801-7
Reducing DWV
trap adapter
HUB × SJ

4803-2
5803-2
DWV spigot
female adapter
SPIG × FIPT

4803
5803
DWV female
adapter
HUB × FIPT

4804-2
5804-2
DWV spigot
male adapter
SPIG × MIPT

4805
5805
Reducing DWV
soil pipe adapter
HUB × SPIG

Bushing

4801-2-F
5801-2-F
DWV spigot
flush bushing/SPIG × HUB

Cap

4817
5817
DWV cap
HUB

Cleanout

4816
5816
DWV spigot cleanout
SPIG × cleanout w/plug

Closet flanges

4851
5851
DWV closet flange
HUB

Couplings

4801
5801
DWV coupling
HUB × HUB

4801-RP
5801-RP
DWV repair
coupling
HUB × HUB

Plugs

4818
5818
DWV plug
MIPT

5826
DWV FTG
plug
SPIG

8-14 *ABS and DWV fittings.* NIBCO INC.

Elbows

4806
5806
DWV 45° ell
HUB × HUB
(1/8 bend)

4806-2
5806-2
DWV 45°
street ell
SPIG × HUB
(street 1/8 bend)

4807
5807
DWV 90° ell
HUB × HUB
(1/4 bend)

4807-V
5807-V
DWV 90° vent ell
HUB × HUB
(1/4 bend, vent)

4807-2
5807-2
DWV 90°
street ell
SPIG × HUB
(street 1/4 bend)

4807-LT
5807-LT
DWV 90° long turn ell
HUB × HUB
(long turn 1/4 bend)

4807-2-LT
5807-2-LT
DWV 90° street long
turn ell
SPIG × HUB
(street long turn 1/4 bend)

4807-3
5807-3
DWV 90° ell
HUB × FIPT
(1/4 bend)

4808
5808
DWV 22 1/2° ell
HUB × HUB
(1/16 bend)

Tees

4811
5811
DWV sanitary tee
HUB × HUB × HUB

4811-2
5811-2
DWV street tee
SPIG × HUB × HUB

4811-14-FX
5811-14-FX
DWV fixture tee
HUB × HUB × FIPT

8-14 Continued.

4835
5835
Reducing DWV
double sanitary tee
HUB × HUB × HUB

4870
5870
DWV tee w/90°
right and left inlet
ALL HUB

Traps

4884
5884
DWV P-trap
w/cleanout
HUB × HUB ×
CLEANOUT W/PLUG

4885
5885
DWV P-trap
HUB × HUB

4892
5892
DWV P-trap
w/union joint
SJ × HUB

4895
5895
DWV P-trap
w/union joint
HUB × HUB

Ty's

Wyes

4812-LR
5812-LR
DWV combination long
radius ty
HUB × HUB × HUB

4810
5810
DWV 45° wye
HUB × HUB × HUB

4834
5834
Reducing DWV 45°
double wye
ALL HUB

8-14 *Continued.*

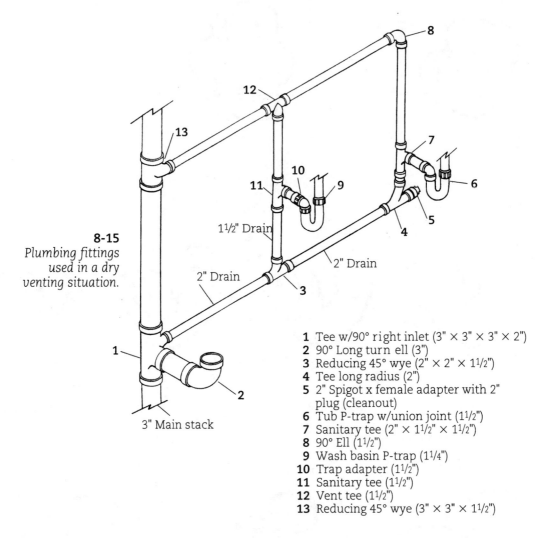

8-15
Plumbing fittings used in a dry venting situation.

13

12

8

7

10

11

9

6

5

4

1½" Drain

2" Drain

2" Drain

3

1

2

3" Main stack

1 Tee w/90° right inlet (3" × 3" × 3" × 2")
2 90° Long turn ell (3")
3 Reducing 45° wye (2" × 2" × 1½")
4 Tee long radius (2")
5 2" Spigot x female adapter with 2" plug (cleanout)
6 Tub P-trap w/union joint (1½")
7 Sanitary tee (2" × 1½" × 1½")
8 90° Ell (1½")
9 Wash basin P-trap (1¼")
10 Trap adapter (1½")
11 Sanitary tee (1½")
12 Vent tee (1½")
13 Reducing 45° wye (3" × 3" × 1½")

As is true in so many areas of bathroom remodeling, it is important to know what tools will be required and it helps to have some simple instructions to guide you through the process. When working with PVC, it is essential to apply a primer before using solvent cement in order to form a good joint. Omitting the use of primer could lead to system failure—and leaks! Primer is not required for ABS. The basic hand tools required are a pipe saw (fine-tooth handsaw with a special blade for plastic), an optional miter box, and a knife or deburring tool for cleaning the pipe ends after cuts.

The following instructions from NIBCO Inc. should help you better understand how to join ABS, PVC, or CPVC fittings into leak-proof permanent joints. Where differences occur, they are clearly noted.

1. Cut pipe squarely Use a miter box or sharp tube cutter with a special blade for plastic. If the end isn't square, the pipe won't seat correctly in the fitting and a weak joint will result.

2. Smooth end of pipe Remove the burrs on the end of the pipe after cutting, or the rough edge will scrape away the solvent during assembly. Use a pocket knife or special deburring tool—but make sure the end is perfectly smooth.

3. Check for interference fit Try the dry joint. The pipe should go in only about halfway; it should not go in all the way to the seat of the fitting. This type of fit is essential to forming a strong, solid joint.

4. Apply primer (PVC and CPVC only) Be sure surfaces are clean and dry. Use only primer specifically designed for PVC and/or CPVC. Apply primer first to the inside of the fitting, then to the outside of the pipe to the depth that will be taken into the fitting when seated. Be careful not to leave a puddle in the bottom of the fitting. Wait 5 to 15 seconds before applying solvent. For ABS, a primer is not required.

5. Apply solvent cement While the surfaces are still wet from the primer, brush on a full, even coating of solvent cement to the inside of the fitting. Again, be careful not to form a puddle in the bottom of the fitting. (Applying too heavy a coat or leaving a puddle in the fitting will usually result in some flow restriction.) Next, apply solvent to the pipe to the same depth as that of the primer. Again—a reminder of the critical importance of using the right solvent cement for the plastic you're installing. There is no "universal" solvent that will give totally satisfactory welded joints on all plastics. Use the right solvent for each kind of plastic.

6. Fit and position pipe and fitting Put the pipe and fitting together immediately, before the solvent evaporates. Use enough force to ensure that the pipe bottoms in the fitting socket. Give the fitting about a quarter turn as you push it on to ensure even distribution and absorption of the solvent. Then hold the joint firmly for about ten seconds (longer in cold weather) to allow the solvent to start bonding the two surfaces. If you position and release too soon, the interference fit will force the pipe out. NIBCO fittings are marked in eighths around the edge of the fitting cups to help you with alignment and positioning.

7. Check for the correct bead Check the ring of cement that has been pushed out during assembly and alignment. If it doesn't go all the way around the joint, it means you haven't used enough cement and the joint could leak.

8. Wipe off excess cement If the bead looks complete, wipe off the excess cement with a clean rag, leaving an even fillet all the way around. This helps the joint cure faster.

The following information applies to all three types of plastics (PVC, ABS, and CPVC). Where differences occur, they are clearly noted.

Don't be intimidated if you have cast iron pipe. Figure 8-16 shows a no-hub coupling connecting plastic pipe to a cast iron drainpipe. These couplings can also be used in many different DWV situations to connect plastic pipe to galvanized pipe. To install a no-hub coupling, first slide the band (shield) over the end of one pipe and push it off to the side. Then roll the rubber gasket back onto itself and fit it onto the end of the first pipe and then roll the gasket down onto the pipe. Then roll the open end of the gasket back up over itself and the pipe, fit the second pipe up against the gasket, and roll the gasket down over it. Finally, slide the shield down over the gasket and tighten the clamps. No-hub couplings come in four popular sizes: 1½", 2", 3", and 4".

Figure 8-17 shows a 1½" line connecting to a 2" line which then joins up to a 3" stack with a cleanout. The cleanout is required at the

8-16
*No-hub couplings connect
plastic to cast iron pipe.*

end of your main stack; be sure to make it easily accessible. Notice all the different fittings it took to accomplish this short transition.

Figure 8-18 features a 3" main line in the crawl space. On the left-hand side of the photo you'll notice a pipe stubbed through the subfloor for the toilet. You can also see three lines feeding into the main line. The lines on the upper and lower right are drain lines; the one on the upper left is a vent line.

8-18
A spiderweb of plumbing.

Figure 8-19 shows typical waste lines for dual wash basins. The trap arms are 1½", the vent is 1½", and the drain with a cleanout is 2".

You might want to install a built-in washing machine outlet box because it conveniently and neatly contains all the plumbing hookups necessary for a washing machine. Figure 8-20 shows the backside of a washing machine outlet box with

8-19
Dual wash basin plumbing assembly.

8-20
Washing machine outlet box.

a 2" trap arm connected to it. The center pipe is the vent line and the line to the right of that is for a laundry tray. You might want to consider adding either a wash basin or laundry tray when designing your plumbing assembly.

If you are replacing an older toilet, measure from the finish wall to the center of the closet flange. Some of the older toilets sat at 10" or 14" on center while the new ones are at 12". If you find yourself in this situation, the offset flange shown in 8-21 might allow you to complete your hookup without a major plumbing redo. A similar situation frequently occurs with rough-in plumbing in basements of new houses, as well as in older homes where the plumbing has been sitting since it was first installed. Be sure to ask your building department before using this product as it might not be allowed in your area.

8-21 *Offset closet flange.*

Other considerations

Before drilling into any floor joist for drainpipes, check with your building department. Normally, you can drill holes in a 2×10 or 2×12 large enough to accept a 2" pipe; however, you need to stay at least 2" away from the top or bottom edges of the joist. Sometimes when you drill through 2×4s in a wall, not much remains of the stud. Additionally, if you locate your piping too close to the edge, you could easily penetrate the pipe with your wallboard fastener. For that reason, it is important that you install stud guards (18-gauge galvanized steel, 1½"×3" or 1½"×5", 8-28A). They are required by code and can eliminate the frustration of having to reopen a wall to repair an accidental puncture, so don't forget them!

The code requires that you provide pipe supports every four feet for horizontal plastic pipes as well as support in unusual situations. You might want to try the economical plastic pipe-hanging strap that is now on the market. Whenever you use plumbing straps, it is a good idea to use roofing nails because they have larger heads.

Remember that all horizontal drains are required to slope down and back toward the main stack by ¼" to every 12". This is also true for vent piping, except vent pipes slope upward. It works out to a 1" pitch to every 4' of drain or vent length, and this pitch is also required on short runs as well. If your drain exceeds a ¼" to 12" grade between the trap and the vent, you might create what is known as a siphon trap, which could suck all the water out of the trap. If this happens, sewer gases and odors could enter your home.

Figure 8-22 shows an improper installation of a drain from a wash basin down toward the main stack. If you look carefully at the very center of the photo, you can see that the 1½" drain

8-22
A prime example of what your plumbing should NOT look like!

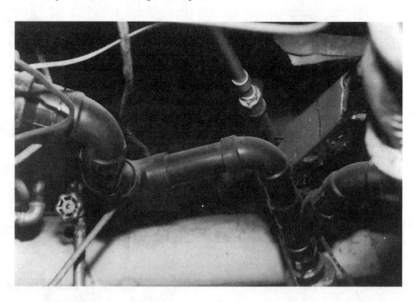

slopes back up before taking a 90° turn down into the stack. Under these circumstances, the sink would drain more slowly than normal because it lacks the proper gravity feed required for natural flow. As you can see, it is very important that you remember the proper slope: ¼" to 12".

An unusual situation is shown in 8-23. The drain and water supply lines to the wash basin had to be installed in the subfloor and then brought back into the wall. This type of installation was required because there was a barrier directly beneath the plate. To resolve this situation, the pipes were placed so the toe kick of the cabinet would neatly conceal them.

8-23
An unusual situation.

Don't be discouraged by such obstacles; a carefully thought-out plan can allow you to meet your goal.

Venting

What do you do with the vent pipes? In most cases, the individual vents (normally 1½") are run up through exterior or interior walls and are finally vented through the roof. In some cases, you might need to route the vent pipe back into the room parallel with a truss, and turn it so it passes through the trusses to tie into another vent.

Now you are ready to go through the roof with the vent pipe. Figures 8-24A and B show the proper steps to take when there is an existing roof covering. Visually examine the hub of the flashing to get an idea of how much roofing material to remove. Before final installation, trial fit your flashing to the roofing material to ensure that you have trimmed away enough. Use a hole saw ¼" to ½" larger than your vent piping to cut through the roof. You might want to use a drill bit extension if you cannot reach the area.

8-24A
Installing the flashing.

8-24B
Securing flashing to roof.

It is very important to make sure that the vent roof flashings are installed properly so you don't experience water leakage. Also be sure to extend the vent pipe up about 12" above the roof. Use galvanized roofing nails to secure the flashing to the roof (8-24B). Cold temperatures can cause some roofing materials to become exceptionally brittle. Take care when bending back the tab in order to nail the flashing. Be sure to consult the building department for the proper height and for other code requirements that might apply to this installation.

You might have an option other than to penetrate the roof with a vent pipe. With the help of a Durgo Air Vent, you can vent the pipe into the attic (8-25). This unit can only be used if a main vent has been installed through the roof. This venting product might or might not be approved for use in your area, so consult your building department before you purchase it.

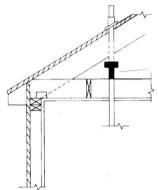

Conventional vent pipe through roof and flashing are eliminated

DURGO Air Vent in attic space

8-25
This device might save you from a rooftop vent installation. ENERJEE LTD.

Now that the drain and venting lines are in, it is time to start on the water supply lines. Actually, the procedures are somewhat similar, but you will be working with copper tubing and fittings. If you already have the galvanized line installed, you can use a copper adapter at the nearest threaded joint. These adapters have both male and female threads, and the threaded ends are produced to conform to standard pipe threads.

When you are installing water supply lines, it is a good practice to keep the hot and cold lines about 8" apart. This distance provides enough room to cut the copper lines. In most cases, you will be working with ½" pipe, but check the plumbing codes in your area to make sure you are in compliance.

Copper water supply lines

Parts Figure 8-26 shows some of the typical copper pressure fittings and reducers that you will use during installation of the water supply lines. Just as for ABS or PVC, there are some common abbreviations used in the industry so you will want to consult the list of abbreviations included.

Pressure fittings

90° Ell C × C   45° Ell C × C   Tee C × C × C   Tee C × C × F   Adapter C × M

Adapter C × F   90° Drop ell   Coupling with stop   Union C × C   Tube cap C
                 C × F   C × F

Fitting terms and abbreviations

C — Female solder cup
Ftg — Male solder end
F — Female NPT thread
M — Male NPT thread
Hose — Standard hose thread

Hub — Female end for soil pipe
Spigot — Male end for soil pipe
No Hub — Used with mechanical coupling
O.D. Tube — Actual tube size
SJ — Slip joint

Fitting reducers

Fitting reducer   Ftg. × C   Fitting adapter   Ftg. × F   90° Fitting ell   Ftg. × C

45° Fitting ell   Ftg. × C   90° Fitting ell   Ftg. × C   Fitting adapter   Ftg. × M
                              Long radius

8-26 *Pressure fittings and fitting reducers.* NIBCO INC.

Figure 8-27 shows some of the basic clamps required by code. They absorb tubing movement or eliminate contact altogether between pipe and framing surface; ribbed design permits faster cooling, and allows pipe to expand and contract freely, with minimum transmission of water line noise. These clamps are made of polyethylene; others are made of metal. Whenever you are working with copper and you choose to use metal clamps, straps, or hangers, make sure that they are made of the same material: copper to copper, for example. Other metals could react chemically with the copper piping.

Pipe clamp w/nail   Suspension
pipe clamp
Insulating
pipe clamp
Standard
pipe clamp

8-27
*Basic clamps
required by code.* Oatey Co.

To get a better idea of how and why fittings are used, take a look at 8-28A through F, six situations of fittings in use.

Clamps or tube straps are shown in use in 8-29A and B.

8-28A *A bathtub and shower valve. Notice the use of stud guard.*

8-28B *Washing machine outlet box; hot water supply line loops around box.*

8-28C *Hot and cold water supply lines for wash basin.*

8-28D *Cold water supply line for toilet.*

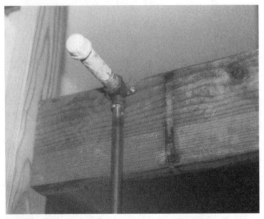

8-28E *A brass 90° drop ell for shower head; don't forget to fasten drop ell with screws, not nails.*

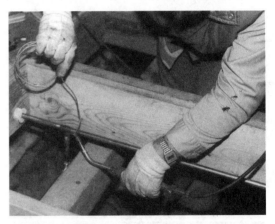

8-28F *Soldering a tee.*

Soldering copper fittings

Soldering is simply heating copper pipe and fittings to a high enough temperature so that they will melt the solder and draw it into, all around, and through the joint. Once the joint has cooled, the strength of that joint is equal to, or even greater than, the strength of the copper pipe itself.

8-29A *Insulated pipe clamps.*

8-29B *Galvanized and copper tube straps.*

Soldering is a simple process. By following these steps and tips, you'll be able to accomplish this job with great pride.

The first thing to do is cut the pipe to length. I find the best tool for this to be a tube (roller) cutter. Place the cutter over the tube and tighten the roller firmly to the tube—but not so tight that it compresses the tube or that you are unable to turn the cutter. Next turn the cutter around the tube. When you have made one complete revolution, tighten the roller. Keep tightening with each complete revolution until the tube is finally cut.

Once the pipe has been cut, the burrs need to be removed from both the inside diameter (I.D.) and the outside diameter (O.D.) of the tube. You can clean the I.D. with a flat metal reamer and the O.D. with emery paper. To achieve good soldered joints, the mating surfaces must be absolutely and unconditionally clean so the filler metal (solder) can *wet* the surfaces easily and evenly. The cleaner the surface, the easier the wetting process. *Wetting* is the process whereby the solder draws itself up and flows evenly in and around the joint, and bonds to the surfaces. If the copper is dirty, the solder balls up and adheres to itself, not to the copper. These areas then cause voids in the solder joints, and create leaks in the system.

8-30A *Fitting brush.* Oatey Co.

8-30B *Cleaning a copper fitting.* NIBCO INC.

8-31A *Fluxing copper water tube.* NIBCO INC.

8-31B *Fluxing copper fitting.*
NIBCO INC.

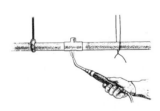

8-32 *Use temporary support of wire or string.* NIBCO INC.

Clean about ½" more of the tube than the depth of the fitting socket. This provides a clean area on which to start the solder and melt it into the joint. The fitting socket should be cleaned to the same standard as the copper tubing. The inside of the fitting is one of the joint surfaces, and it is very important that this area also be clean. Even though it is shiny and new, clean the fitting socket with an emery cloth or with a special wire brush made especially for this purpose (8-30A and B). Be careful not to overclean, especially when using emery cloth; copper is a soft metal and it doesn't take much to reduce the size of the tube, which you don't want to do! Just clean the parts without removing metal. Powered wire brushes are available if you are cleaning enough fittings to make a power brush economical.

If there are small dents or depressions in either the fittings or the tube, toss the fitting away, cut off the damaged area of the tube, or cut all new tubing.

You are now ready to solder the joints, but you need one more ingredient to start the process: solder flux. Flux usually comes in a paste form and contains a mild acid which, when applied, covers the area to be soldered and protects it from oxidation. The mild acid is slightly corrosive and has a cleaning action.

Flux should be applied with a clean brush. Apply in a thin, even layer and use only enough flux to properly cover the surfaces to be joined. Too much flux does not improve the joint; in fact, it interferes with the soldering process (8-31A and B).

Assemble joints as soon as they are cleaned and fluxed. Align the tube and fitting so they are straight and square. They should be supported horizontally as well as vertically while you are soldering. Failure to provide proper support can cause misalignment which can affect the soldered joint by changing the space between the tube and the fittings. If only temporary support is required, then support the tube with wire or string until the joint has set (8-32).

Now you are ready for the final steps: heating the joints and applying the solder in just that order. First, you will need a torch that runs on propane or a similar fuel, and lead-free solid wire solder. You might be able to rent a torch at your local rental center. Set the torch for a small flame—it will take you a little longer, but it's easier to use and you'll have better control. Heat the tube first, then move the flame back and forth to heat the fitting and the tube alternately (8-33A and B).

Your flame should be held far enough away from the fitting that the sharp point of the inner cone of the flame just touches the metal. The heat will then be evenly spread by the larger outer envelope of the flame.

While heating the area to be soldered, touch it with the solid-wire solder from time to time to see if it melts. Do not melt the solder in the flame but rather by contact with the heated joint. When the solder begins to melt, even a little, move the flame to the heel or center of the fitting. Manipulate the flame so that the entire fitting is hot and at the same time feed the solder into the joint (8-34). When the joint looks full, remove the flame—do not overheat. To be sure of the joint, some plumbers will remove the heat and apply solder all around the joint a second time. This can be done as long as the tube is hot enough to melt the solder.

If you want to produce a clean-looking joint, use a damp cloth to wipe away any excess solder and flux. Do this at once, while the joint is still hot. (This step is not required.) The joint will cool very quickly in still air.

Repairs & other considerations

If your tubing gets damaged during your remodeling project—and it certainly can—don't get too excited. It can easily be repaired, as shown in 8-35.

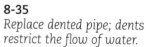

8-35
Replace dented pipe; dents restrict the flow of water.

Before the wallboard covers the piping, the plumbing inspector might require you to test the DWV and water supply lines. The best way to do this is to install plugs into and caps over all openings, turn the water lines on, and fill all drain lines. Then inspect each fitting for leakage.

Hook up the waste and overflow drain to the tub and install the tub in place (8-36 and 8-37). Clear and helpful diagrams are included in the packaging of your waste and overflow drains. Be sure to follow the manufacturers' instructions.

8-36 *Underside of bathtub with P-trap connected to waste and overflow drain.*

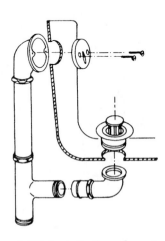

8-37 *Installation of waste and overflow drains.*
American Standard Inc.

If you live in a radon problem area and are installing a bathroom in the basement, you need to seal all cracks and openings between the dirt and your plumbing pipes. You can caulk around the toilet flange and at the drainage and vent pipes going up a wall. There is a tub trap enclosure on the market that will seal off the bathtub trap from the dirt and still allow the trap to be accessible.

If you plan to install a preformed shower base, now is the time to do it. Figure 8-38A and B illustrate typical shower drain assemblies. The instructions accompanying the product you purchase might show a different installation. Follow the manufacturer's directions.

Install drain to the shower floor. Make sure latex or silicone caulking is applied to the underside of drain body flanges and secure it as shown. Do not use oil base caulking for any plastic type drain. May cause drain to break or distort.

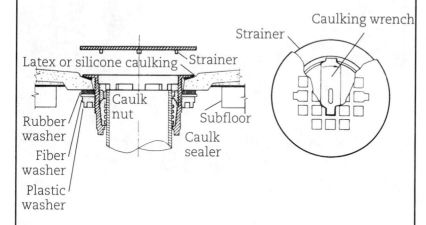

Caulking wrench

Strainer

Latex or silicone caulking — Strainer

Caulk nut

Subfloor

Rubber washer

Fiber washer

Plastic washer

Caulk sealer

8-38A
Plastic self-caulking drain.
The Swan Corporation

For self-caulking (speedy seal)—Using the caulking wrench provided, screw in caulking nut (clockwise) until it is tight enough to compress sealer. Install strainer by snapping it in the drain body.

Install shower floor by sliding metal drain cup over drain pipe. Slide caulk sealer over drain pipe. Complete installation by snapping strainer into place.

Latex or silicone caulking — Strainer

Rubber washer
Fiber washer
Brass locknut
Drainpipe

Lead

Subfloor
Drain body
Oakum

8-38B *Pressed-in drain.*
The Swan Corporation

The person in 8-39 is using a soil pipe cutter to score and snap a cast iron pipe. This tool can be rented at your local tool rental store.

Tool tips

Plumbing   111

8-39
*Use the proper tool to cut a
soil pipe.*

In 8-40, a Hole Hawg (right angle drill) is being used to cut a
hole for the toilet. The self-feeding bit simplifies the work of
boring a pipe-sized hole in wood. The Hole Hawg is a powerful
tool and must be securely held and braced to prevent operator
injury or damage to the tool. If you are cutting holes in studs,
rest the pipe handle against a stud to help steady the tool.

8-40
Hole Hawg right angle drill.

For boring holes for water supply lines, you can use a standard drill and spade (flat) wood bit. These bits utilize high speed for efficient cutting and perform poorly at slow speeds. Auger bits are preferred by many electricians and plumbers. An auger bit with a self-feeding screw point will pull the bit through the material, so hang onto that drill! For cutting existing galvanized or ABS/PVC pipes, consider using a reciprocating saw as shown in 8-41. Be sure to wear goggles and use only the blade recommended for the material you are cutting.

This chapter is filled with useful information that you need to complete your bathroom remodeling project. It wouldn't hurt to reread the chapter—it's possible you'll get some new ideas from a second reading.

Now it's time to move on to the electrical phase of the project. Be sure to read the next chapter carefully!

8-41 *Reciprocating saw.*
Milwaukee Electric Tool Corporation

CHAPTER 9

The electrical system

NOW THAT YOU HAVE MADE IT through the plumbing chapter, it is time to dig into the electrical work. You might choose to hire an electrician, and that's OK, but before you make that decision, read this entire chapter. It's possible that your plans do not call for you to move or add any electrical fixtures. If you do plan to make some electrical changes, this chapter provides some easy steps to help you accomplish this phase of the job.

There are two very important facts to keep in mind when working with or around electricity. **NEVER work with the electricity on.** *Always* disconnect the electricity before you begin the project, either by removing the fuse or by tripping the breaker in the main panel. If you have any doubts or you are not sure, then use a tester and check the line you are about to work on. It is also important to make sure that your wiring complies with code, either national, state, or local; check with your building or electrical department. Even your choice of lighting for a closet might be limited by code—it pays to check first.

New products

Before going right into the electrical, let's talk about some new products. If you decide to purchase and install any new products, you might have to add a new line from the power source (breaker box) or you just might have to relocate the wiring. Always follow the manufacturer's instructions for final hookup.

Have you ever considered a phone in the bathroom? If you are not sure at this time, then go ahead and put the phone line in anyway. The best location for the phone is near the toilet, so bring the phone line up into a single gang (outlet/switch) box on a wall that is close to the toilet and put a blank cover over the box. This way, if you decide later to put the phone in, you will be ready to do so.

IRON-A-WAY, Inc.

9-1
When choosing an ironing center, be aware that there are many options available. Some contain a storage shelf, a light, and an outlet for the iron while others contain only an ironing board.

Another item you might want to consider is a wall-mounted hairdryer located near the vanity. If you have a laundry in the bathroom, consider adding a built-in ironing center (9-1). If you like warm towels, you might want to have an electric towel warmer.

There are lights to consider. If you decide to install a light in the tub/shower area, make sure the light meets code and is a moisture-proof unit. You might prefer to use a ventilating fan/light combination unit, as shown in 9-2. There are also products on the market (fans and fan/light/night-light units) that turn on automatically, triggered either by motion or humidity or both.

Lights & exhaust fans

Broan Mfg. Co., Inc.

9-2
This fan/light also features a night-light for extra safety.

When choosing an exhaust fan, be sure the fan can adequately handle the moisture and odors in the room. The more CFMs (cubic feet per minute) the fan has, the better the unit will work. I recommend using units with 90 to 160 CFMs depending on the conditions and size of the room. Do you have a steam room or a whirlpool bath? Less expensive fans have lower CFMs and cannot handle the steam generated by such items. Check the sone rating of the fan also. The lower the sone number, the quieter the fan will be. There are also heat lamps with exhaust fans built in as one unit.

What about fans that have multiple uses? They can boost the efficiency of dryer venting or provide adequate venting in spa or shower areas where building codes might not allow exhaust fans to be used directly. Figure 9-3 shows such a fan system venting both the shower and the water closet area. If you live in a radon problem area, you might want to install a fan specifically designed for radon mitigation.

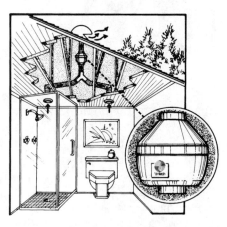

9-3 *A fan system that can accommodate more than one bathroom and multiple venting points.* FANTECH, Inc.

Heat How is your existing bathroom heat? Is it time for a change or for something new? The heater in 9-4 is conveniently mounted on an otherwise unusable wall. Also consider the direction of heat flow when mounting your heater. Chapter 15 details the installation of such a unit. At this stage of the job, it is important to provide wiring in the right place (9-5). If you have cold feet, you might consider a heater that will fit in the toe kick space of a vanity.

If—like me—you enjoy padding around the house in bare feet, this is the time to consider radiant heat in the floor. There are kits available that include all the parts to complete the system,

9-4
When installing a wall-mounted heater, consider the direction of heat flow and the possibility of mounting it on an otherwise unusable wall as shown in this photo.

9-5
You will want to purchase your wall-hung heater before you do the electrical so you can properly site the wiring.

including a wall-mounted thermostat, floor temperature sensor, and spacer strips that allow for easy mounting of the electric cable to either wood or concrete subfloors (9-6A). The installation guide outlines the final wiring connections. The

The electrical system   117

9-6A *Spacer strips allow easy installation of electric cable to wood or concrete subfloors.* Gyp-Crete Corp.

9-6B *Therma-Floor Easy-Mix is poured over cables and smoothed and flattened with finishing tool.* Gyp-Crete Corp.

only thing left to do is to pour the floor mix over the cables (9-6B) and smooth the surface with concrete finishing tools. Once the floor has hardened (within three hours), you can walk on it. In about three to five days, you can apply your finish floor. The entire process (according to the manufacturer) from start to finish takes approximately four hours.

Electrical symbols & parts

If you ever had an opportunity to view a set of architectural plans, you might have noticed symbols and not understood them. Figure 9-7 shows some of the standard symbols and their meanings. Using standard symbols makes electrical plans easy to read. A solid line shows wires in ceilings or walls, and a dotted line shows wires in or under the floor. When drawing your bathroom plans, you will want to use standard symbols.

Symbols for 120-volt appliances

⊕ Ceiling light fixture

⊢⊕ Wall light fixture

⊃○ Duplex receptacle

WP ⊃○ Weatherproof duplex

≡○ 240-volt receptacle

↳S Single-pole switch

↳S₃ 3-way switch

↳S₄ 4-way switch

▬ Electrical service panel

▭ Meter

DW ≡⬠ Dishwasher

SP ≡⬠ Sump pump

WP ≡⬠ Water pump

GD ≡⬠ Garbage disposal

VF ≡⬠ Vent fan

FF ≡⬠ Furnace fan

AC ≡⬠ Air conditioner

W ≡⬠ Clothes washer

H ≡⬠ Portable space heater

Symbols for 240-volt appliances

WH ≡⬠ Hot water heater

R ≡⬠ Range

D ≡⬠ Clothes dryer

AC ≡⬠ Central air conditioning

H ≡⬠ Heater

9-7 *Standard electrical symbols.*

It's possible your bathroom has metal electrical boxes, and that's OK because they are still on the market. Figure 9-8 shows four basic boxes. The octagon is used for the overhead or sidewall installation of lighting and for support of other types of fixtures. The square is normally used as a junction box. It can also be used for single or double outlets (receptacles) or switches when used in conjunction with special covers as shown in 9-9.

9-9
Combination square-drawn and tile covers. RACO INC, subsidiary of Harvey Hubbell Incorporated

Switch boxes normally contain wiring devices (outlets or switches). The handy box (sometimes called a utility box) is used as a junction box, but can also be used for wiring devices. Whenever you use a metal box, it is important to use wire connectors to bring wire into the box (9-10). Remove one of the

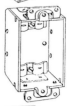

Octagon

Square

Switch

Handy

9-8 Box types. RACO INC, subsidiary of Harvey Hubbell Incorporated

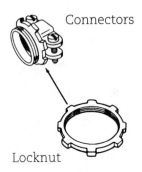

Connectors

Locknut

9-10 *Wire connectors.*
RACO INC, subsidiary of Harvey Hubbell Incorporated

knockouts and install the wire connector so that the connector is on the outside of the box, and the locknut is on the inside. Once secured, you can then feed the wire through the connector and tighten the clamp screws. Some metal boxes have built-in clamps; in this case, remove the knockout, insert the wire, and tighten the clamp. Also make sure that all your ground wires are tied together and grounded to the box, using either a ground clip or a ground screw as shown in 9-11.

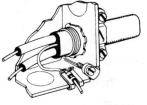

Ground clip

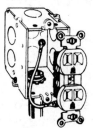

9-11 *Grounding.* RACO INC, subsidiary of Harvey Hubbell Incorporated

Even though you have metal boxes, you can still use plastic nail-on boxes as shown in 9-12. Again, be sure that all your ground wires are tied together.

9-12
Plastic boxes.
RACO INC, subsidiary of Harvey Hubbell Incorporated

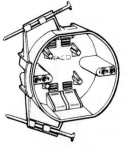

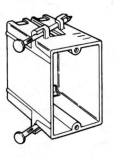

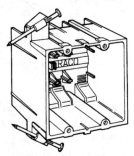

New work
ceiling box with
captive nails

New work single-
gang box with
captive nails

Two-gang
work box with
captive nails

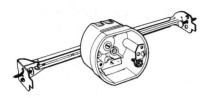

Setup box
Adjustable bar hanger

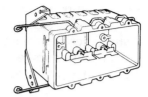

Three-gang work box
with captive nails

When you need to install a new outlet or switch in an existing wall but you do not want to open the wall, consider using cut-in boxes as shown in 9-13. There are two different styles and they both work well.

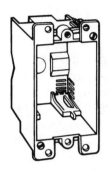

9-13
Old work single gang box.
RACO INC, subsidiary of Harvey Hubbell
Incorporated

Saddle holds box
behind wall. Clamps
grip cable.

Wire size & capacity

Electrical wire is sized by numbers: the smaller the wire, the larger the number, and vice versa. When remodeling your bathroom or incorporating a laundry, you will use wires sized from 14 to 8.

Wires sized 14 and 12 are used in standard 120-volt circuits for lighting, outlets, switches, and other small appliances. Wires sized 10 and 8 are normally used in 240-volt circuits for electric dryers, water heaters, and other major appliances. It is not enough just to know the number size—you also need to know the amps (amperes) and watts that correspond to each size of wire. For example:

Wire size	Amps	Watts	Wire size	Amps	Watts
14	15	1800	10	30	3600
12	20	2400	8	40	4800

It is very important when installing electrical wiring that you use the proper size fuse(s) or breaker(s) to protect the wire against overloads or short circuits. For example, if you are working with number 12 wire, which carries a 20-amp rating, then you need to use a 20-amp fuse or breaker.

The wire can only handle so many watts before it becomes overloaded and blows fuses or kicks off breakers. When using a number 12 wire on a 120-volt circuit, you need to know it can only handle 2400 watts before it becomes overloaded. Knowing how many watts go into the line is very important. To give you a better idea of what 2400 watts equals—if you turn on 24 100-watt light bulbs all at the same time, that would equal 2400 watts (24×100 watts) based on 120 volts. It is common practice, however, for safety's sake, to plan on only using 80 percent of a circuit's capacity. In this case, a 2400-watt circuit would have a maximum capacity of 1920 watts.

To better understand electricity, it is essential to understand the three basic measurements of electrical power: amps, volts, and watts. To make it simple, moving electricity creates a current called amperes (amps). When electricity moves under pressure, it is known as voltage. When the main power source comes into your home, the voltage fluctuates between 114 and 126 volts. Even though the National Electrical Code calculates electricity on 115 and 230 volts, you'll find that many professionals, packaged products, and other how-to and professional books refer to voltage as 120 volts and 240 volts.

When you take these two elements—amps and volts—and multiply them together, you get the number of watts. For example, 120 volts times radiant heat at 6.7 amps equals 804 watts. What if you don't know the amps but you want to? Simply divide the watts by the voltage. For example, a wall-mounted hair dryer at 1200 watts divided by 120 volts equals 10 amps. There is one more thought on the subject of watts— one watt used for a period of one hour equals one watt-hour, and 1000 watt-hours equal one kilowatt.

All the information covered so far concerning wire size and rating relates to copper wiring, and I will continue this throughout the chapter. If you prefer to use aluminum wire, be sure to check the codes for your area—but be aware that it does not conduct electricity as efficiently as copper. In order to achieve with aluminum wire the same amperage rating as copper, you must go up one wire size. For example, a copper wire at number 14 would be a number 12 in aluminum.

Wire is manufactured in coded colors. Regardless of the color of the wire, when you work with existing wiring, it is a good idea to use a voltage tester to determine whether or not a wire is hot, and whether the white wire is indeed the neutral wire. **There is one exception to the rule that the white wire is always neutral:** *If the power source goes through a light fixture and then to the switch, you may use the white wire as a hot black wire. Whenever you use a wire in this type of situation though, it is required by code that you place a piece of black tape around the white wire to identify it as a hot wire.*

Red and blue wires are used for hot wires; and green, green and yellow, and bare copper are grounding wires. Two or more insulated color-coded wires combined in a non-metallic (plastic) sheath create different types of cables. (The most common of these cables used in residential electrical installations is known as *Romex*.) Cables are stamped with numbers and letters, such as these typical classifications: *Type NMB 12-2G* or *Type NMB 12-3G*. These stamped numbers and letters mean the following:

* Type NM means *nonmetallic*.
* B refers to insulation up to 90°C.
* 12 means it is a size 12 wire.
* 2 means two insulated wires (black and white).
* 3 means three insulated wires (black, red, and white).
* G means it has a ground wire.

Always connect the black wire to a dark or copper-colored terminal on switches, outlets, and to the black wire of lights and fixtures. Connect the white wire to the light or silver-colored terminal of all outlets and to the white wire of lights and fixtures.

Wire specifications

Panel box & new circuits

It might be a good idea if you are planning a major remodel of your bathroom, especially if you plan to add today's modern luxury-type fixtures, to check out your electrical service. Many older homes have 60-amp or 100-amp panels. That was sufficient for an earlier time period, but times change and so do our needs. You might have to upgrade your service to a 150- or 200-amp main service panel to fit those needs.

The power source—three wires—enters your home through the meter. After the two black wires (hot—120 volts each) from the meter are connected to their proper terminals (main disconnect) in the panel box, the white (neutral) wire from the meter is connected to the neutral bar in the panel, which is bonded to the cabinet. When the entire system is properly grounded to a copper grounding rod (driven 8' into the ground) and a cold water pipe (consult your building or electrical department for their grounding procedures), you will be able to create the new circuits needed for your project. Keep in mind that some panel boxes have ground connections on the neutral bar while others have ground connections on a separate terminal bar in the panel.

A 120-volt circuit is one breaker. The hot wire (normally black) is attached to the breaker, the white wire is attached to the neutral bar, and the ground wire (bare) is connected to the ground bar (for service panels, these are normally the same bar).

For a 240-volt circuit, a double breaker (two 120-volt circuits) is required. One black wire (hot) will connect to one breaker, and a white wire (hot) will be connected to the other breaker. The ground wire is connected to the ground and/or neutral bar in the panel box.

GFCI, outlets, & switches

New on the scene is the requirement for ground fault circuit interruptors (GFCIs) in new bathrooms and for hot tubs. This outlet is a safety device that monitors the equal flow of electricity through the hot (black) wire and the neutral (white) wire. It will shut itself off automatically (in about $^{25}/_{1000}$ of a second) if a current leakage to ground exceeds 5 milliamps (1 milliamp equals $^{1}/_{1000}$ of an amp) in the circuit. This reduces the danger of current leakage and the possibility of shock hazard if you touch an improperly grounded appliance or light fixture.

There are three types of GFCIs available. The portable GFCI plugs into existing grounded outlets. There is also a built-in GFCI (9-14). Finally, there is a GFCI breaker that fits into the service panel just like a standard breaker, except the neutral wire from the circuit cable connects to the neutral lug of the breaker, and the neutral pigtail on the breaker connects to the neutral bar in the panel. Be careful not to confuse the white pigtail with the white wire in the cable.

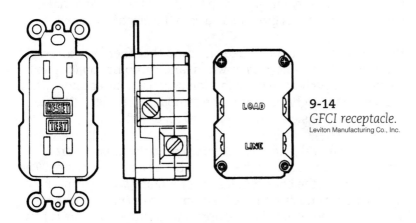

9-14
GFCI receptacle.
Leviton Manufacturing Co., Inc.

It certainly makes good sense to use GFCI outlets in rooms (or on fixtures in rooms) where water and electricity are both together, such as a bathroom. It is also important to know that *a GFCI must have its own individual circuit.* If it is on a circuit that has a neutral wire sharing another circuit, the GFCI might not properly perform its safety function.

A GFCI device is available with built-in ground fault protection that can be installed to provide GFCI protection only through its own outlet, or it can be wired to feed through devices (other outlets) protecting all or part of a branch circuit. While we are on the subject of GFCI receptacles, take a moment to look at 9-15. This outlet can replace standard switch and outlet devices and still provide the GFCI protection which is required by the National Electrical Code (NEC) to be used in bathrooms.

There are new styles of outlets on the market today that might fit the decor of your new bathroom, so you will want

9-15 *Combination switch and GFCI outlet.* Leviton Manufacturing Co., Inc.

to check them out before you purchase a standard outlet. A three-hole grounding outlet is required by the NEC in remodels and new construction. If you are thinking of replacing an existing ungrounded two-hole outlet with the new style, be aware that your electrical system might not be grounded, so the new three-hole outlet wouldn't accomplish anything. If you use a three-hole outlet in an ungrounded system, you must take a ground wire to either a cold water line or back to the service panel. Otherwise, if the outlet box is metal, ground the outlet to the box and make sure the metal box is grounded back to the electrical panel.

When choosing an outlet, keep in mind that there are three basic types: side-wired, back-wired, and combination (duplex). Personally, I prefer the combination because I never know what the situation might be during the remodeling project. Chapter 15 shows the basic wiring hookup to an outlet.

Remember that the hot (black) wire goes to the brass-colored screw and the neutral (white) goes to the silver-colored screw. The green screw at the bottom is for the grounding wire. The back-wired or push-in outlets have holes in which to insert the wires. The back of the outlet also features a strip gauge that shows how much insulation to strip off the end of the wire. Also look for the word *white* printed on the backside—that is the side for the white neutral wires. As you look at the outlet, notice the vertical plug holes which indicate that this is a 15-amp outlet. If the left-hand hole has a horizontal **T**, then it is a 20-amp outlet.

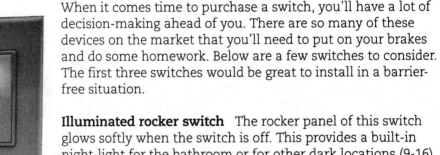

When it comes time to purchase a switch, you'll have a lot of decision-making ahead of you. There are so many of these devices on the market that you'll need to put on your brakes and do some homework. Below are a few switches to consider. The first three switches would be great to install in a barrier-free situation.

Illuminated rocker switch   The rocker panel of this switch glows softly when the switch is off. This provides a built-in night-light for the bathroom or for other dark locations (9-16).

9-16 *Illuminated rocker switch.*  Leviton Manufacturing Co., Inc.

Pilot light rocker switch This switch is the same as above but in reverse. The switch lights up when it is on, acting as an indicator light to let you know the switch is on.

Passive infrared occupancy sensor switch This switch can help to save energy by turning on incandescent or fluorescent lights when you enter a room and turning them off when no motion is detected.

Slide dimmer and ceiling fan speed control This preset device provides a separate rocker switch to allow on-off switching without disturbing a preset brightness level or fan speed (9-17).

Rotary dimmer This product is available in two different variations—a push-on/push-off model that requires rotation of the dial for full-range dimming, and a model that rotates on to the desired brightness level and then rotates toward the off position for dimming.

Toggle dimmer This product provides full-range lighting control and can be used in combination with a standard toggle switch for a coordinated look. It has positive on/off action and is available with an illuminated clear toggle.

9-17 *Slide dimmer and ceiling fan speed control.*
Leviton Manufacturing Co., Inc.

Single-pole switch This is the most commonly used switch in the home. Its primary function is to turn on and off. You might have switches of the older style which make a loud clicking sound when you operate the toggle. If this is the case, you might want to consider replacing them with quieter switches. The toggle is marked *on* and *off*.

Three-way switch This type of switch is used in pairs to control a light or outlet from two separate locations. It is great for bathrooms with two doors. The switch has three terminals (screws): one black or copper-colored, and two brass or silver-colored. There are no *on* and *off* markings on the toggle.

Four-way switch A four-way switch works in conjunction with three-way switches to control lights or outlets from three or more locations. It has four brass-colored terminals and no *on* or *off* markings on the toggle.

Tips to remember

Depending on the code for your area, you might be required to ground switches. If that is the case, then you can use single-pole switches with a ground screw attached. Outlets located within 6' of any wash basin must be GFCI protected (National Electrical Code). You might be required to have only GFCI outlets in your bathroom. Check with your building or electrical department.

If you included a laundry in your bathroom, your washer will require a 20-amp circuit. Extra outlets can be on the same circuit. The dryer will require a minimum 30-amp circuit (remember, this is a 240-volt circuit).

Depending on the appliances, fixtures, heat, etc., you include in your bathroom, you might need more than one 20-amp circuit. Some of the items you choose to install might require a 240-volt circuit instead of a 120. Check the items carefully.

Whirlpool baths and hot tubs are either plug-in or wired in directly (hardwired). Whatever the case, the outlet or junction must be on a GFCI-protected line, and at least one convenience outlet must be located a minimum of 5' from the inside lip of the unit and not more than 10' away (NEC).

Set your outlet boxes so they are convenient for you. Place switch boxes 48" off the floor to the center of the box. Remember to locate the box on the same side of the doorframe that the doorknob is on.

Whenever your wires enter or leave a box, take time to secure the wire with staples within 12" of the box (9-18). It is also required that a staple be placed every 4½' thereafter. In this case, scrap materials were used as spacers to give the proper height to the light fixture above the medicine cabinet.

When bringing a new wire into any outlet box, leave at least 6" of wire extending out of the box. That 6" is a comfortable amount to work with when installing fixtures, outlets, or switches.

Remember to use the proper size wire connector for the size of wire you are using. Firmly twist the two wires together in a clockwise direction with a pair of linesman pliers, and snip any excess wire if the ends are uneven. Then tighten the wire

connector snugly. This is known as a solderless connection (9-19). Once the connections are made, push the wires and wire nuts to the back of the outlet box.

When installing fixtures that have adjustable hanging extension bars, be sure to fasten the ends of the bars with staples, nails, or screws. In addition, make sure that they are securely fastened to the framing material (9-20).

If you drill a hole through a framing member for a wire and you get within 1¼" of the front of the stud, be sure to fasten wire protectors over this area, as required by the NEC, to protect the wire from accidental damage during installation of the wallboard or any other type of wallcover.

9-19 *A solderless connection.*

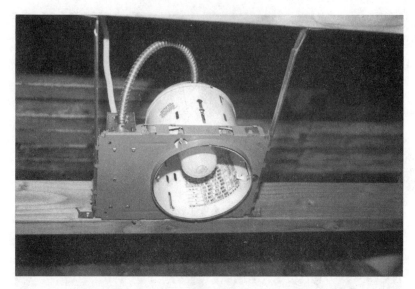

9-20
Make sure extension bars are securely fastened to framing material.

It is always a good idea to test the electrical system before installing any wallboard. Hook up the entire system and install temporary pigtail lamp holders (9-21) anywhere you have light fixtures. This is a good way to test switches. As for outlets, it is best to purchase a receptacle circuit tester. They are inexpensive and simple to use, and they're great for fault identification in 3-wire, 120-volt circuits when testing for open ground, reverse polarity, open hot, open neutral, hot and ground reversed, hot on neutral, and hot open.

9-21
Temporary pigtail lamp provides light to hang wallboard.

When fastening your ground wires together, it is a good idea to use a crimp connector to achieve a solid connection. One last note—whenever possible, make sure that your ground wire is attached to both the switch and the light fixture. It is possible that your switch and fixture do not have ground terminals. If that is the case, either buy new ones with ground terminals or if they are in metal boxes, fasten ground wires to the boxes. In plastic boxes, coil the ground wire and push it to the back of the box. Be sure to check the codes in force in your area concerning ground wires for switches and fixtures used in plastic boxes.

Fishing for an outlet

The time might come when you need to add a new outlet or rewire an existing one, and this is when ingenuity and creative planning really come into play. One tool needed to accomplish this task is an electrical fish tape. To use the tape, start by drilling a 1" (minimum) hole up through the subfloor and bottom plate of the wall into the cavity of the same stud space as the existing outlet or the cut-in box you want to wire. Push the fish tape down through the bottom of the existing outlet box (or into the hole cut in the wallboard for the cut-in box) until it hits the bottom plate. If you're lucky, you'll hit the hole you drilled in the bottom plate! Otherwise, take a piece of wire with a hook formed in it (a coat hanger) to "fish" in the stud space through the hole you cut from below until you "catch" the fish tape. Attach the new wire to the tape and pull it up through the wall to the outlet box. Alternatively, if you have a second pair of hands, snake the fish tape up through the hole you drilled and have your assistant catch the fish tape with a hooked piece of wire.

Wiring diagrams

The following diagrams for switches, outlets, and fixtures will show you how to connect the wiring, separately or in combination. For your particular wiring job, find the diagram which is similar to your project and then wire as illustrated.

Appliance outlets Figure 9-22 shows a surface-mounted dryer outlet. Also available are recessed outlets. These large outlets are designed to deliver 240 volts for the heating coils and 120 volts for standard items such as the timer and the pilot light.

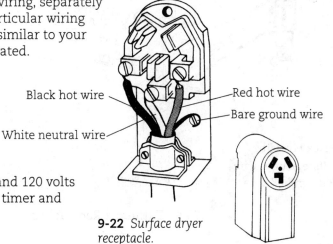

Black hot wire

Red hot wire

Bare ground wire

White neutral wire

9-22 Surface dryer receptacle.

Ground fault circuit interruptors GFCIs are installed like standard duplex outlets (9-23). Some models have "pigtails" for connections; others have normal screw terminals. Be sure to follow the manufacturer's installation instructions.

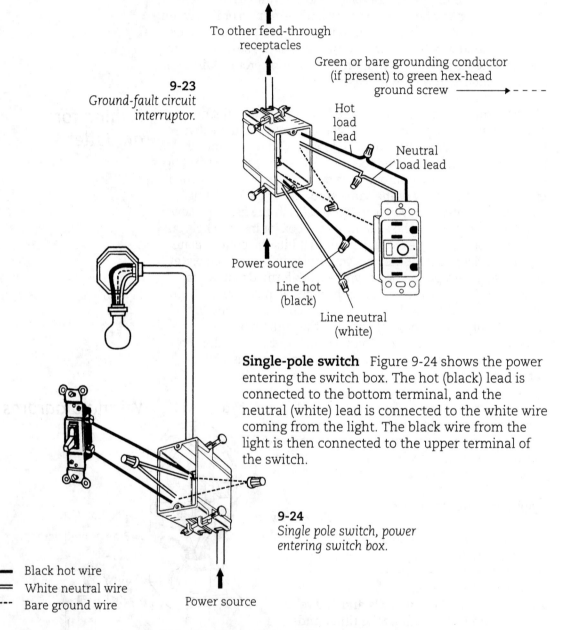

To other feed-through receptacles

Green or bare grounding conductor (if present) to green hex-head ground screw ⟶ - - - -

9-23
Ground-fault circuit interruptor.

Hot load lead

Neutral load lead

Power source

Line hot (black)

Line neutral (white)

Single-pole switch Figure 9-24 shows the power entering the switch box. The hot (black) lead is connected to the bottom terminal, and the neutral (white) lead is connected to the white wire coming from the light. The black wire from the light is then connected to the upper terminal of the switch.

9-24
Single pole switch, power entering switch box.

━━━ Black hot wire
═══ White neutral wire
------ Bare ground wire

Power source

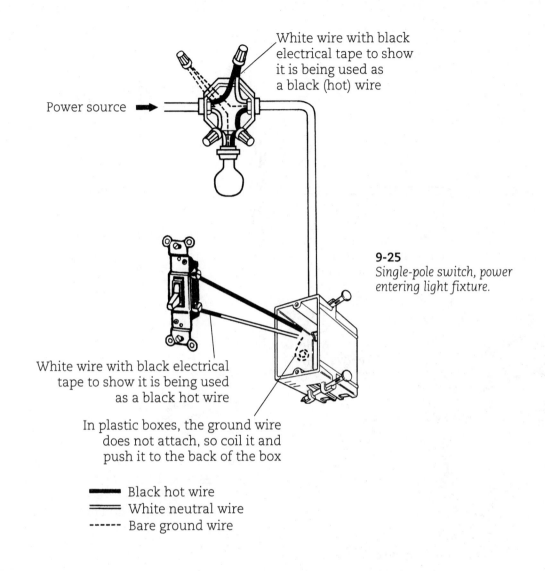

White wire with black electrical tape to show it is being used as a black (hot) wire

Power source →

9-25
Single-pole switch, power entering light fixture.

White wire with black electrical tape to show it is being used as a black hot wire

In plastic boxes, the ground wire does not attach, so coil it and push it to the back of the box

▬▬▬ Black hot wire
═══ White neutral wire
------ Bare ground wire

Single-pole switch   Figure 9-25 shows the power entering the light fixture. The hot (black) lead is connected to the neutral (white) lead of the switch at the brass colored terminal. The white must be marked black to indicate that this is a hot lead.

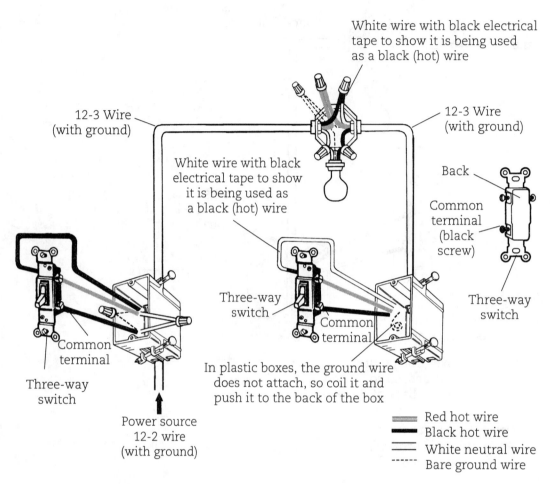

White wire with black electrical tape to show it is being used as a black (hot) wire

12-3 Wire (with ground)

12-3 Wire (with ground)

White wire with black electrical tape to show it is being used as a black (hot) wire

Back

Common terminal (black screw)

Three-way switch

Three-way switch

Common terminal

Common terminal

Three-way switch

In plastic boxes, the ground wire does not attach, so coil it and push it to the back of the box

Three-way switch

Power source 12-2 wire (with ground)

Red hot wire
Black hot wire
White neutral wire
Bare ground wire

9-26 *Three-way switch, power entering switch box.*

Three-way switch Figure 9-26 shows a three-way switch with power going into the switch box and the light fixture between the two switches.

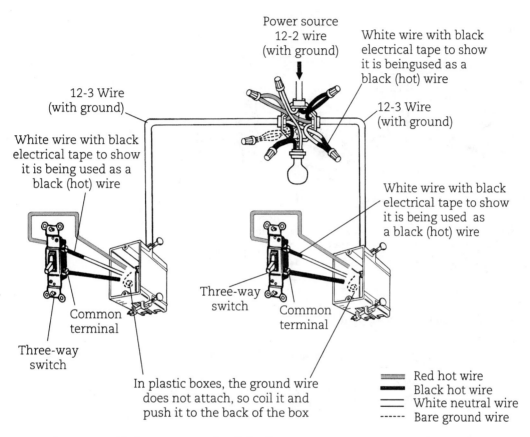

Power source
12-2 wire
(with ground)

White wire with black
electrical tape to show
it is beingused as a
black (hot) wire

12-3 Wire
(with ground)

12-3 Wire
(with ground)

White wire with black
electrical tape to show
it is being used as a
black (hot) wire

White wire with black
electrical tape to show
it is being used as
a black (hot) wire

Three-way
switch

Common
terminal

Common
terminal

Three-way
switch

Three-way
switch

In plastic boxes, the ground wire
does not attach, so coil it and
push it to the back of the box

━━━ Red hot wire
━━━ Black hot wire
── White neutral wire
------ Bare ground wire

9-27 *Three-way switch, power entering light fixture.*

Three-way switch   Figure 9-27 shows a three-way switch with
power going to the light fixture. Again, the light fixture is
between both switches.

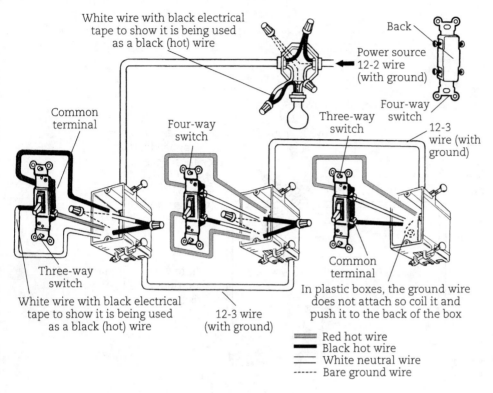

White wire with black electrical tape to show it is being used as a black (hot) wire

Back

Power source 12-2 wire (with ground)

Common terminal

Four-way switch

Four-way switch

Three-way switch

12-3 wire (with ground)

Common terminal

Three-way switch

White wire with black electrical tape to show it is being used as a black (hot) wire

12-3 wire (with ground)

In plastic boxes, the ground wire does not attach so coil it and push it to the back of the box

━━━ Red hot wire
━━━ Black hot wire
═══ White neutral wire
------ Bare ground wire

9-28 *Four-way switch, power entering light fixture.*

Four-way switch Figure 9-28 illustrates a four-way switch with power going into the light fixture. Notice that the four-way switch is between the two three-way switches.

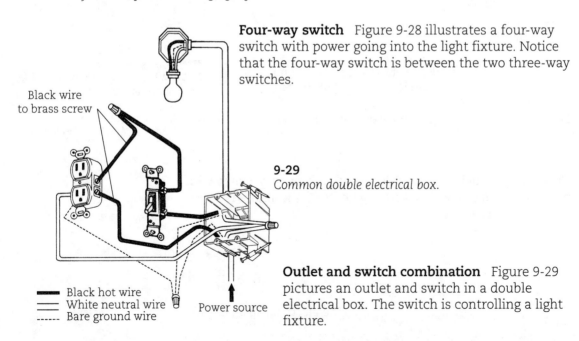

Black wire to brass screw

9-29
Common double electrical box.

━━━ Black hot wire
═══ White neutral wire
------ Bare ground wire

Power source

Outlet and switch combination Figure 9-29 pictures an outlet and switch in a double electrical box. The switch is controlling a light fixture.

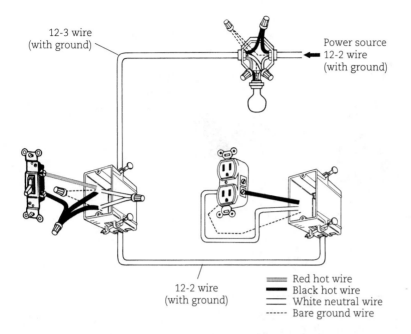

12-3 wire
(with ground)

Power source
12-2 wire
(with ground)

9-30
Power entering light fixture, feeding switch, then feeding outlet.

12-2 wire
(with ground)

▨ Red hot wire
━ Black hot wire
═ White neutral wire
------ Bare ground wire

Outlet and switch combination   Figure 9-30 shows an outlet and switch in separate boxes. The power is being fed through the light fixture.

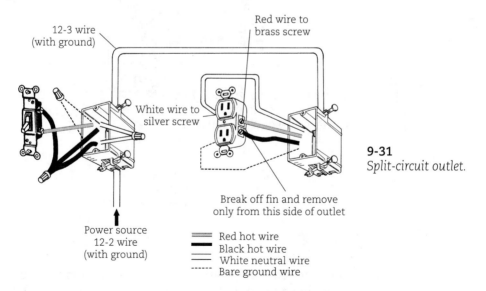

12-3 wire
(with ground)

Red wire to
brass screw

White wire to
silver screw

9-31
Split-circuit outlet.

Break off fin and remove
only from this side of outlet

Power source
12-2 wire
(with ground)

▨ Red hot wire
━ Black hot wire
═ White neutral wire
------ Bare ground wire

Outlet and switch combination   Figure 9-31 is a split-circuit outlet. The switch controls the top half of the outlet while the bottom half of the outlet is always hot. To accomplish this, it is important to break off the fin (9-32) from the power side of the outlet, and you also need a 12-3 wire between the switch and outlet.

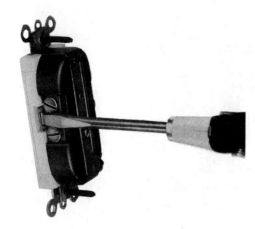

9-32
Screwdriver fits into slot in fin for easy removal.
Leviton Manufacturing Co., Inc.

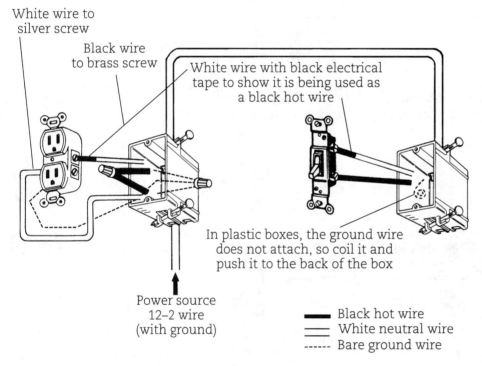

White wire to silver screw

Black wire to brass screw

White wire with black electrical tape to show it is being used as a black hot wire

In plastic boxes, the ground wire does not attach, so coil it and push it to the back of the box

Power source 12–2 wire (with ground)

▬▬▬ Black hot wire
═══ White neutral wire
------ Bare ground wire

9-33 *Switch-controlled outlet.*

Outlet and switch combination Figure 9-33 shows a switch controlling the entire outlet and power coming into the outlet box.

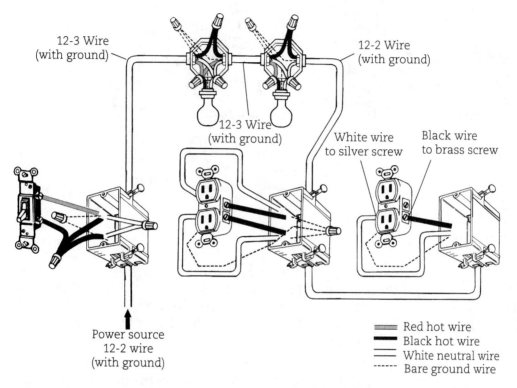

12-3 Wire
(with ground)

12-2 Wire
(with ground)

12-3 Wire
(with ground)

White wire
to silver screw

Black wire
to brass screw

Power source
12-2 wire
(with ground)

━━━ Red hot wire
━━━ Black hot wire
─── White neutral wire
----- Bare ground wire

9-34 *Wiring for single-pole switch with lights and outlets.*

Outlet and switch combination   Figure 9-34 has a switch
controlling two lights with power continuing through light fixtures
to feed two outlets. The power is going to the switch box. Notice
where the 12-3 and 12-2 wires are being used.

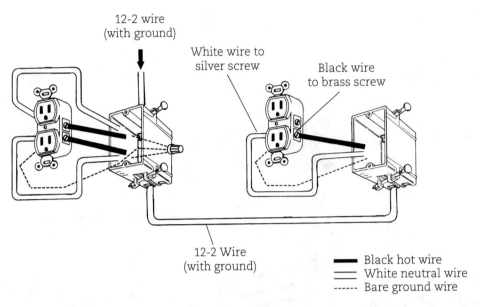

12-2 wire
(with ground)

White wire to
silver screw

Black wire
to brass screw

12-2 Wire
(with ground)

—— Black hot wire
═══ White neutral wire
------ Bare ground wire

9-35 *How to wire outlets.*

Outlets   Figure 9-35 shows two outlets where the power is fed to the first outlet. If you want to continue to feed yet another outlet, then attach the wires to the upper terminals of the second outlet and continue. Remember to attach the black wire to the brass terminal (screw).

The diagrams included in this chapter are only a small sampling of the possible combinations. The light fixtures in the diagrams are for the purpose of illustration. They could as well be fans or heat lamps—I'm sure you get the idea. Remember to take your time, turn the electricity off before you begin any work, and follow the codes in your area.

Now it is time to move on to the wallboard chapter. This is where it all starts to come together!

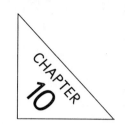

Wallboard techniques & finishing

WALLBOARD IS THE TRANSITIONAL STAGE of the remodeling job during which your bathroom is transformed from a skeleton to a completely covered surface. It is important to have a clear vision of how you want your bathroom walls to look once they are finished; this determines the products and procedures you will use.

Take time to research and select the appropriate wallboard materials to use in different areas of the bathroom. Using the proper materials results in long and satisfactory performance. Again, it is important that you follow the manufacturers' recommendations for use when choosing these products, and follow their instructions when installing them. You might also want to write the Gypsum Association, 810 First Street, N.E., Suite 510, Washington, DC 20002, for literature containing their recommendations regarding the different types of gypsum products, their specific applications, and detailed installation instructions. You might also want to write the United States Gypsum Company for a copy of their excellent reference book on how to do wallboard and plaster construction. The *Gypsum Construction Handbook* (528 pages) can be ordered for $12 directly from the United States Gypsum Company, Dept. 193— Handbook, 125 South Franklin Street, Chicago, IL 60606-4678.

Wallboard products

Gypsum wallboard is the most popular wallcovering for walls and ceilings in the bathroom—especially when the final finish will be paint or wallpaper. Gypsum is a mined mineral, gray to white in color, which is crushed, dried, and ground to a powder that is commonly called plaster of paris. The processed powder is then mixed with water and other ingredients and sandwiched

Gypsum wallboard

between two sheets of specially manufactured paper to form various types of gypsum wallboard, commonly called drywall. Regular gypsum wallboard is available in ¼" to ⅝" thicknesses. The ½" size is the most popular, although the ⅝" product might offer better performance in some situations. It comes in a standard width of 4', and the length varies from 6' to 16'; 4×8 or 4×12 sheets are most commonly used. Along the two lengthwise edges, the wallboard face is slightly tapered. As the two edges meet during installation, a shallow recess is created to accommodate joint reinforcement (tape and joint compound).

Even though wallboard is a relatively lightweight product, a 4×8 sheet is often too heavy and awkward for one person to handle. Regular gypsum wallboard is also not water-resistant, so it is not recommended for use in bath and shower areas where it could come in direct contact with water.

Water-resistant wallboard

Water-resistant gypsum wallboard, commonly called *green board*, is specially processed for use as a base for ceramic or plastic tile and other nonabsorbent finish materials. The gypsum core contains a special moisture-resistant chemical to make the wallboard water-resistant. The multilayered face and back papers are also chemically treated to withstand the effects of moisture and high humidity. The panel is easily recognized by its distinctive green face.

Similar to regular gypsum wallboard, it comes in ½" and ⅝" thicknesses and a standard width of 4'. The length varies from 6' to 16', with 4×8 or 4×12 sheets most commonly used.

Although this product is water-resistant, it is not waterproof. It is not recommended for use where there will be severe exposure to water or to continuous high-humidity conditions such as those found in saunas, steam rooms, gang shower rooms, or swimming pool enclosures. In addition, if you plan to install an impervious finish (such as ceramic tile) in a tub or shower area, this product is not recommended for use over a vapor retarder (a situation that could be encountered on an exterior insulated wall). However, if you are installing a fiberglass tub and shower enclosure or a similar product that can guarantee no water penetration, then water-resistant gypsum wallboard will serve very well.

The Gypsum Association recommends one practice that creates a satisfactory vapor barrier between the gypsum board face and a tiled surface. Briefly, their recommendation is to apply a uniform skim coat, not less than ⅟₃₂" thick, of water-based Type 1 ceramic tile adhesive over the water-resistant gypsum board and allow it to dry before the installation of tile. A silicone caulk product can also be used as grout between tiles to seal the surface. For areas above and beyond the tile area, apply a vapor retardant paint or primer over the wall surface following the paint manufacturer's recommendations. If you plan and prefer to use an impervious finish, you might want to consider using a cementitious backer board instead of water-resistant wallboard.

Cementitious backer board

Known to many as *cement board* (and also manufactured with glass-fiber mesh reinforcement), cementitious backer board was developed to provide a permanent base for ceramic tile.

This product has been approved for wet area use in tub and shower enclosures and in showers over wood and steel studs. It can also be used on floors over structurally sound subfloors and for counter and vanity tops where the thin-set method is used.

Cement board is a lightweight concrete panel composed of aggregated Portland cement and coated glass-fiber mesh reinforcement. It contains no gypsum or paper so it will not disintegrate or delaminate if it gets saturated (as gypsum board or gypsum plaster might), nor will it swell or rot as do wood products. It is unaffected by water, moisture, or steam, and will not decay, warp, or soften.

Cement board comes in thicknesses from ¼" to ½", widths from 32" to 36", and lengths from 4' to 8'. It can be scored and snapped, like gypsum wallboard, and is fastened to the wall with nails or screws.

I have included some illustrations to help you understand the installation of these products and their particular uses. Figure 10-1 shows the installation of cement board on interior walls that would be used in both shower and tub areas. Notice how the cement board and tile are held up off the shower pan, regardless of the shower pan's material or fabrication method.

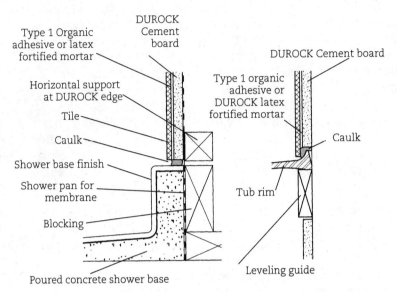

Tub and shower-single layer board

DUROCK Cement board

Type 1 Organic adhesive or latex fortified mortar

DUROCK Cement board

Horizontal support at DUROCK edge

Type 1 organic adhesive or DUROCK latex fortified mortar

Tile

Caulk

Caulk

Shower base finish

Tub rim

Shower pan for membrane

Blocking

Leveling guide

Poured concrete shower base

10-1
Installation of cement board on interior wall.
United States Gypsum Company

Once this area has dried, a mildew-resistant silicone rubber caulk can be used to scale the gap. 10-2 shows a typical bathtub installation. The gray area is the area of concern, the *wet* area, and this is the place to install cement board. Notice the joint where the two types of wallboard come together; it is taped in the same fashion as all other joints.

To summarize, the basic wall covering products are used as follows:

Gypsum wallboard Used for smooth and textured walls and ceilings where there will be virtually no water or long-term moisture exposure.

Water-resistant gypsum wallboard Used for tub and shower areas; provides very good results with ceramic or plastic tiles when properly installed and maintained, and excellent moisture protection when using fiberglass (or similar) tub/shower enclosures.

Cementitious backer board A premium product for use in any wet areas to be covered by ceramic tiles.

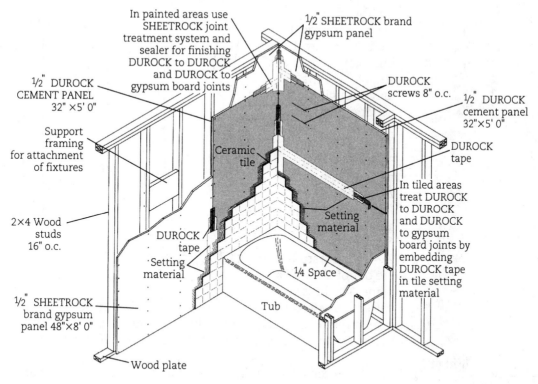

10-2 *Typical bathtub installation.* Drawing courtesy of United States Gypsum Company

Before you get started, examine your framing to check for trouble spots before you begin to install wallboard. Carefully look at the headers above doors and windows. Often you'll find the corner of a stud sticking out beyond the framing stud. Use a chisel to shave down the high spot. Check where studs meet both top and bottom plates to make sure they don't extend beyond the plates. This applies to both single and double plates (10-3). Again, correct this problem by chiseling off the high spot. Sometimes framing members get out of alignment; correct these areas before hanging any wallboard. Check the trimmers in doorways and around windows. If they stick out farther than any studs, you might have to remove the trimmers and reposition them correctly. If the trimmer is too wide, then it needs to be removed and cut down to size before reinstallation.

Preventive measures

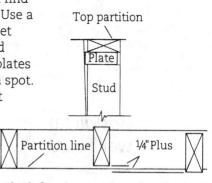

10-3 *Check framing members for alignment.*
United States Gypsum Company

Another framing area to check is bowed studs. One way to find them is to take a straight 2×4 that is long enough to hold horizontally against at least 8' of wall (if the wall is more than 8' long). Place the narrow edge of the 2×4 against the wall frame and you'll be able to see gaps between the straight 2×4 and any studs that are out of the wall's plane. The best way to

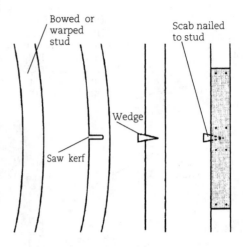

10-4 *Correcting bowed framing members.*
United States Gypsum Company

correct bowed studs is to cut the bowed stud partway through (sometimes completely in half), install a wedge, pull the stud in to straighten it, and scab a 1×4 onto both sides of the stud (10-4).

Check the ceiling joists (floor joists for the upper story) to make sure one is not lower than the others. If this condition exists, plane the joist so it is even with the others. If it is curved upward and not flush with the other joists, attach a furring strip.

Finally, watch out for bridging that sticks down farther than the joist. It should be cut flat to the face of the joist (10-5).

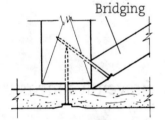

10-5 *Bridging that is not flush with the face of the joist can puncture the face of your wallboard.*
United States Gypsum Company

I highly recommend that you not "float" any wallboard, i.e., leave an end unattached because there is no nailer. Try to mount a backer or nailer of some sort to which you can securely attach the wallboard all around its perimeter.

Installing wallboard

Now that you have selected the appropriate type(s) of wallboard for your project and have corrected any framing irregularities that could interfere with a smooth wallboard installation, it is time to cover those walls. First, however, you need to make some important decisions about that installation.

All the basic wallboard products can be installed with screws, nails, and adhesive. I recommend that you use screws and adhesives rather than wallboard nails. Wallboard nails grip with friction but can loosen as wood shrinks, which might pop nailheads above the surface and create problems in the future.

When fastening ½" wallboard to wooden studs, use Phillips bugle head W 7×1¼" screws (10-6). For cement board, use Rock-On Hi-Lo type S 8×1¼" (or 1⅝") screws (10-7).

10-6 *Recommended fastener for gypsum wallboard products.*
ITW Buildex and Illinois Tool Works Inc.

10-7 *Recommended fastener for cement board.*
ITW Buildex and Illinois Tool Works Inc.

10-8 *Cross section of wallboard correctly dimpled. Notice the nailhead is in the center of the dimple.*
United States Gypsum Company

If you would really prefer to nail, use only nails designed for wallboard. For ½" wallboard, use 1⅝" wallboard nails and a wallboard hammer as shown in chapter 4.

Always hold the wallboard firmly against the framing as you attach it; don't depend on the fastener to bring the wallboard snugly up against the framing members. When nailing, always start in the center of the sheet and work your way out to the edges. Drive the nails with the wallboard hammer so the last blow forms a shallow dimple around the nail (10-8). Be careful not to break the wallboard paper while dimpling the nailhead, but if it should happen, drive another nail 2" above or below the first nail.

I recommend that you also use wallboard adhesive, especially with nails, as it helps to eliminate the popping of nails at a later date. Apply the adhesive in a bead that is about ⅜" in diameter and ¼" thick to all the framing surfaces (except the plates) the wallboard will touch. Run a double bead of adhesive on framing members that will back up a wallboard joint. Properly installed, the adhesive will be forced out to the outside edges of the framing by the wallboard as it is fastened to the framing members (10-9). In order to attain the proper thickness of the adhesive bead, it is important to cut the nozzle of the adhesive tube according to your intended application—walls or ceilings

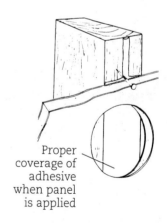

Proper coverage of adhesive when panel is applied

10-9 *The wallboard will spread the adhesive evenly as it is securely fastened to the framing members.*
United States Gypsum Company

(10-10). Using the adhesive gun at the correct angle will also help you to apply the adhesive properly (10-11).

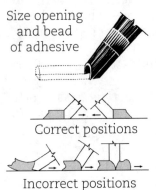

Size opening
and bead
of adhesive

Correct positions

Incorrect positions

for walls   for ceilings

Nozzle cuts

10-10 *Adhesive cartridge tip preparation.*
United States Gypsum Company

10-11 *Proper nozzle opening and adhesive gun position.* United States Gypsum Company

Nailing schedule

Whether you choose screws or nails and fasten them with or without adhesive, it is important to space those fasteners so they securely attach the wallboard to the framing members. To do this properly, you need to follow a *nailing schedule* that fits your specific applications. It is very possible that your building department has a nailing schedule as part of its building code. Check with them so you can work to their nailing specifications.

Nails When nailing a ceiling without adhesive, space your nails no farther apart than 7" on center. On sidewalls, nails should not exceed 8" on center (10-12). On edges and ends of wallboard, nail at least ⅜" away from the edge but no farther than ½".

When nailing using adhesive, it is important to know the spacing of your framing members—16" or 24" on center. You also need to know if any of the walls (partitions) is a support wall (load-bearing). For example, your exterior walls are load-bearing walls. If you are in the basement or on the first floor of a two-story house or on the first floor with man-made roof rafters (not factory-engineered trusses), the center wall of your home should be load-bearing. Once you know this, you can

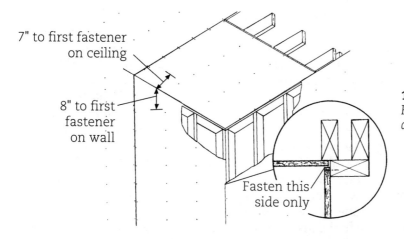

7" to first fastener on ceiling

8" to first fastener on wall

Fasten this side only

10-12
Floating interior angle—detail. United States Gypsum Company

select the appropriate nailing schedule. If your framing members are 16" on center, nail ceilings and load-bearing partitions 16" apart, and non-load-bearing partitions 24" apart. If your framing is 24" on center for ceilings and load-bearing partitions, nail 12" apart, and for non-load-bearing partitions, nail 16" apart. Again, it is important to check with your building department for the nailing schedule that applies in your area.

Corner beads Nail no more than 9" apart with nails opposite each other.

Screws When using adhesive and working with framing members that are 16" on center, drive your screws 16" apart for ceilings and 24" apart for load-bearing and non-load-bearing partitions. For framing members that are 24" on center, ceilings and load-bearing partitions should have screws placed 16" apart, and non-load-bearing partitions should have screws placed 24" apart. Edges and ends should be fastened using the same schedule.

If you are not using adhesive, screws should be placed 12" apart on ceilings and 16" apart on sidewalls. If you are attaching water-resistant wallboard, the screws should be 12" apart on both ceilings and walls. If you plan to apply tile to water-resistant gypsum wallboard, the screws should not exceed 8" apart. Again, check with your building department for their recommended spacing.

Vertical corners and ceiling Some contractors feel that incomplete nailing along inside corners where wallboards meet (sometimes called a *floating interior angle*) allows (some) relief, which in turn might prevent the surface cracking that can be caused by normal structural stresses (10-12). While structural stresses do exist, I believe that extra measures should be taken during the framing stage to minimize movement. Take the time to make sure that whenever one framing member rests on—or against—another, it is completely nailed. Examples of this are joists on double plates, or places where walls come together, as in a partition or at corners. Also, do not frame with green material, and allow materials to dry at room temperatures for about a week. Under these circumstances, wallboard can then be securely fastened in the inside corners. I have followed this procedure for years and have never experienced stress or surface cracks.

The preferred way to hang wallboard where a ceiling meets the wall is to hold back the ceiling nails 7" from the wall, and the sidewall nails 8" down from the ceiling (10-12).

Wallboard installation

When all your electrical outlets are in place, it's time to tuck the outlets or switches into outlet boxes. Be careful not to grab the sides of switches or outlets—they could be hot!

Always begin wallboard installation with the ceiling. Measure the length so that each end of the wallboard lands in the center of a framing member—this is true for both walls and ceiling. Stagger the joints as shown in 10-13. (Notice the use of water-resistant wallboard—green board—in the tub/shower area and around the sink area.) Wallboard should be mounted so it horizontally spans the framing members on both ceilings and walls.

Measure wallboard and cut it with a utility knife, using a T-square as shown in 10-14 to ensure straight

10-13 *A correct installation of wallboard products.*

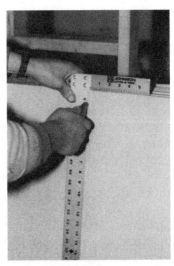

10-14 *A T-square ensures fast and accurate cuts in wallboard.*

cuts. Score the finish side, then bend it back and cut the backing. Some professionals will cut and snap the wallboard, but I prefer cutting the back paper from the backside so it does not tear away from the gypsum. Rasp the ends with a wallboard rasp, if necessary, and fasten the wallboard in place on the wall using nails or screws (as discussed earlier). It will probably take two people for this job.

If you have any electrical boxes in the ceiling, take the time to precisely measure for these items. "Measure twice, cut once." Transfer your measurements to the wallboard and cut with a circle cutter or keyhole wallboard saw. Make accurate cuts around fixtures so the final trim pieces will cover any gaps. Always cut from the finish side of the wallboard.

Do not force the wallboard into place. If the fit is too tight, take it down and shave the edge with a wallboard rasp; be careful, though, as gaps between joints should not exceed $\frac{1}{16}$" to $\frac{1}{8}$".

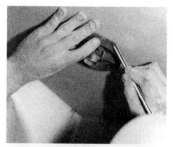

The basic installation procedure is the same for the walls. Start with the upper part of the wall and work down toward the floor. Raise the wallboard until it touches the ceiling and fasten it in place. When installing water-resistant wallboard in the tub and shower area, keep it up off the tub or shower pan about $\frac{1}{4}$". On the remaining walls, remember to cut out for outlet boxes and any other fixtures. When cutting for the plumbing, cut a hole for the shower head and tub spout just large enough to go over the stem assembly, but do not fasten the wallboard in place yet. Instead, take the faucet template, turn it around, and slide it over the stem assembly so you can trace around it. Remove the wallboard, cut out the traced area with a keyhole wallboard saw, and then finally install and fasten your wallboard (10-15). When assembling your new faucet, don't throw away the template; it will come in handy to cut the hole in the wallboard for the finish trim. Faucet housings and pipe escutcheons (finish trim) should liberally cover the gypsum wallboard or tile behind them, which should be cut close to the pipe. Be sure to caulk cut edges and openings around pipes and fixtures with a flexible water-resistant caulk or adhesive.

10-15 *Cutting hole for faucet assembly.*

Continue your installation, cutting around openings, plumbing pipes, and miscellaneous items (10-16). Check your nails or screw heads to make sure they don't break the surface of the paper.

10-16
Typical items you need to cut around during wallboard installation.

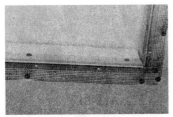

10-17 *Typical installation of nail-on corner bead.*

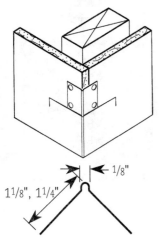

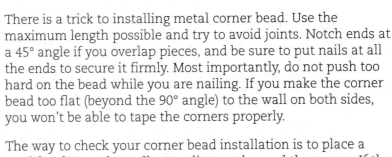

← 1/8"

1 1/8", 1 1/4"

10-18 *Exposed nose of corner bead.* United States Gypsum Company

Once the wallboard is in place, install corner bead over all outside corners. You have a couple of choices here: you can install tape-on corner bead, which is embedded in joint compound and installed at the time you are taping, or you can use nail-on metal corner bead, which I believe yields a corner that is less prone to surface cracking at a later date. Cut the bead to fit and nail it to the corner. Be sure to nail down both sides of the corner bead (10-17).

There is a trick to installing metal corner bead. Use the maximum length possible and try to avoid joints. Notch ends at a 45° angle if you overlap pieces, and be sure to put nails at all the ends to secure it firmly. Most importantly, do not push too hard on the bead while you are nailing. If you make the corner bead too flat (beyond the 90° angle) to the wall on both sides, you won't be able to tape the corners properly.

The way to check your corner bead installation is to place a straightedge on the wall extending out beyond the corner. If the corner bead was installed correctly, the straightedge will not touch any part of the corner bead except the actual bead (the corner itself) and this should hold true for both sides of the corner bead (10-18). The exposed nose of corner bead protects your corner from damage and provides a guide for your taping knife to ride along as you apply joint and finish compounds.

Before you begin to tape the joints, you must decide if you want smooth or textured walls, or if you want to install wallpaper or tiles. Keep in mind that smooth walls take more time and require an extra coat of finishing compound during the taping process. Many professionals apply texture to walls and ceilings to eliminate that extra coat, but don't let that be the deciding factor in your bathroom project. If you want smooth walls, then insist on them.

If you choose to handle the taping job yourself, then you should purchase two kinds of *mud*: an all-purpose joint compound (or taping compound), and topping compound. Purchase them both in premixed form.

I recommend that you purchase your first joint and topping compounds in pails, and then purchase any additional compound in a box. You can pour the box into the pail after the pail becomes empty. (Be careful to not let babies or toddlers play around any large buckets as drownings can occur.) Even though both are ready-mixed products, you need to stir them before use.

The drill you choose to power the mixing paddle should have a low rpm so you don't burn out the motor. Hold the bucket securely between your feet so it doesn't spin. By adding a minimal amount of clean tap water (½ to 1 cup of water per pail), you can mix the compound to a consistency that is comfortable to use. Be careful not to overthin. Check the consistency by placing a wallboard finishing knife into the compound. The compound should just stick to the knife point; when you tip the blade, the compound should slowly slide toward the edge of the blade without actually falling off. If the compound is too thick, you won't be able to work with it. If it is too thin, it will fall off the knife before you get it to the wall. With this in mind, always stir the compound first and then add water as needed.

Always apply all-purpose taping compound first, and use topping compound for the finish coats. You also need fiberglass or paper wallboard joint tape. The paper tape, used by many professionals, is preferable. However, first-timers might find the glass-fiber tape with pressure-sensitive adhesive backing easier to use. This tape is pressed onto the wall without using any joint compound, but it is finished in the same fashion as other paper tape (discussed later in the chapter).

Tools The basic tools you need are a 12" mud pan for holding the joint or topping compound, a 4" knife for the first coat, a 6" knife for the second coat, and a 10" knife for the third coat. Optional tools are a tape holder, which I highly recommend, and an inside corner taping tool. Finally, you'll need a pole sander for upper walls and ceilings, and a hand sander for inside corners and the lower walls (10-19).

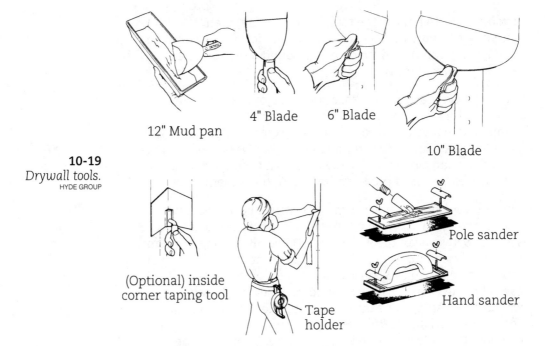

10-19
Drywall tools.
HYDE GROUP

12" Mud pan

4" Blade

6" Blade

10" Blade

(Optional) inside corner taping tool

Tape holder

Pole sander

Hand sander

To achieve best results with your knife, apply medium pressure and hold the knife at a 45° angle to the wallboard. When using your mud pan, remember to dip the knife sideways into the pan and load only half of the blade. Draw the blade out over the metal edge of the mud pan in order to clean the backside of the blade. It is important to keep the backside clean.

As you work with the compound, the mud will begin to dry on the blade, wall, and in the mud pan. Be sure to scrape any dried compound from the blade that might have been picked up from the wall. Also scrape the inside walls of the mud pan and throw away any dried compound. These dried bits of compound will leave scratches in the wet compound as you draw the knife over it. This is annoying, and will interfere with your ability to achieve a smooth surface, so keep your blade clean at all times.

Applying compound is the messiest part of the job, and I believe it is best handled by a professional. However, if you choose to tackle this yourself, follow these steps. Professional tapers might have a different approach, but I have found that finishing joints in this particular order neatly conceals all cut ends of tape and yields smooth joints.

First coat—joint compound Start with the short vertical joints (those that are perpendicular to and intersecting with the horizontal joints) and apply an even, thin coat of joint compound the entire length of the joint using a 4" blade (10-20). Center and lightly press the tape into the compound with your fingers. Starting at the top of the joint, draw your blade firmly over the tape to lightly embed the tape in the compound. Be sure there is a sufficient amount of compound under the tape to prevent blistering on the top. If blistering should occur, lift the tape in this area with the corner of your knife and apply more compound, finishing by drawing your blade over the tape.

10-20
First coat of mud.

While drawing your blade, remove excess joint compound from both edges. This is important as you need a fairly smooth surface when you are ready to apply the second coat.

If this is the first time you have treated wallboard joints, I recommend you let this coat dry for at least half a day before you tape the horizontal joints (10-21). As you do horizontal joints, overlap the tapes where they intersect with the previously-applied vertical tapes. Continue until all the horizontal joints—except the inside corners—are complete.

10-21
Embedding tape.

Now that all short vertical and horizontal joints are done, you can start on the inside corners. Because you started with the vertical joints, begin now with the horizontal corners—the ceiling. Using your 4" knife, apply compound to both sides of the corner from wall to wall. Fold the tape along the center crease and lightly push it into position with your fingers or the 4" knife. As with the other joints, lightly embed the tape in the compound and remove any excess compound from around the edges. Be careful not to cut the inside corner fold of the tape with the corner of your blade. Wait until these corners dry for a day before you apply tape in the same manner to the vertical inside corners (10-22). Start at the ceiling and apply compound right down to the floor. The tape follows the same procedure. If you chose to finish exterior corners with tape-on corner bead, apply it with joint compound the same way you finished the inside corners.

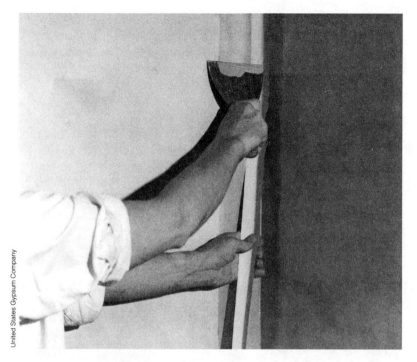

10-22
Finishing inside corners.

While the tape dries on the corner joints, apply compound to each nail or screw dimple (*spotting*) and wipe off any excess compound with your second stroke (10-23). The compound should be level with the surface of the wallboard. If you scrape or see the head of a fastener as you are applying the compound, sink the fastener in a little deeper, again taking care not to break the paper face of the wallboard. Then reapply your compound.

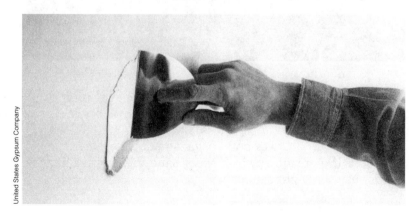

10-23
Spotting fastener heads.

Wallboard techniques & finishing

Even though you plan to cover the wallboard in the tub/shower area with tile or an enclosure of some sort, finish this area as you would the rest of the walls. This will ensure a smooth, even surface for application of your tile or enclosure. Spot the fastener dimples right down to the floor.

If there are no damp compounded areas where the corner bead(s) intersect with horizontal joints, apply compound to the outside corners. I prefer to use a 6" knife for the first application. Just as you did on the inside corners, start at the top and work down toward the floor (10-24). Before you spread compound on the other side of the bead, run your knife up the length of the bead itself to remove any excess compound. Once this is done, you can apply compound to the other side, again removing any excess along the bead and taking care not to disturb the side you finished first.

10-24
Fill coat application for corner beads (outside corners).

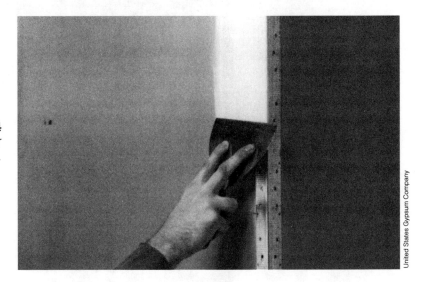

United States Gypsum Company

Second coat—topping compound When the joint compound is dry, you can apply your second coat. Before you begin, carefully scrape off bumps, ridges, and other imperfections with your 4" knife. Check both inside and outside corners and fasteners. If there are any high spots, sand them with a hand sander using 100-grit sandpaper.

Stir the topping mix just as you did the joint compound. The topping compound can be a different color, which makes it easy to see where you started your second coat. Use the 6" knife on all inside and outside corners and fastener heads, and the 10" blade on all vertical and horizontal joints (10-25).

United States Gypsum Company

10-25
Fill coat application (second coat).

The real secret to applying compound is to alternate the second coat so you do not overlap wet applications. For instance, if you are applying compound to an inside corner, do one side only. Then on the other side of the inside corner apply topping compound to a horizontal joint over to the next corner on the other side of the wall. You should be able to alternate the second coat all the way through the job.

Third coat—second coat of topping compound The second coat of topping goes on just like the first coat. Again, clean the ceiling and walls by scraping with a wallboard knife, taking care not to dig into the paper. This time, apply the compound to the sides of the corners that were not done the first time, and work through the job alternating applications as before. Apply a third coat to each fastener; each application should spread over an area slightly larger than the previous coat and feather the edges (10-26). To feather the edges on an inside corner, take pressure off the blade closer to the wall and lift the blade slightly. At the same time, put pressure on the blade where it hits the wallboard. This helps to bring the compound out to the width of the blade you are using.

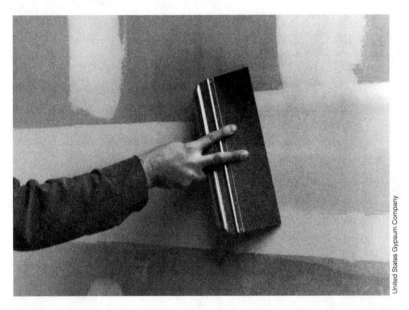

10-26
Finish coat application (third and possibly fourth coats).

United States Gypsum Company

Final coat—finish application Make sure all the topping compound is completely dry, and scrape the areas to remove any little bumps. Lightly sand the imperfections. Avoid sanding so much that you sand into the tape, and be careful not to roughen the surface of the paper.

When sanding into the corners, take care to not sand a groove into the corner. If you are using sandpaper especially designed for wallboard, you can eliminate this problem by removing the ear on one side of the pre-cut sandpaper, which removes the sandpaper on the edge of the sanding block (10-27).

Cut the ear off along dotted line.

10-27 *Cut the ear off on one side of the sandpaper.* HYDE GROUP

160   *Bathroom Remodeling*

Check that all taped joints are level with the surface of the wallboard. Hold your 10" blade across the joint, perpendicular to the wall, to see if the blade "rocks" over the joint. If it does, the joint has a hump. To resolve this problem, apply compound to both sides of the centerline of the hump, feathering it out as far as possible. This might take five or six coats, and the compound must dry between each coat. Check other areas that might need a final coat and again check to make sure all edges are feathered. If the edges are too high, either apply compound over the area or sand carefully.

At this point, you might want to consider *skim coating* the entire surface with compound if you plan to use glossy paint or if you want smooth walls. A skim coat is a thin coat of joint compound over the entire surface of the wallboard to reduce surface texture and suction variations. Caution should be taken during skim coating to eliminate gaps or tool marks. The walls or ceiling surface should be lightly sanded or sponged, but be careful to leave a thin film of the compound to seal the wallboard paper (10-28).

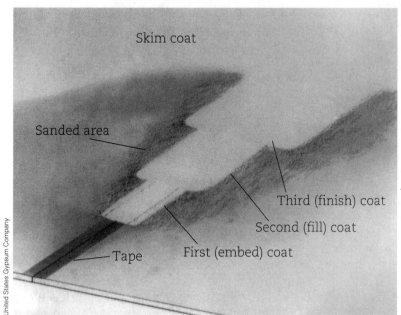

Skim coat

Sanded area

Third (finish) coat

Second (fill) coat

First (embed) coat

Tape

United States Gypsum Company

10-28
Levels of gypsum board finishing, including skim coat.

Once you are completely satisfied with the smoothness of your walls and are through sanding, take a damp sponge and remove any sanding dust. When the walls and ceiling are dry, it wouldn't hurt to take one more look for any imperfections.

When this process is completed, you are ready for the next step: smooth walls, textured walls, or wallpaper.

Smooth walls

If you plan to paint the walls and want a smooth surface, apply a quality heavy latex base primer. Once the primer has dried thoroughly, examine the walls. The primer will reveal imperfections that were not noticeable before, so this is the time to make corrections. The primer might raise the fibers of the wallboard paper. If this occurs, use your sanding block with 200- to 300-grit paper and go back over the walls again, sanding these areas very lightly. Check them for smoothness, wipe off any sanding dust, and, if you prefer, prime the repaired areas again. Once the walls are dry, you are ready to apply your finish paint. Always purchase a good quality of paint—for a bathroom, I recommend a semi-gloss (not flat) latex enamel. Apply two coats and always follow the manufacturer's directions as found on the back of the paint can. Also, be sure to paint far enough into the tub or shower area. I recommend that you prime the tub or shower walls where you plan to use tile or an enclosure kit, even if the wallboard is water-resistant. Be sure to allow the recommended drying time between coats.

Make sure you also allow adequate drying time before you attempt to install fixtures, outlet covers, and adhesive for rubber cove base.

Textured walls

If you have decided to texture your walls, you need to choose the size of the texture and decide whether you are going to roll it on or *knock it down* (flatten with a wallboard knife). The size of the room will play a part in the nap of the texture. There are many options from which to choose, and you might even want to create your own pattern. If you wish, you can apply a very fine spatter to the walls and knock down just the ceiling. Before spraying on the wall finish, experiment on a scrap of wallboard until you find a texture you like. Practice with the equipment until you can spray on an even small- to medium-sized spatter texture and achieve a good appearance when you knock it down with a wallboard knife. After the surface has been spattered, wait about 10 to 15 minutes and very lightly flatten the top of the spatters with a wallboard knife. Your finish pattern depends on how long you let the sprayed texture set up before you knock it down. Again, be sure to experiment on a scrap of wallboard.

The wall texture is sprayed on with a hopper that uses air pressure (10-29). For this system, you will have to mix the wall texture. An alternative is to purchase premixed wall texture and apply it with a hand-held pump spray gun. The pump shown in 10-30 produces multiple spray patterns and works well on small jobs such as bathrooms.

10-29 *Units similar to this can be rented.* HYDE GROUP

10-30
· *Model 4205 and 4405P Spray Texture Gun.*

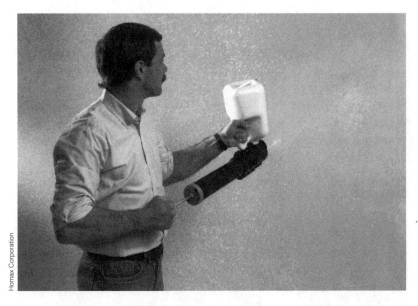

Hornax Corporation

Figures 10-31 through 10-35 show various textures. These commercially used patterns are listed below with a brief explanation of how to achieve the same look.

Fog and spatter This texture is sprayed on and can be applied in three sizes: heavy, medium, and light. It is also known as *orange peel* (10-31).

10-31
*Fog and spatter, or
"orange peel."*

Knock-down and skip-trowel Both textures are sprayed on. To achieve a knock-down look, wait 10 to 15 minutes after spraying for the compound to set up and then very lightly flatten only the tops of the spatter using a flat blade. The skip-trowel pattern is achieved by spattering the compound at low pressure to create larger spatters. After waiting 10 to 15 minutes for the compound to set up, knock down the spatters but apply more pressure than for the knock-down pattern (10-32).

10-32
Knock-down and skip trowel.

Roller texture A roller texture is applied by hand. Thin ready-mix compound to the consistency of latex paint, depending on the desired texture. Completely wet the roller with the compound and apply it to the surface as evenly as possible. Short-nap rollers produce a lower stipple for a finer pattern, and a longer nap produces a higher stipple for a coarse pattern (10-33).

10-33
Roller texture.

Crow's foot Apply the compound in the same fashion as for the roller texture. When the material has dried to a dull wet finish, stamp the surface with a texture brush that has been pre-wetted with texture material (10-34).

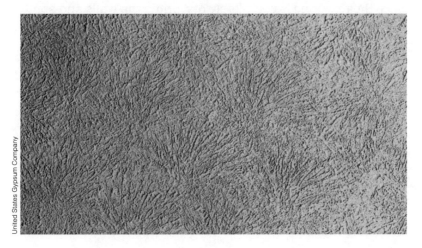

10-34
Crow's foot.

Swirl finish Apply the compound in the same fashion as for the roller texture. When the surface has dried to a dull wet finish, use a wallpaper brush in a circular motion to achieve the desired swirl texture (10-35).

10-35
Swirl finish.

United States Gypsum Company

These are just some of the many textures available and techniques that will help you accomplish your desired pattern. Don't be afraid to mix your patterns—use one pattern for the walls and another for the ceiling. As I suggested earlier, experiment on a scrap of wallboard before tackling your new walls or ceiling.

Once the texturing is completely dry, prime the walls and apply your paint.

Wallpaper

Wallpaper comes in a wide array of colors, patterns, and textures. The best wallcovers for bathrooms are made of vinyl, which is easy to maintain and very durable; but patterns in vinyl might be limited. Vinyl-coated papers come in a wide range of patterns, but their backings tear easily. You might want to look at vinyl wallpapers that have fabric backings of polyester or cheesecloth; these are very durable.

When purchasing wallpaper, be sure to purchase enough for the entire job, because dye lots or printing runs can vary. Even so, check each roll before installation to be sure the patterns and colors match.

Your dealer will have specific recommendations on how to prepare the walls for wallpaper installation. In most cases, the best method is to seal new wallboard with PVA (polyvinyl acetate) primer or paint it with an oil-based topcoat, and then apply sizing.

I don't recommend hanging wallpaper over walls that have not been prepared properly with primer or an oil-based topcoat and then sizing. Removal of the wall covering at a later date could damage the face of the wallboard.

If you want to hang wallpaper but already have textured walls, you have several choices: you can sand the texture, which I don't recommend; you can skim-coat the walls; or you can install lining paper. If you already have wallpaper, it is best to remove it first. If you cannot remove the paper, then use wallpaper primer over the existing paper and apply sizing. For glossy paint, lightly sand the surface to a dull finish, apply flat paint, and then apply sizing. These treatments might take some time, but be patient. To achieve a great-looking wallpaper job, dedicate 90 percent of the work to preparation.

Paint

All new walls need to be primed. You can use PVA primer to seal wallboard. I like to use enamel undercoater as a primer and a latex semigloss paint for the finish. Flat paints do not wash easily and are more subject to wear. For smooth and textured walls, I recommend using a ½" lamb's wool roller. These rollers hold a lot of paint and distribute the paint evenly, yet with a slight texture, on the wall surface.

Avoid purchasing less expensive paints because they contain fewer solids (the effective raw materials used to manufacture paints) and will not stand up to normal bathroom wear. For small bathrooms that are subjected to excessive moisture, your paint dealer can add an anti-mildew chemical to the paint to prevent mildew. Remember to read and follow the manufacturer's instructions on the back of the paint can, and to work in a well-ventilated room.

Are you tired of walking on grubby subfloors? Now that the walls are done, the floor probably looks even worse! Hang in there—next up is the floor covering, and your project will really take on a finished look!

CHAPTER 11

Flooring

ALL YOUR WALLS ARE NOW FINISHED AND PAINTED and you are ready to install the floor covering. This is a critical stage of the job and requires some investigative work on your part. You need to decide what type of floor covering you want: resilient (vinyl), nonresilient (ceramic tile), carpet, or hardwood.

Each type of floor covering has an optimum time for installation. For example, it is much easier to install resilient (vinyl) floor covering in an open room, so it really helps to postpone cabinet installation until after the vinyl is down. On the other hand, nonresilient (ceramic tile) and carpet floors should be laid after the cabinets are in, and hardwood floors can be installed before or after the cabinets. When you install flooring after the cabinets are in, it is important that you maintain the height of the toe kick under the cabinet. The best way to do this is to raise the cabinet the thickness of the finish floor, including, if necessary, the thickness of the carpet padding. A piece of plywood the proper thickness and the same width and depth of the cabinet works well to raise the cabinet. Doing this will have an impact on the plumbing and might also affect the back splash.

Different floor coverings require different preparation of the underlayment. Follow the manufacturer's specifications for the floor material you plan to install. You also need to be aware of the different types of adhesives to be used on wood, cement board, or concrete surfaces such as you would encounter on slab or in a basement bathroom. The purpose of this chapter is to introduce you to the types of products and underlayments to use, and to detail the proper procedures to follow for a professional-looking installation.

Resilient flooring

There are two kinds of resilient vinyl floors: *tiles* and *sheet goods*. Floor tiles come in either 12" by 12" or 9" by 9" sizes. Sheet flooring comes in rolls, usually 6' or 12' wide. Before you install any vinyl floor tiles, contact your local building department to see if vinyl tiles comply with regulations in your area.

Most vinyl sheet flooring falls into one of two categories, depending on the styling process used: printed-pattern and inlaid-color floors. The printed-pattern floors (or *rotovinyls* as they are called in the flooring industry) consist of a backing material, a layer of foam cushioning (not comparable to the cushion floors used in the 1970s), the color and pattern (which are printed on by the rotogravure method), and a clear *wear layer* on top to protect the color and pattern.

Once this type of flooring is installed, it has to be sealed, or coated, at all seams with a special sealer or coating (solvent) made for that particular product. The solvent actually welds the two pieces of flooring together to keep out dirt and moisture.

The inlaid-color floors don't have a printed pattern. Instead, the pattern is built up by using thousands upon thousands of colored vinyl granules which are then fused together by intense heat and pressure before the wear layer is applied. This process gives a rich look to the floor, and it is impervious to dents and damage (such as tears and gouges), but it can be difficult to work with because of its stiffness. Inlaid color floors come in 6' wide rolls only, and professional installation is recommended by the manufacturer.

Today's floor coverings come with beautiful designs and patterns, and even some that simulate glazed quarry floor tiles (11-1). After you've chosen between printed rotovinyl and inlaid vinyl flooring, you have to select the kind of wear layer (top coat) you want. Again, you have a couple of choices: vinyl or urethane. Each flooring manufacturer has its own terminology regarding wear layers, and the performance of these wear layers will vary from manufacturer to manufacturer; discuss with your floor covering retailer the exact manufacturer definitions of wear layers.

The factory-applied wear layer essentially replaces the need for wax, dramatically reducing the amount of time you'll spend on floor care. Up to a point, the vinyl and urethane wear layers perform identical functions—protecting both the color and the pattern. This protection also makes the floor easier to clean, but there the similarities end. A urethane wear layer is a lot harder and will keep its like-new appearance much longer than

Finishes

11-1
This vinyl flooring simulates floor tile.

Armstrong World Industries, Inc.

its vinyl counterpart. It also offers the glossiest shine and the toughest stain and scuff resistance. When the original luster on the vinyl begins to look dull, a coat of liquid polish applied with a sponge mop will restore the shine for cosmetic purposes. A urethane surface might also lose some of its gloss, depending on traffic patterns but it, too, can be restored with polish.

Backing

Resilient floor backing also varies from product to product and can affect the ease of installation. Perimeter-installed floors have a flexible, tear-resistant backing which can be stretched over most types of preexisting floors and underlayments. This type of floor covering is only secured around the perimeter.

Felt-back floors, on the other hand, can be installed over a more limited range of underlayments and need to be glued entirely using a mastic (adhesive). An understanding of these backing differences, as well as the type of floor backing that is right for your particular application, can save you both time and money, whether you plan to install the floor yourself or have a professional do it for you.

Nonresilient flooring

Nonresilient flooring includes ceramic mosaic, paver, and quarry tiles, as well as terazzo, stone, slate, and brick. When selecting a floor tile, be sure that the tile is durable enough to withstand wear and tear. Glazed tile, because of its glass-like surface, scratches easily. If you choose such a floor tile, make sure that its finish isn't so slick it is dangerous to walk on.

Unglazed tiles that are porous, such as clay, mosaic, paver, or quarry tile, and other nonresilient porous materials, need treatment with a special stain-resistant sealant. This product provides protection against most greases, oils, and chemicals. Your local tile dealer can advise you on the proper sealant to use, and give you specific care instructions.

Hardwood and carpeting

My best recommendation on this subject is not to install either hardwood or carpeting in any bathroom. If you do decide on hardwood, finish it with a marine-type varnish and try to keep it out of areas of direct contact with water. Ask your local paint dealer for advice on finishes.

If you decide on carpet, again, keep it out of areas of direct water contact, or consider an outdoor type of carpet. Outdoor carpeting has a backing that is made of a closed-pore type of vinyl or latex foam, which keeps out moisture. Over concrete floors, such as in a basement, you might want to consider rubber-backed carpet that has a nonskid backing and is water-resistant.

Warranties

It is very important to read the warranty from each manufacturer carefully and check for the following:

- What is the length of the warranty once the floor covering has been installed?

- Under what circumstances will the manufacturer replace or repair the floor covering?

- Does the floor covering have to be installed by a professional in order to be covered under the warranty?

- Is there a guarantee against wear, loss of gloss, or discoloration?

A warranty should add to, not detract from, the value of the floor you are considering. Knowing what a floor warranty covers can prevent unpleasant or costly surprises later.

Underlayment

Before you install any new floor covering, it is important that the surface (underlayment) you plan to cover (whether it is concrete, plywood, or an existing vinyl floor) be smooth, structurally sound, and generally clean. If the surface is dusty and dirty, you won't achieve the proper bond that is essential for a good installation. If the surface has depressions or foreign deposits, they, too, should be corrected or removed because they can eventually telegraph through the new flooring. As you can see, a certain amount of preparation is necessary for a professional-looking job.

Over the years, I have learned to recommend against a couple of practices. For instance, do not use particleboard as an underlayment. This product swells when it comes in contact with water over a period of time. Second, I do not recommend the installation of a new floor covering directly over an existing floor covering. It is difficult to achieve the proper bond between the new floor and the existing one, which can cause separation or lifting. In many cases, however, you can install new over existing floor coverings if the existing flooring has been properly cleaned with a product such as TSP (tri-sodium phosphate). For environmental reasons, you might not be allowed to use TSP in your community. If that is the case, then contact your local paint store for an environmentally safe product.

The best results in floor covering installations are achieved when existing flooring and underlayment have been replaced with new underlayment. This process gives added protection when dealing with manufacturer's warranties.

Laying over existing flooring

If your current floor covering contains asbestos, you might be able to bypass expensive removal and disposal procedures by installing a new underlayment and floor covering over the existing asbestos product. Before you do this, however, be sure to check with your building department and the applicable governing agencies to make sure this is acceptable.

If your existing floor covering was a product of the 1970s and has a true cushion backing, then it would be best to remove the floor covering rather than to install a new underlayment over it. Again, you will want to check with your building department.

A ⅜" underlayment is thick enough to do the job. However, if you need to use a thinner underlayment in order to achieve a good match-up with adjacent existing floor covering (carpeting in doorways), consider fastening it to the existing floor covering with adhesive in conjunction with ringshank nails or screws. You might want to choose a thicker underlayment to lay over existing flooring—be careful, though, that you don't get too high a floor. Check the threshold of the doorway where it meets either a hallway or another room; you want to make a good transition from the floor in one room to the floor in another. Also check to see if you can open and close the door and if the toilet flange needs alterations or if a wax bowl ring will be enough for proper installation of the toilet.

If you are using ¼" underlayment, select a product that will meet the manufacturer's specifications and warranties. There are new products on the market which are unlike traditional underlayment materials. Some are fabricated with marine grade adhesives and will not warp, buckle, or delaminate. These underlayment systems might require professional installation, and they are not recommended for use under ceramic tile applications. Your floor covering dealer can help you select the proper underlayment for your specific flooring application.

The surface of a concrete subfloor should be dry, smooth, and structurally sound. It also should be free of depressions, scales, or foreign deposits of any kind. All concrete subfloors on or below grade level, particularly those that are less than two years old, should be tested for moisture with a bond test. First, remove any foreign material such as oil, grease, paint, varnish, and any other special surface treatments and then install a small section of the flooring measuring at least 36" square. If the surface is large, then install several test patches at intervals. This test should not be conducted at temperatures less than 50°F.

Laying over concrete

If the patches are securely bonded after 72 hours, you can conclude that the concrete surface is dry and sufficiently clean of foreign material to permit a satisfactory installation of the resilient flooring. If it took an unusual amount of force to lift the patches from the surface and you notice adhesive clinging to both the back of the flooring and the concrete surface, you can consider it to be a secured bond and the surface will not need further cleaning. These test areas, however, will need to be cleaned (before you can install your finish flooring) by scraping off the adhesive with a razor scraper.

If your bond test fails (i.e., the floor material does not tightly adhere to the concrete), you probably have a moisture problem. Water could be coming from a variety of sources, and you might be able to address the problem fairly easily, for example, by adding rain gutters. However, the situation could be much more complex. You will want to bring in an experienced professional for advice before you attempt to solve this problem on your own.

A dusty or chalky surface on a suspended concrete subfloor should be swept clean and sealed with a primer coat. A thin, even layer of the proper adhesive for a concrete floor applied with a smooth-edged trowel may be used as a primer before installing materials with an adhesive.

A dusty concrete floor on or below grade can be a sign of alkali salts; again, a bonding test should be made. A concrete floor that shows signs of alkali salts might need to be neutralized before you can install any floor covering. Consult a professional who can handle this job for you.

Sometimes a rough concrete floor can be smoothed with wet sharp sand and a floor machine equipped with abrasive stones. If you have rough spots, they could be smoothed by using a latex underlayment. Scaling, crazed, and cracked concrete surfaces will not make a good base for resilient flooring. Such surfaces should be given a top coat of either latex-bonded concrete or epoxy. Avoid using self-leveling gypsum-based concrete toppings—some flooring manufacturers will not warrant their resilient floor covering if it is installed over such products. Also, don't install a wooden underlayment over concrete; it can trap moisture, creating all kinds of problems later on.

Again, as for any other underlayment or concrete subfloor, the surface must be smooth, structurally sound, clean, and free of depressions, foreign deposits, and particles. Make sure that all screws and nails are installed just below the surface of the underlayment.

Use an American Plywood Association (APA) trademarked plywood rated as an underlayment for vinyl or other resilient-finish floorings. Other unrated products are available, but you will need to research these products carefully with specific emphasis on their warranties. The product should have an Exposure Durability Classification (Exterior or Exposure 1) and should have a fully sanded face (surface). Other recommended APA plywoods are Underlayment A-C, B-C, or C-C Plugged or C-C Plugged EXT when marked *sanded face*. Your lumber dealer can give you a list of APA and other recommended plywoods, or contact the American Plywood Association, 7011 South 19th Street, Tacoma, WA 98411.

If your existing floor covering does not contain asbestos, and you have removed the floor covering and underlayment as detailed in chapter 6, you are ready to install new plywood underlayment.

Basically, follow the same procedures in reverse to install underlayment. Install felt paper between the subfloor and the underlayment to serve as a vapor barrier and to prevent squeaking floors. It can also help you to achieve a good match-up with carpeting in doorways. Before you lay down the felt paper, however, take a moment to notice the direction in which the subfloor runs; your underlayment should run in the same direction. Notice where the subfloor seams are so you can overlap them with underlayment. You do not want one seam on top of another. The minimum seam overlap for plywood is 2" extending beyond the subfloor seam. I recommend, however, that you extend the underlayment to the next floor joist. That way, you have a solid framing member to which you can fasten the underlayment.

While you are looking at the subfloor, follow the nailing pattern to learn the locations of the floor joists, and mark on the walls

Plywood underlayment

Installation of plywood underlayment

(near the floor) the location of each joist. If it is at all possible, locate all underlayment seams in the center of a framing member. To avoid a seam running down the center of the doorway, cut your underlayment to fit into the opening in a full piece (11-2). You might also have to cut a little off the bottoms of the doorstops, jambs, or casing in order to install underlayment or floor covering.

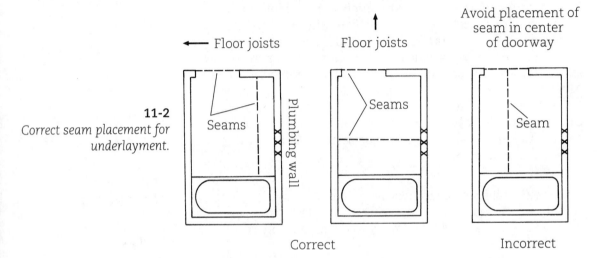

11-2
Correct seam placement for underlayment.

When installing the underlayment, loosely butt the seams, and stay away from the walls and tub about ³⁄₁₆". If you are going to nail, use a ringshank nail that is long enough to penetrate the floor joists at seams and at least ½" into the subfloor in the field. Personally, I like to fasten the entire underlayment to the subfloor using 1½" deck screws. Drive the screws just below the surface of the underlayment. In general, you will want to space screws 3" apart on center around the perimeter and along seams, and 4" to 6" apart in the field over the floor joists. Check with your building department, however, for their recommended nailing schedule. Drill for the toilet flange (if necessary), and fill all screw holes, gouges, gaps, chips, sunken edges, and seams more than ¼" wide with a quick-setting, nonshrinking compound (11-3A and B).

Sand out any imperfections and sweep or vacuum the area, making sure that all dust is removed from the plywood surface.

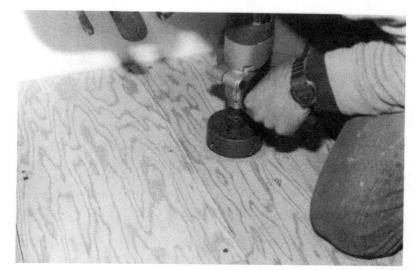

11-3A
When drilling for toilet flange, be sure to hold side handle of drill for complete control.

11-3B
Fill all seams, screw holes, and other depressions with compound.

Now is a good time to check the floor for any imperfections that might have been overlooked. Note: If you use nails instead of screws, you might consider not filling the nail holes. If a nail works loose, it can force the patching compound up and form a small bump under or in the finish floor which invites premature wear. Be sure to drive the head of the nail just below the surface of the underlayment or—better yet—use deck screws.

Installing sheet goods

One of the most important parts of installing finish flooring is to make sure the pattern looks square in the room. There are two main areas that require special attention: in front of the tub and in the doorway. Both of these areas are very noticeable, so it is important to make sure that any "grout" lines in the pattern of your floor covering are parallel to both the tub and the door at the same time.

If the tub and the door are not parallel, then the secret is to keep some space between any object (walls, tub, cabinets, door opening, etc.) and the next grout line in the flooring pattern. One way to achieve this is to cut the grout line off using a straightedge and a utility knife (11-4A). Before you cut anything else, also check out the pattern from side to side. Again, don't let grout lines get too close to the walls unless you can bring the line so close that the toe of the base molding will cover it completely (see 11-4B and C).

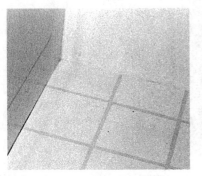

11-4A *Grout line against front of bathtub has been cut off.*

11-4B *Grout lines are parallel both to wall and rough door framing.*

11-4C *Grout line close to wall should be covered by base molding or cut off.*

The installation I'm describing in this chapter is a cut-and-fit method of applying resilient flooring. Some installers refer to this method as *freehand*, and prefer to use a pattern (cut exactly to fit) method. If this is your first time, I recommend using the pattern method, especially when the flooring material is thick. All you need is building paper and masking tape. Cut the paper to fit the shape of the room and then transfer the pattern to the sheet goods. Tape the pattern down and cut. Be careful not to cut anything of value that might be underneath the floor covering. One advantage to this method is that you can lay the pattern out on your new floor material and move it around until you reach the best layout for your room.

For those who prefer the cut-and-fit method, let's continue with cutting the flooring along the length of the wall. So far, you've cut the tub and doorway areas; only the sidewalls remain. On the sidewall, the floor covering will curl up the wall in the shape of a **U** (11-5A). Be careful as you approach an inside corner like this, or you can damage the backing. If you cut the flooring in the bottom of the **U**, it will be too short. What you need to do is push the floor covering simultaneously down and into the corner to close the gap of the **U** so you can approach a 90° angle. What you are actually doing is creasing the floor covering into the corner where the wall meets the underlayment.

11-5A
Inside corner detail.

At this point you have two options. One is to use a stiff straightedge to push down on the floor covering and into the corner (where the wall meets the underlayment), at the same time that you cut the floor covering. Apply pressure to the straightedge and cut the floor covering on the wall side of it with a utility knife, continuing along the length of the wall (11-5B).

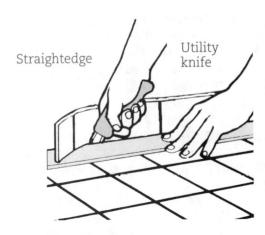

Straightedge

Utility knife

11-5B
Use a straightedge; a 2×4 does not work for this operation because of its thickness.

When bathrooms are small, I prefer to use the alternate option, a heavy-duty 3" angle scraper (putty knife) instead of a straightedge. Use the angle scraper to push down on the floor covering and into the corner. Again, cut on the wall side of the scraper and continue the length of the wall.

A special tool is also available for purchase or for rent that will cut the flooring in this type of situation, but I have found the method I described above to be the easiest for me.

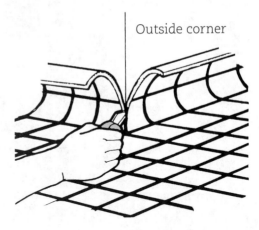

Outside corner

11-6A *Trimming an outside corner.*

To trim an outside corner, start at the top of the flooring material where it overlaps the corner and cut the material down to the floor using a sharp razor blade (11-6A).

To fit an inside corner, use a utility knife and carefully cut out V-shaped sections down into the corner until the flooring lies flat on the floor (11-6B). Take your time and make small cuts as

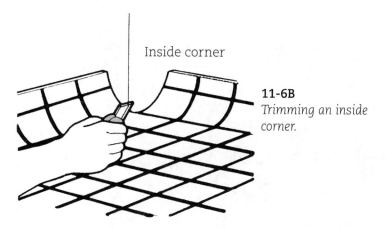

Inside corner

11-6B
Trimming an inside corner.

you trim the corners, and be sure to use sharp tools; dull blades can damage the flooring material.

Once you have cut the floor covering to size, you are ready to apply mastic. It is not necessary to remove your newly-cut flooring to apply the mastic. Instead, roll it back half of the room size and sweep the underlayment and the backside of the floor covering. Use a trowel (see chapter 4 and the back label of the mastic container for the proper notch size) to spread adhesive on the open half of the room (11-7A and B) and roll the floor covering down onto the mastic. Now roll back the other half of the flooring, but when you roll it back, roll it back beyond the area just glued down (11-8). This ensures that when you trowel the mastic onto the other half of the underlayment, it will overlap the mastic applied first.

11-7A *To spread adhesive, start at farthest exposed underlayment and work back toward rolled floor covering.*

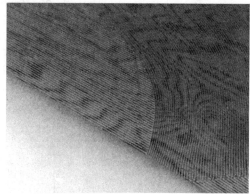

11-7B *Properly troweled mastic; notice grooves.*

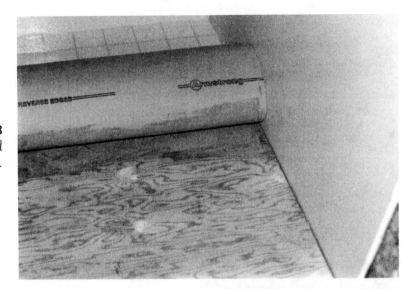

11-8
Retrowel over mastic exposed when you roll back flooring.

Once you complete the installation of the floor covering, use a roller (11-9) and roll with slight pressure from the center to the outside perimeter. This helps bring any air bubbles out from under the floor covering. Finally—and this is very important—use masking tape to seal the edge where the flooring meets the tub. This will keep dirt out until you are ready to use silicone (rubber) caulk (chapter 16).

11-9 *Roll floor to release trapped air bubbles.*

Nonresilient installation

Quarry tile or any other nonresilient product can be installed over most floor surfaces that are dry, clean, firm, and level. *Don't lay tile over a springy floor.* If the floor needs leveling, shore up sunken areas and fill irregularities by applying a quick-setting nonshrinking compound with a trowel, then cover it with exterior grade APA (at least ⅜" thick) plywood or cement board. For a plywood underlayment, follow the instructions contained in this chapter. For cement board, apply a setting bed of latex-modified mortar over the plywood subfloor using a ¼" square-notched trowel. You must fasten the units of cement board every 6" to 8" both in length and width over the entire area while the mortar is still workable.

Make sure that the joints do not line up with the underlying subfloor joints. Allow approximately ⅛" of space between panels, and fill with latex-modified thin-set mortar using a flat-edge trowel. It is not necessary to tape these joints, but taping does provide a flat, uniform surface. Regardless of the above recommended installation instructions, follow the manufacturer's specifications for installation of the cement board product you purchased.

Basic tile installation is described in detail in chapter 13. Make sure floor tiles are firmly set by sliding a flat board across the surface while tapping it with a hammer. Figure 11-10 shows a cross section of a tile floor using a cement board product as underlayment.

When installing any nonresilient product, use cement board as the underlayment for these products. When installing over an existing subfloor, be sure to check that the subfloor is sound and solidly fastened.

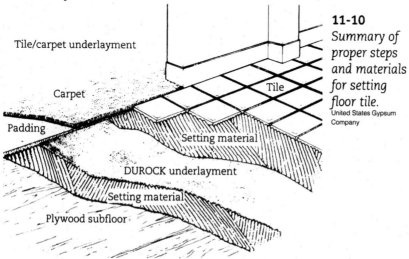

Tile/carpet underlayment

Carpet

Tile

Padding

Setting material

DUROCK underlayment

Setting material

Plywood subfloor

11-10
Summary of proper steps and materials for setting floor tile.
United States Gypsum Company

Flooring   183

Special applications

There are other areas of concern when installing nonresilient products under specific circumstances. For instance, you might decide to install a hot tub just outside your bathroom and you want to tile over an existing concrete patio. Or you might live on the upper level of a condominium and want to apply tile over the concrete subfloor. Your tile dealer can provide you with the guidance you will need under these special conditions, or write the Tile Council of America, Inc. (P.O. Box 326, Princeton, NJ 08542-0326) for brochures and detailed information. Some of their information might require payment of a small fee.

How do you feel? Doesn't it feel good to be walking on that new floor? If you think it's coming together now, stay tuned because the cabinets are next!

Cabinets
& countertops

I WOULD VENTURE A GUESS that many of us would love to create a bathroom so big we could get lost in it. And we would fill it with enough cabinets (12-1) that we wouldn't know where to start looking for a new bar of soap. Wouldn't that be great? In reality, unless you are building a new home or addition, you will have to live with what you have—so let's make the most of it.

12-1
A total decorator look achieved with traditional bathroom cabinetry.

KraftMaid Cabinetry, Inc.

In order to incorporate the cabinets into your plans, you need to know their sizes (height, width, and depth). Manufactured cabinets share typical layouts and dimensions; get an illustrated brochure or list of cabinets and their dimensions from your local building supply store, and browse through it. As you will see, there are a lot of choices. From vanity combination drawers to contemporary overhead lights, you will be able to coordinate everything, both in color and style. Exploring all the possibilities of design offered by a complete cabinetry line is a really exciting part of planning a new bathroom.

Take the time to check out all the different types of door styles, lighting, mirrors, wall cabinetry, accessories, and hardware. Also explore the types of wood and the finishes that are available. This will all take time, but it is a very necessary part of planning for your finished bathroom.

There are a few measurements you need to know as you select your cabinets. A wash basin requires a vanity that is a minimum of 24" wide. A bathroom cabinet, including the top, has a finished height of 32", while a kitchen cabinet is 36". Depending on your height, you can install any cabinet that is comfortable to use, especially the sink cabinet. It is OK to install kitchen cabinets in a bathroom, but remember that a kitchen cabinet is also 24" deep, 3" more than a typical bathroom vanity.

If you are planning a barrier-free bathroom, then the counter can be no higher than 34" above the floor. To allow for knee space, the wash basin cannot be deeper than 6½". The bottom edge of mirrors must be no higher than 40", and lever-type faucets, which are easy to use, should be installed (12-2).

You don't want to crowd your bathroom with so many cabinets that you have no room to walk. If you want to hang a wall cabinet above the toilet, I would recommend using a vanity wall boutique which protrudes from the wall from 4⅝" to 8"; wall cabinets protrude 12". A vanity wall boutique will look more in balance with the toilet tank.

If you install a vanity base drawer unit on a wall near the door, you will find when you open the drawer that it is very close to the door casing. Manufacturers sell a 3" *vanity filler* that can be very useful in situations like these. I recommend pulling the cabinet away from the sidewall about 1" and trimming the filler down to size. It is also easier to mount the filler onto the cabinet stile before attaching the unit to the wall (12-3).

While you are planning your cabinetry, be sure to take note of any unfinished ends that will be exposed. Cabinet manufacturers sell finish panels to match all their finishes, so be aware that you might need to buy one or more.

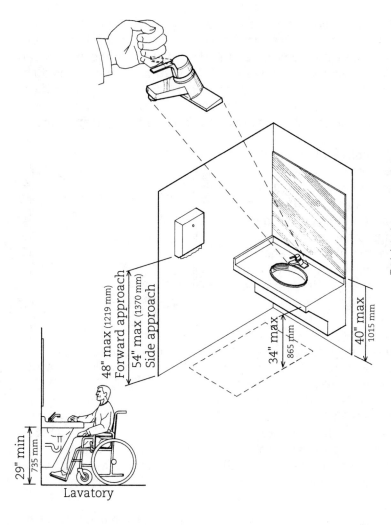

12-2
Barrier-free bathroom measurements.
East. Paralyzed Vet. Assoc.

48" max (1219 mm) Forward approach

54" max (1370 mm) Side approach

34" max 865 mm

40" max 1015 mm

29" min 735 mm

Lavatory

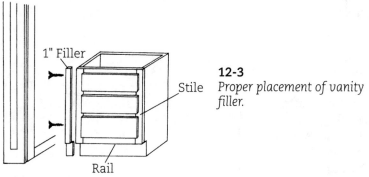

1" Filler

Stile

12-3
Proper placement of vanity filler.

Rail

Cabinets & countertops   187

There are a couple of other areas to watch out for. Try not to locate a cabinet too close to a tub, because it can be difficult to clean up water between them. Also, the moisture can adversely affect the finish on the cabinet. If you have no choice, install a smaller-width vanity with a smaller wash basin. It is best if you can keep the vanity at least 6" away from the tub so that if water does get into this area, you will be able to clean it up.

12-4 *Cabinet organizers provide convenience and organization.* CLOSET MAID - Clairson International Corporation

If you have a laundry room located under the bathroom, you might want to install a laundry chute. Your building department might have some recommended dimensions for such a chute. If you do install a laundry chute, be sure to do it in such a way that small children will not have access to it. If you have the space, you might also want to install storage baskets or roll-out shelves in the cabinets (12-4). If you plan to locate the laundry area in the bathroom, you might want to plan space for a laundry bin and storage shelves (12-5). There are many pre-made storage systems that are affordable, adaptable, and easy to install. Take the time to research them as you plan your bathroom.

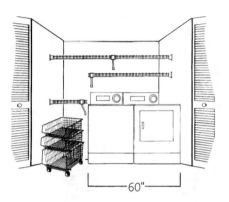

12-5 *A simple way to organize laundry products, including towels.* CLOSET MAID - Clairson International Corporation

Required tools

The tools you will need to install upper and lower cabinets include:

- Handsaw.
- Drill and countersink bit.
- Screw gun.
- Tape measure.
- Level.
- Hammer and rubber mallet.
- Trowel.
- Pry bar.

- Two **C** clamps.
- Carpenter's square.
- Stepladder.
- Stud finder.

Hardware needs include:

- Screws with coarse threads (1⅝" to 3" long).
- Finish nails (brads).
- A putty stick that matches your choice of finish.
- Toggle bolts (used to fasten to wallboard when you are unable to fasten to a stud).
- Adhesive as recommended by the cabinet manufacturer.
- Wooden shims (essential to your project; they will be used to help level both base and wall cabinetry).

Helpful hints

- It can be helpful to remove doors and drawers from the units before installing the cabinets.

- Always predrill your holes.

- Use a countersink bit in stiles or rails.

- Always use clamps when installing two cabinets side-by-side.

- Use cardboard or a piece of wood at both ends of the clamp to protect the face frame edges from damage.

- Whenever possible, conceal your installation screws behind hinges when fastening cabinets together.

Preparation

Before you begin to install any cabinets, upper or lower, take the time to check your walls and floor to see if they are level and even (12-6). As you can see, there is some work involved but careful attention to these details will ensure a quality installation.

Uneven spots on the floor and walls can adversely affect cabinet installation. Wall unevenness can cause misalignment of cabinets, resulting in racking of doors and drawer fronts. To make the cabinets plumb, true, and square, it might be necessary to shim them (put thin pieces of wood behind, between, or under them) during installation. Use a straight length of 2×4 and a carpenter's level (12-6), to check the floor

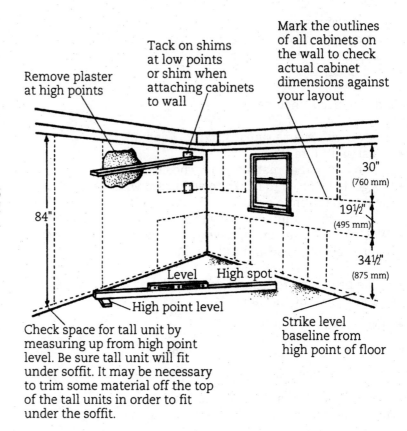

Remove plaster at high points

Tack on shims at low points or shim when attaching cabinets to wall

Mark the outlines of all cabinets on the wall to check actual cabinet dimensions against your layout

12-6
Preparation of walls and floors. KraftMaid Cabinetry, Inc.

84"

30"
(760 mm)

19½"
(495 mm)

34½"
(875 mm)

Level   High spot

High point level

Check space for tall unit by measuring up from high point level. Be sure tall unit will fit under soffit. It may be necessary to trim some material off the top of the tall units in order to fit under the soffit.

Strike level baseline from high point of floor

and walls in the cabinet area for high spots. When you locate the highest point on the floor, mark a level baseline on the wall in the area(s) where the cabinets will be installed. Also mark cabinet outlines on walls to check their actual dimensions against your layout. Use a stud finder (or tap on the walls) to locate studs, and mark their positions.

Installing cabinets

Install recessed medicine and upper cabinets first, beginning with the upper corner cabinet (if any). Measure up from the floor baseline to mark the baseline of your upper cabinets. If you are installing more than one cabinet, it helps to have a second pair of hands, or use a T-brace (made from rough lumber) to support the base of the cabinets as you install them.

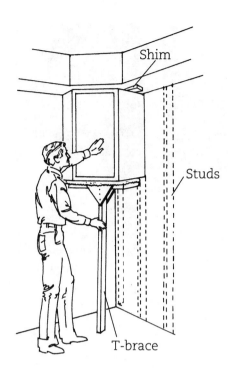

Shim

Studs

T-brace

12-7
A T-brace holds upper cabinet in correct position.
KraftMaid Cabinetry, Inc.

Make sure your screws are long enough and that you hit solid framing material (backing or members). If the upper cabinet has an exposed unfinished side, you will need to glue on a finish panel. Take your time to carefully fit this panel. Once you are satisfied with the fit, trowel on the adhesive and use ½" finish nails (brads). Countersink the nails and camouflage the holes with a matching putty stick.

Installing lower cabinets

If possible, install the lower cabinets *after* resilient flooring has been put in place; it is much easier to install floor coverings in an open room than to cut around cabinetry. Figure 12-8 illustrates the use of **C**-clamps and shims to install side-by-side cabinets. Figures 12-9 through 12-12 illustrate the steps involved in the installation of lower cabinets. Use a framing square to make sure your cabinets are perpendicular to the wall (12-9). Make sure the cabinets are level both parallel (12-10A) and perpendicular to the wall. Don't forget to use shims to achieve a level installation, so the doors and drawers will open and close properly. Shims might be required for leveling both at the back of the cabinet and under the toe kick (12-10B through 12-11B).

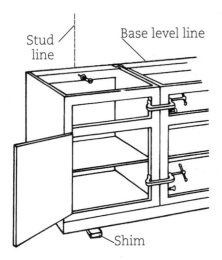

Stud line

Base level line

Shim

12-8 *Use of shim and **C**-clamps.*
KraftMaid Cabinetry, Inc.

12-9 *Framing square ensures cabinets are perpendicular to wall.*

12-10A *Check for level both parallel and perpendicular to wall.*

12-10B *Shims might be required for leveling at back of cabinet.*

When fastening a screw through the toe kick of the cabinet, be sure to use a long screw and predrill your hole. Work carefully, because the toe kick is made of very thin material. Screws should be installed at a sharp angle at the ends of your cabinet's toe kick (12-11A). Trim the shims, no matter where they are located (12-11B).

12-11A
Use a long screw and predrill your hole.

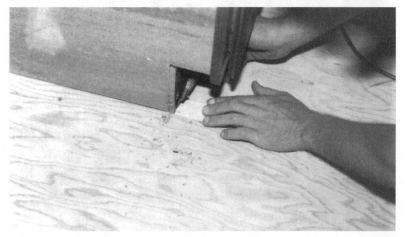

12-11B
Trim the shims.

Before you glue the finish panel onto the exposed side of a cabinet, be sure to cut out the toe kick. Using the toe kick as a guide, scribe the prefinished panel to provide a cutting guide (12-12).

12-12
Cut out toe kick in prefinished panel.

Installing countertops

Figures 12-13 through 12-17 show the installation of a countertop. You can purchase countertop material that is 25" wide and up to 12' long. Draw a level line on the wall to the level of the cabinet to guide your cleat placement (12-13). Then mount ¾" furring strips across the top of the cabinet to raise the countertop enough so the laminate's finished edge will not interfere with door and drawer operation (12-14). Make sure when you attach the countertop material to the furring strips that you countersink the screws and putty the holes (12-15).

12-13
Draw a level line to guide cleat placement.

12-14
Furring strips achieve proper counter height.

The recommended overhang for countertops is 1", but if you
want a ¾" by 1½" wooden edge instead of a laminate edge, then
overhang the countertop by only ¼" (12-16). I recommend that
you glue your edge to the countertop with wood glue in
addition to countersinking the finish nails.

12-16
*Installation of hardwood
edge.*

Periodically check to make sure your wooden counter edge is even with your rough countertop. When applying a wooden edge, it is good practice to predrill your holes to prevent splitting. Countersink your finish nails far enough that the hole will hold putty. To ensure tightly mitered corners, apply pressure when you predrill and sink your nails, and be sure to use glue. Take care not to get any glue on the surface of the wood. If this happens, quickly use a wet clean white rag to wipe off excess glue. Once the edge and top are complete, sand the top with a finish sander, and dust the top thoroughly (12-17).

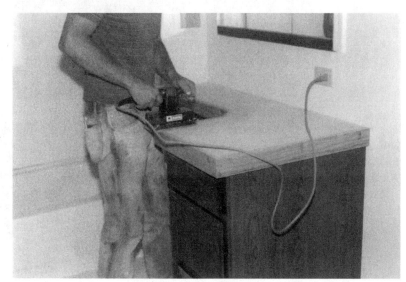

12-17
Be sure to clean off sanding dust!

Installing plastic laminate

If you plan to apply plastic laminate over your countertop, take time to carefully trial fit the laminate before gluing (12-18A). Use a carbide scoring tool and a straightedge to cut the laminate so it overhangs the edges by about ⅜". While applying pressure to the straightedge, draw the tool toward you, scoring the finish side at least three times in the same spot (12-18B). Continue to apply pressure to the straightedge while you lift up the discard piece (12-18C). Lift hard and fast—the laminate will snap with a loud noise (don't be alarmed) and break away.

When spreading contact cement, be sure to follow the manufacturer's instructions on the backside of the can, and

12-18A
Trial fit plastic laminate to wall and inside corners before cutting.

12-18B *Score laminate.*

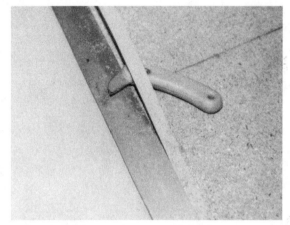

12-18C *Apply pressure to straightedge as you snap laminate.*

work in a warm, well-ventilated room. Use rollers to ensure that the glue completely covers the surfaces of both the countertop and the backside of the laminate (12-19A and B). You might want to have a disposable drop cloth underneath the laminate while you roll the contact cement.

12-19A
Make sure glue completely covers surface.

12-19B
Use a paintbrush to apply glue close to wall.

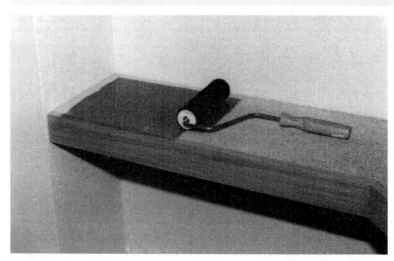

I recommend the use of old venetian blind slats to hold the glue-coated laminate up and off the glue-covered countertop until you are satisfied that the laminate is correctly positioned. This is a job that has to be done right the first time; once the two glued surfaces come in contact with each other, a bond is made and you will be unable to lift up the laminate to make any adjustments. After the contact cement has dried for the recommended time, spread out your venetian blind slats over the countertop, hump-side up (12-19C). Carefully lay out the laminate—the venetian blind slats will keep it away from the contact cement until you are sure of its positioning (12-19D).

12-19C
Spread out venetian blind slats hump-side up!

12-19D
Carefully lay out the laminate.

Working from the wall out, remove a couple of blinds and press the laminate down onto the countertop. Be careful not to rub the laminate tightly against a slat or you won't be able to pull it out. I find that working about 2" away from the slats really helps to avoid this situation. Repeat the process and slowly work your way to the outer edge. Using an extension roller, press the laminate down onto the countertop, applying a firm, even pressure (12-19E). Make sure you roll over all areas of the laminate, with special attention to the edges, to ensure a tight bond.

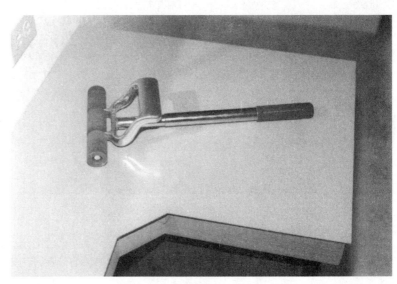

12-19E
Roll over all areas of the laminate.

The final step is to rout the edge, cutting off the ⅜" overhang (12-20A). I prefer to use a carbide (not steel) bit when routing the edge. Periodically check the roller on your router bit for buildup of contact cement. If you are using a standard router, you won't be able to rout the edge up against the wall or in small angles. Use a laminate scoring tool and a straightedge to remove the laminate in the areas where the router will not fit (12-20B). Take your time and work very carefully—you don't want to chip the laminate.

A disc sander can then be used to remove most of the rest of the material (12-20C). Select a large enough disc pad (3") so it extends out beyond at least one side of the drill; otherwise you won't be able to get the tool close enough to the wall.

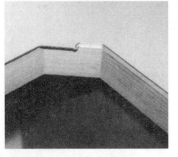

12-20A *Routing the edge.*

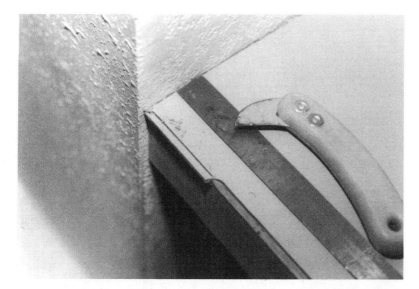

12-20B
Use laminate scoring tool with straightedge.

12-20C
Use a disc sander to finish the job.

Careful handwork with a sharp chisel or a file might be required where the counter meets the wall (12-20D). To finish the edge, first use a flat file (fine pattern) and then a hand sanding block with 100-grit sandpaper to sand the edge where the laminate meets the wooden edging. When you are satisfied with its smoothness, finish the edge. When choosing your

12-20D
Finished laminate countertop.

finish, remember that oils really bring out the woodgrain. If scratches should appear after an oil has been applied, then sand again using a higher grit sandpaper and reapply the oil.

Depending on the shape and length of the countertop, you might have to create a seam by butting one piece of laminate up against another. Achieving a perfect seam is next to impossible, but it can be done with patience. A product is available in a wide range of colors that you can use to fill the void between the two pieces of laminate. You might want to experiment with the product a little to understand its characteristics. If necessary, you can mix colors to match exactly the color you need. Follow the manufacturer's instructions and clean off any excess with a solvent. This product dries very fast, so work quickly!

Installing tile

One way to make the countertop in your bathroom look rich is to install tile. Before you begin, however, read chapter 13 for the basics of installing tile. It is also very important that you experiment with the tile and your desired pattern by laying out a dry run of the tile.

If you wish, you can use ¾" exterior-grade plywood for a countertop. If you do use wood, be sure to seal all cut or exposed edges to avoid water damage. Keep in mind that wood substrate materials used in wet areas are subject to deterioration from moisture penetration. I highly recommend the use of cement board instead of plywood. Install it to the manufacturer's specifications. Figure 12-21 shows a cross section of tile-covered countertop with cement board for underlayment.

When you lay out the tiles for your dry run, work from front to back so that cut tiles will be up against the wall and less noticeable. If the counter has a wash basin, work from the sink edge outward. If there is no wash basin, start in the center. Adjust your layout to arrive at the best-looking pattern with the least amount of cut tiles (12-22). If the countertop is between walls, adjust the tiles so both ends will have tiles cut to approximately the same size.

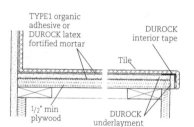

Countertops

12-21 *Cross section of tile-covered countertop.* United States Gypsum Company

American Olean Tile Company

12-22
A tile countertop adds color to your bathroom decor.

The key to achieving a professional tile installation is to be patient and take your time. Once this step is completed, you will be ready to install the back splash that will complete your countertop. This procedure is described in chapter 13.

By now, you should be feeling good about what you have achieved. The next chapter discusses tub and shower enclosures. This is an area where you can display your personality!

Tub & shower enclosures

T UB AND SHOWER ENCLOSURES can drastically change the appearance of your bathroom. You can do this simply by the selections you make for your tub and shower enclosure and door. There are many styles and colors from which to choose. Keep in mind that some enclosures have to be installed by a professional contractor. Because there are so many choices, I will focus on the basic installation of molded fiberglass panels and tile.

First, however, I would like to introduce a couple of products worth considering. For those who prefer tile, SwanTile might be just the product for you. It is a 3- or 5-panel fiberglass wall system that looks and feels like an expensive grade of tile. It is easy to install and maintain and will not develop cracks or discolored grout lines. The unit comes with two shampoo shelves and a built-in soap dish. The surface is chip- and scratch-resistant and the color is molded throughout (13-1).

13-1 *SwanTile: The look and feel of expensive ceramic tile.*

The Swan Corporation

The other product is called Swanstone, a solid material that also has the color molded throughout. It comes in 1-, 2-, or 3-panel units and can be combined for installation over almost any shower floor situation. It can be cut or shaped easily for special effects or for a custom fit. You can get a wall panel trim kit that adds an elegant edge detail to any shower area. Accessories include corner molding strips and a corner soap dish. A matching shower floor is also available.

One of my favorite tub and shower enclosures is made of press-molded fiberglass with a high-gloss finish manufactured in standard colors: white, beige, blue, pink, and bone. Known as Tubwal Model TW-32, this system comes complete with five fiberglass panels (plus two apron strips for installation down the front of the tub) as well as all the necessary materials for installation. The TW-32 adjusts to fit tub sizes 29" to 32" deep, 57" to 62" wide, and is designed to go with any make of tub on the market today: cast iron, steel, acrylic, or fiberglass. It is an ideal and stylish way to upgrade any bathroom quickly (13-2).

The Swan Corporation

13-2
High-gloss fiberglass panel system has tough polyurethane finish.

Molded fiberglass panels are easy to work with, but I would like to share with you a few tricks to make your installation proceed smoothly.

Fiberglass panels

Installation hints
- Be sure to protect the surface of the tub.

- Always trial fit your pieces.

- Grind off any imperfections that might be found around the edge on the backsides of the panels.

- Begin with the back wall and trial fit the two edge panels as they fit into the corners. The panels should go in vertically; use a level on the sides of the panels. If the panels lean into the corners (i.e., the corners are not straight), then level the panels, mark them at the bottom where they meet the tub, and cut them off so the panels drop to the tub squarely and yet are level at the same time. This is important; the tub surround should be level all the way around the tub, and the panels should match evenly at both ends of the tub. If they are not even, it will be obvious once the shower door is installed, because the tub surround will be higher at one end of the tub than at the other, and the level shower door will emphasize that fact. If you put the panel in straight and the tub is crooked, you will have a noticeable gap at one side of a panel when you apply caulk. You might have to "fudge" your level a little bit to ensure that the panels match evenly at both ends of the tub, and this procedure could take some time. No matter what tub enclosure you purchase, be sure to read and follow the instructions supplied with the unit by the manufacturer.

- After you have applied your adhesive, rest the panel on the edge of the tub and keep the top of the panel away from the wall. Press firmly from the bottom up. Keep in mind that you only have one opportunity to correctly mount these panels. If the panel should go on the wall crooked, it is extremely hard to remove it for adjustments.

Windows
If you have a window in the shower area and you are using one of these shower kits, don't panic.

1. Remove the casing (if any) on both sides of the window.

2. Measure carefully and cut the window area out of the center panel using a jigsaw. Be sure to cover the bottom of the foot

of the saw with masking tape to protect the finish surface of the panel.

3. Install the center panel and the window trim kit especially designed for your unit.

4. Recut the casing (if part of the window is above the enclosure) so it rides on top of both the window trim and the panel; then install the casing. Figure 13-3 shows a properly installed fiberglass window trim kit.

There is one final consideration. In every place where one panel overlaps another panel, apply latex caulk with silicone right where they meet. If you use caulk that is the same color as the unit, you will have a professional-looking job.

13-3 *Matching window kits are available.* The Swan Corporation

While you are installing your new tub/shower surround, take a look at your plumbing supply, the tub/shower valve. It is possible that the unit needs replacing, so now is the best time to do it. Don't make the mistake that many do—they install a new tile or fiberglass shower surround only to discover a month later that the valve needs to be changed. As discussed in chapter 6, you might be able to repair or replace the valve from the backside through an access panel, but this is not always an option.

A fiberglass unit is available that allows you to replace the valve while maintaining the surface of the existing wall. This single piece comes pre-plumbed and in a full range of colors to match or complement any color scheme or existing walls. The "Shower Tower" is designed for easy installation during any remodeling project with a standard shower head or hand-held shower. Figure 13-4 shows it installed over tile.

If the unexpected occurs

13-4 *"Shower Tower" works on any wall surface.* The Swan Corporation

Tile

Choosing ceramic tile allows you the opportunity to express your individual tastes in creating one-of-a-kind designs. There is no limit to the variety of looks that you can achieve using a mix of sizes, shapes, and colors. What's more, ceramic tile is easy to install. With product innovations like thin-set adhesives, special trim pieces, and easy-to-use grouts, you can achieve professional results in less time (13-5).

13-5
Decorating with tile increases value of your home.

American Olean Tile Company

Selecting tile

Whether you plan to install the tile yourself or have a professional do it, take the time to visit local tile dealers. They can help you lay out the job and select the correct tile for your project. When you purchase any tile, be sure it is all from the same production run, and check for uniform color and texture.

Because products change, it is a good idea to purchase extra tiles, especially if you have an additional project in mind. Also, the need to replace damaged tiles in the future could arise. Before you purchase any tile, I recommend that you bring a sample home, because the color of the tile under showroom lights might appear different under your home lighting. In fact, it is a good idea to bring home more than one piece. This will give you a better picture of the look you want to achieve.

Remember your local tile dealer or contractor can answer any questions you might have—you just need to ask.

There are many tile products from which to choose, but there are four main tile categories: glazed wall, paver, quarry, and ceramic mosaic. Quarry, paver, and ceramic mosaic come in both glazed and unglazed finishes. The glazed tile has a glass-like surface that can be shiny, matte, or textured. High-gloss tile is generally used in areas where scratching is unlikely to occur, such as walls or tub/shower enclosures in bathrooms.

Tile categories

Unglazed quarry tile develops a natural gloss as it ages, giving it a soft shine. It also maintains its natural color, which runs throughout the body of the tile. Unglazed mosaic, paver, and quarry tiles are more durable so they are commonly used for floor and outdoor applications.

The American National Standard Specifications for Ceramic Tile (ANSI A137.1-1988) lists descriptions of many different types of tile and definitions of many tiling terms. The list is available from the Tile Council of America (TCA), Inc.

You can use most tiles for projects such as walls, countertops, bathing platforms, showers, tub enclosures, and floors, but it is important to use the tile specified for a particular use as recommended by the manufacturer.

While wall and floor tiles can exceed 12 square inches in size, ceramic mosaics (the smallest) are less than six square inches. Tile comes in all shapes; the most popular are square, rectangular, hexagonal, and octagonal dots. (Figure 13-6 shows an array of trim tiles.) They come in a huge array of colors, from the palest pastels to the boldest primaries. You can choose tiles with designs or solid-colored tiles, or you can use a combination of the two to create a unique look in your bathroom.

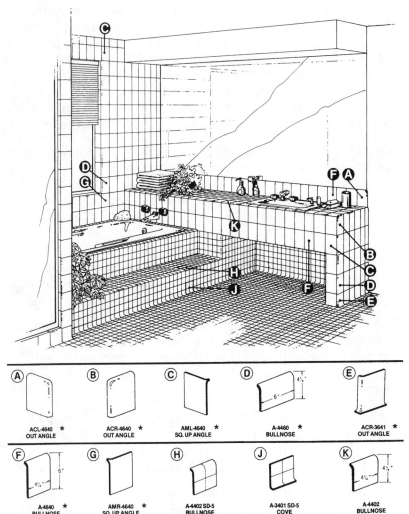

13-6
*Diagram of tile trim shapes
and their uses.*
America Olean Tile Company

Ⓐ ACL-4640 ★ OUT ANGLE	
Ⓑ ACR-4640 ★ OUT ANGLE	
Ⓒ AML-4640 ★ SQ. UP ANGLE	
Ⓓ A-4460 ★ 4¼" 6" BULLNOSE	
Ⓔ ACR-3641 ★ OUT ANGLE	
Ⓕ A-4640 ★ 6" 4¼" BULLNOSE	
Ⓖ AMR-4640 ★ SQ. UP ANGLE	
Ⓗ A-4402 SD-5 BULLNOSE	
Ⓙ A-3401 SD-5 COVE	
Ⓚ A-4402 4¼" 4¼" BULLNOSE	

Selecting the correct grout—the material used to fill the spaces between the tiles—is just as important as the tiles you choose. Portland cement is the base for most grouts, and they are available in a variety of colors that can be used to coordinate or contrast with tile colors. Grouts are also modified to provide specific qualities such as whiteness, mildew resistance, uniformity, hardness, flexibility, and water retentivity. A latex product can be added to the grout to help it spread easier and to speed up the curing time (13-7).

Printed through the courtesy of the Materials & Methods Standards Association A rubber faced trowel should be used when grouting glazed tile with sanded grout.	GROUT								
	Commercial Portland Cement		Sand-Portland Cement	Dry-Set	Latex Portland Cement (3)	Epoxy (1)(6)(3)	Furan (1)(6)(3)	Silicone or Urethane (2)	Modified Epoxy Emulsion (3)(6)
	Wall Use	Floor Use	Wall-Floor Use	Wall-Floor Use					
GLAZED WALL TILE (More than 7% absorption)	•			•	•	•		•	
CERAMIC MOSAICS	•	•	•	•	•	•		•	•
QUARRY, PAVER & PACKING HOUSE TILE	•	•	•		•	•	•		•
Dry or limited water exposure	•	•	•		•	•	•	•	•
Wet areas	•	•	•	•	•	•	•	•	•
Exteriors	•	•	•	•	•(4)	•(4)	•(4)		•(4)
Stain Resistance (5)	D	D	E	D	C	A	A	A	C
Crack Resistance (5)	D	D	E	D	C	B	C	A Flexible	C
Colorability (5)	B	B	D	B	B	B	Black Only	Restricted	B

(revised 1992)

(1) Mainly used for chemical resistant properties.
(2) Special tools needed for proper application. Silicone, urethane and modified polyvinylchloride used in pregrouted ceramic tile sheets. Silicone grout should not be used on kitchen countertops or other food preparation surfaces unless it meets the requirements of FDA Regulation No. 21, CFE 177.2600.
(3) Special cleaning procedures and materials recommended.
(4) Follow manufacturer's directions.
(5) Five performance ratings — Best to Minimal (A B C D E).
(6) Epoxies are recommended for prolonged temperatures up to 140F, high temperature resistant epoxies and furans up to 350F.

13-7 *Grout guide.* Tile Council of America, Inc.

There are also non-cement-based grouts such as epoxies, furans, and silicone rubber that offer properties not possible with cement grouts. However, these products require special skills and should be installed by a professional tile setter.

Pregrouted tile panels are available for tub and shower tile applications. Ceramic mosaics are mounted on sheets for easy installation. Your tile dealer can help you explore the options and innovations that can help speed up your tiling project.

As I mentioned in chapter 4, you might already have at home some of the tools needed for a tiling project. The basic tools include:

• Straightedge and tape rule.
• Chalk line.

- Carpenter's level and square.
- Scraper.
- Sponge and white cleaning rags.
- A couple of plastic buckets.

Specific tools required are:

- A tile cutter.
- A rubber grouting float or squeegee.
- A notched trowel.
- Tile nippers.

You can rent or purchase these items from your tile dealer.

Before we get into the basics of setting tile, I want to suggest that you write the Tile Council of America, Inc. (P.O. Box 326, Princeton, NJ 08542-0326) for brochures and detailed information on installing tile. Some of this information is free while some might require payment of a small fee. The information you receive, however, is well worth a small price.

Basic tile installation

The information below (in part or in whole) was supplied courtesy of the Tile Council of America, Inc. The five basic steps to tile installation are from TCA's brochure, *How to Install and Maintain Ceramic Tile.*

The basic installation of tile is the same regardless of the surface—countertop, floor, tub/shower, or walls. What differs are the backing (what the tile is glued to) and the type of adhesive. That information is described in related chapters as well as this one. When in doubt, contact your local tile dealer and consult your building department. Keep in mind that installation of tile must conform to local building codes, ordinances, trade practices, and climatic conditions.

Before installing any tile, remove any protruding objects (fixtures, baseboards, nails, screws) as well as any loose or damaged plaster, wallpaper, paint, or grease. Newly plastered walls should be sealed.

Lay out the project Using a level, plumb, and/or chalk line, draw or snap perpendicular lines in the center of the area to be tiled. If the area is large, section it off in squares, making sure that the horizontal starting points are in one continuous line.

Lay a loose course of tile—without any adhesive—along each line. Adjust the tile to the left or right of the lines so you have equal cuts at each end. If you are applying tile to the floor, you might want to start your centerline next to the door directly over the threshold. The most visible portion of the floor is usually just inside the door, so it is important to ensure that the grout lines are both parallel and perpendicular to the threshold.

For a tub or shower installation, you have to decide if you are going to carry tile just outside the tub or shower pan or end it flush. If you decide to continue the tile on the outside, how much of the tile should you bring out? You might be limited by wall space or construction details. Once you have decided, then draw a vertical line (13-8). Set the tile just to cover that line.

Before you can draw the horizontal line, you need to make some decisions. Just how high do you want to install the tile? Begin with the plumbing wall and decide if you want to install tile just below the shower head or above it. If you choose below, make sure the tile ends just below the finish trim (flange) of the shower neck (13-9). Once you have determined tile placement near the shower head, draw a horizontal line around the perimeter of the tub/shower area.

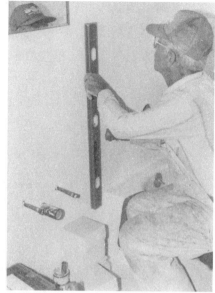

13-8 *Vertical pencil line guides tile placement.*

Another important factor to consider when deciding the height is what will happen to the last row of tiles, the ones that actually sit just off the tub or shower pan. The correct way to set tiles is to individually cut each tile in the bottom row because this allows you to make minor adjustments if the tub or shower has moved out of plumb during installation, or if an existing bathtub has moved over time because of settling of the house. However, you will want to adjust the overall height of the tiles so you don't cut off more than half a tile or cut within ½" of the tile's edge. While this small amount is not impossible to cut, it's not easy because the edges of the tile are very hard. I find that a cut of about 1" in on the tile works well and gives the best overall final appearance. Cut the tiles so there will be about a ⅟₁₆" gap between them and the bathtub or shower pan. This gap will be sealed later with caulk.

13-9 *Proper installation of shower flange above bullnose of tile.*

Apply the setting material With a notched trowel, apply mastic. Make sure you are using a trowel with the correct size of notch. Read the instructions on the back label of the can of mastic or see chapter 4, 4–13.

Apply the mastic to an area small enough that you can comfortably attach the tiles before the mastic sets up. Also, when applying adhesives, stay below the finish line (top row) by about ¼". That will prevent the adhesive from oozing out and onto the wall when you actually set the tile.

Set each tile Everyone sets tile a little differently. When I set tile in a tub/shower area, I prefer to start in the center of the top row on the back wall. Use a slight twisting motion and press the finish tile (bullnose) firmly into place starting in the center of the row and working in both directions. Work your way down the wall (13-10A and B).

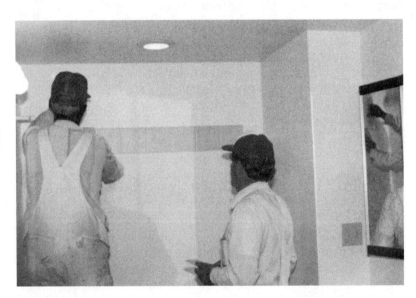

13-10A
First course of bullnose-edged tile is set.

Align the tiles so all the joints are uniform and straight. If you are using self-spacing tiles, the tiles will have lubs or knobs on the sides that automatically space the tile for grout joints. Even so, check the joints for even spacing; you could have an over- or undersized tile that could throw the joints off. If you do not have self-spacing tiles, purchase and use tile spacers to achieve

13-10B
Work your way down the wall.

even grout lines. As you progress down the wall, cut the tiles for the sides. Figure 13-10C shows a stationary tile cutter in use—but this professional should have used a piece of cardboard underneath to protect the floor!

13-10C
Cutting tile with stationary tile cutter.

When you get to about the second or third row up from the tub, decide where to install a soap dish. I recommend installing the soap dish to the left or right of center or out of the path of the spray from the shower head. If you are using ceramic tile, then use a ceramic—not metal—soap dish. You can glue the soap dish to the mastic, or leave an unfinished spot (13-11A), complete the tile installation including cutting in the last row, and then come back and install the soap dish using clear silicone (13-11B and C). Remember that a soap and grab dish really doesn't have any support to carry a load. If you need a grab bar, then install one as described in chapter 16.

13-11A *Cut tile looks best on top.*

13-11B *Clear silicone holds the soap dish securely.*

13-11C *Use masking tape to hold soap dish in place overnight.*

Once the back wall is complete, you can start the sidewalls all the way to the floor. Check periodically to make sure that the rows of tiles are straight both vertically and horizontally as they surround the tub. Also check for loose tiles by pushing in on one of the tile's corners. If the tile is loose, the corner will push in and the opposite corner will pop out, which means that either the mastic dried or there wasn't enough mastic to begin with. Apply sufficient mastic to the tile and reinstall it.

13-12 *Cuts in tile around shower valve and tub spout.*

Cut tiles to fit The plumbing wall requires a little more time as you will have several cuts to make (13-12). There are three ways to make cuts in tile: you can use a carbide ceramic hole saw with a drill (13-13A), a carbide rod that fits in a hacksaw (13-13B), or tile nippers (13-13C). Nippers come in handy when you only have to nip off a small piece. Only use tools designed for cutting ceramic tile! If you have to drill a hole near the edge, take care that you don't break the tile.

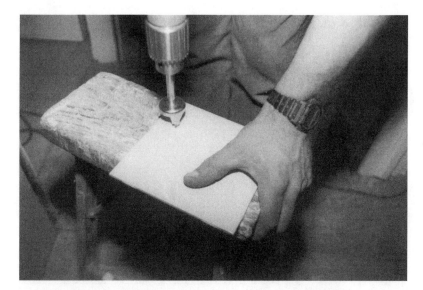

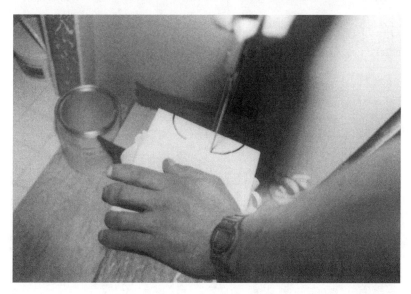

Whenever you cut tile, it is best to knock down the face edge with a hand-held sanding block covered with 80-grit sandpaper. Edges that will be hidden do not need to be smoothed.

When you approach a corner, come as close as possible. You will have to smooth the edge of the piece coming into the first

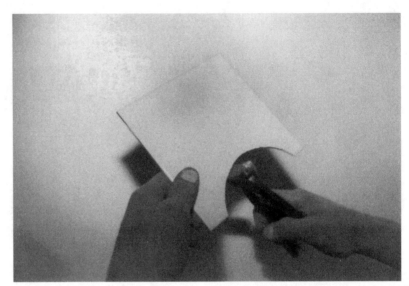

13-13C
Tile nippers.

13-14 *Do not force the fit!*

tile (13-14). Do not force the fit; forcing can move a row of tiles and distort your grout lines. Use bullnose tiles to finish the perimeter and an outside corner to finish the corner where two bullnoses will meet (13-15).

13-15
Hold bullnose edge slightly back from vertical outside wall corner.

If you have a vanity countertop that needs a back splash, tile it now using both bullnoses and outside corners. Always start with an outside corner and work in toward the inside corner (13-16A and B).

Apply grout After the required setting-up time has passed, as specified on the back of the mastic container, you are ready to grout. If you have installed caulk in the corner where the finish flooring meets the tub, first apply a strip of masking tape from the tub to the floor over the caulk to protect it.

Mix the grout according to the manufacturer's instructions, always adding powder to liquid. You might want to use a special liquid latex additive that makes the grout easier to spread and speeds curing. Stir the mixture manually to obtain a workable mix, with complete and visually uniform wetting of the grout powder. Let it stand for about 15 minutes, remix, and use it immediately. It is not recommended that mixed grout be used after an hour. The grout should be free of lumps and possess a consistency such that when it is taken from the bucket, it will hang onto a rubber grouting float.

Using a rubber grouting float at a 30° angle, spread the grout diagonally across the joints, spreading only as much as you can handle comfortably. Once the grout is spread, go over the area a few times with a side-to-side motion until the gaps are packed, and scrape off the excess grout with the edge of the float (13-17). If you are unsure about how large an area to do, start with a sidewall.

13-16A *Bullnose corner used for tile back splash.*

13-16B *Do not cut outside bullnose; only tiles in inside corner are cut.*

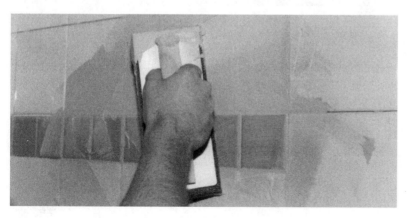

13-17 *Work grout into all grout lines.*

Take a clean wet sponge and thoroughly wring it out. Then wipe over the freshly grouted tile and remove any grout that is standing on the surface of the tile. Clean your sponge often (13-18). Clean the grout off the walls right away. Don't make the mistake I made on my first tile job when I got into the business twenty years ago. I grouted the entire tub/shower area, and because it was about lunchtime, I went to lunch. About an hour later I returned to clean the excess grout. Five hours later I was finally finished—just about the time the customer was coming home!

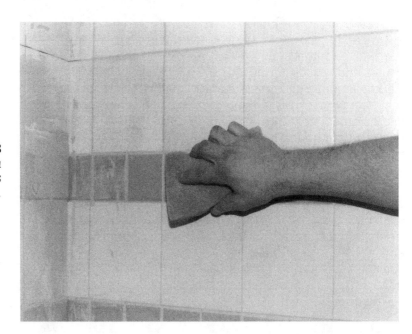

13-18
Take care not to put too much pressure on grout lines as you clean.

If you (like me) want uniform grout lines, then let the area you just cleaned sit for about ten minutes while you begin to clean another area. Return to your first cleaning site and with minimal pressure wipe over the grout lines with your damp sponge, first horizontally and then vertically. Move quickly through this process. Be sure to clean your sponge frequently and then go on to the next wall. Before you know it, you'll be done. About 10 to 15 minutes after your last cleaning, a cement haze will form on the tiles (13-19). Clean this off with a clean white rag or cheesecloth. Be careful not to disturb the grout

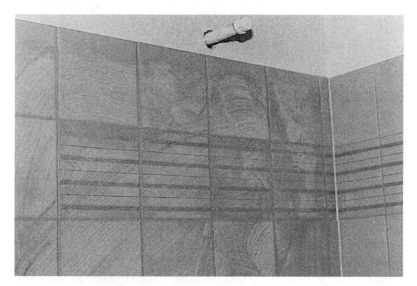

lines. Once the grout has hardened for 24 hours, vacuum the dust and grit from the floor around the tub and/or shower pan. Now you are ready to apply caulk as described in chapter 16.

As a house or tub settles, the grout in the joint between the tub and tile wall might crack or crumble occasionally (13-20). If this happens, remove the old grout with a grout remover or other sharp-pointed tool, being careful not to chip the tile or tub. Dry the joint thoroughly, and fill it with a flexible caulking compound.

Loose tiles can be easily replaced. Scrape the old bonding material and grout from the backs and sides of the tiles. Apply adhesive, set in place, let dry for 24 hours, and grout. If there are many loose tiles, you might have a serious water problem.

Tile can also be combined with hardwood floors. Figure 13-21 illustrates a case where water from a leaking shower pan destroyed the flooring next to the shower. The damaged area was opened up, a filler was placed on top of the subfloor so the tile would match the existing hardwood floor, and a coordinating tile and grout were installed. If you have a problem area in your bathroom, you might want to think about how tile can be used creatively to solve that problem.

Tile & grout repair

13-20 *This tile repair job is small and inexpensive now; it could grow to be a major headache!* Calvin Lea, Chromastat

13-21
A unique design.

Shower rods

Basically, there are two types of shower rods: compression and screw-in. If you choose to install a compression-type rod, do not overtighten it as you can crack the tiles. If you have a fiberglass tub/shower surround, it might be necessary to install the rod above the panels for the same reason, but this will depend on the thickness of the fiberglass.

If you want to install a screw-in type of shower rod in tile, be sure to use a ceramic or masonry drill bit and drill slowly so you do not crack the tile. Don't take the easy way out by trying to drill screws into grout lines (it's easy to crack tiles and difficult to seal properly). Drill screws into the solid surface of the tile. Again, do not overtighten the screws. You might want to install the rod above the tile or fiberglass tub/shower surround.

Shower doors

Once the tile and caulk are completely cured, it is time to install the tub/shower door. There are many types of doors on the market today. The door you select can make a dramatic statement in your bathroom (13-22). Choose a door with the least amount of maintenance; if possible, a trackless door or one with an L-track.

13-22
A shower door can enhance your bathroom's decor.

The biggest problem with tub/shower doors is the leakage around the track if it is not properly sealed. Also, the track needs regular and thorough cleaning—especially a track that is designed for bypassing doors as shown in 13-23. Figure 13-24 shows a tub/shower door that has no track—the panels of the shower door tip in at the bottom toward the tub to deflect the water back into the tub and to help keep water off the sill of the tub. You can also get doors in a bifold style instead of bypass. These tub/shower doors are also manufactured for shower stalls and can be used to good advantage in bathrooms where space is at a premium.

If you decide to install the tub/shower door yourself, be sure to follow the instructions that come with your unit. Be patient and take your time, working through the directions step by step.

Glass companies make and install custom tub/shower doors. Figures 13-25A through D show professionals installing a custom-made shower door—an option worth considering. Notice in 13-25A and B that a level is used while installing the

13-23 *Proper maintenance and cleaning could have prevented this eyesore.*

13-24 *This shower door keeps water in tub with no track to clean.*

Tub & shower enclosures 223

13-25A

13-25B

13-25C

13-25D

door hinge assembly. This is important, as it ensures that the shower door will close properly. Figure 13-25D shows double shower valves and two soap dishes mounted high, out of the path of the water spray.

The door in these figures is being installed on top of tile. As I mentioned during the framing chapter, you need to install backing so that you can install your door system without using plastic anchors. If you are installing a door in an existing bathroom and you are not sure if there is any backing, proceed slowly. Drill through the tile with a ceramic drill bit and stop just when you get through the tile. Finish up with a small bit— you will be able to feel if you are drilling into solid material (wood). If no wood is evident, continue with your ceramic bit and insert plastic anchors.

It is important not to overtighten a screw in tile. If you do, you will crack the tile.

Follow the manufacturer's directions on caulking the tub/shower unit, and be sure to let the caulk cure for at least 72 hours before using. If your tub/shower unit has been installed by a professional, he will apply caulk as part of the job. Chapter 16 also describes in detail where to caulk.

It's hard to wait 72 hours before using your tub or shower, but you can put that time to good use by heading off to the next chapter to install doors, windows, and finish trim.

CHAPTER 14

Doors, windows, & base moldings

The WALLS HAVE BEEN PAINTED, the tile is set, and the cabinets are ready to be filled, but there are still some important areas that need to be completed, such as installing the door, the window, and the base moldings. This chapter walks you through these installations and shares some tips finish carpenters use to achieve that professional look.

Doors

From experience, I have found that installing a door blank into an existing jamb is a difficult and very time-consuming project. It can be done, but it is very unlikely that you would encounter this situation in a bathroom remodeling project. Because of this, I highly recommend that you purchase a prehung door. These units include the door hung on its frame, all hinges and doorstops, and prebored holes for the handle and strike (14-1). Before you can purchase any door, however, you need to determine which way you want the door to swing; and before installation, you need to decide on the type of floor covering you plan to use.

Generally, it is not a good idea for a door to swing into any hallway. Depending on where the bathroom is located, however, it is possible that the door will have to swing out. Most likely, the door will swing into the bathroom and up against a wall, so make sure you allow enough room for the door. You don't want the door to swing in and hit the toilet or a vanity cabinet. In some cases, a door can be installed either for a left- or right-hand swing; in others, the layout might call for a pocket door—a door that slides back into the wall.

The type of floor covering you select also makes a difference in your door installation. For instance, if you install a door that swings into the bathroom over vinyl flooring, you'll want to cut off a portion of the bottom of the jambs and drop the entire unit closer to the floor covering (14-2). Some manufacturers provide

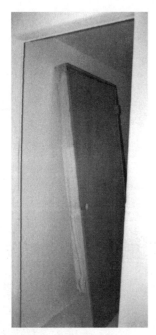

14-1 *Looking through rough opening at prehung door.*

up to 1½" of space from the bottom of the door to the bottom of the jambs. This provides a ¼" to ½" clearance above carpet, depending on the thickness of the carpet and pad you choose to install. If you are planning to drop the door as close to the floor covering as possible, be sure to trial swing the door to verify that the door clears the floor covering on its entire swing.

14-2 *Gap between floor covering and bottom of door.*

The tools needed to install a door include:

- Tape measure.
- Level.
- Finish hammer.
- Circular saw.
- Handsaw.
- Miter box.
- Stepladder.
- Utility knife.
- Nail set.
- Masking tape.
- Straightedge.
- Two spring clamps.
- Twelve-inch masking paper.

Materials needed are:

- Pine or cedar shims.
- Finish nails, including 2½" (8d) for installing the jambs; 1¼" (3d) for the doorstops; and 1¾" (5d) for the casings. Depending on the wall thickness, you might need 2" (6d) nails.

Before you begin, place a level on the floor in the door opening to make sure that the floor between the jambs is level. If the floor is uneven, don't install the door to follow the floor. If you do, the door will not perform properly after it is installed. In addition, you will see an uneven gap at the top, and after the casing (molding) has been installed, you'll be able to see that the door was put in crooked.

If the floor slopes from one side of the frame to the other, you will need to cut the bottom of one of the jambs to drop the top of the doorframe so the gap above the door will be even (14-3). The trick is to check the gap on the hinge side of the door at the top of the frame, and adjust the jamb on the bore side of the door to the same measurement.

14-3 *Uniform gap between top of door and bottom side of frame.*

To install the frame, first remove the doorstops on both jambs but leave the stop on the top of the frame (14-4). This will be removed later, but for now, it helps to keep the door from swinging freely and possibly damaging the hinge side of the door.

I find it is easier to install a door if I work from the doorstop side. With that in mind, place the door in the rough opening. Begin by inserting shims from both sides of the door opening between the backsides of the jambs and the framing of the rough opening at the top corners (14-5), then at the bottom near the floor, and finally near the handle and hinges (shims can be positioned either above or below the strike area). Figure 14-6 shows where all the shims should be located.

14-4 *Removing side doorstops provides room for nailing, prevents damage to stops.*

14-5
Notice positioning of finish nails.

Remember that the shims are tapered, thick at one end and thin at the other. If you were to place two shims on top of each other, thin end to butt end, you would get a uniformly sized piece of wood (14-7A). By sliding one past the other, you can control their thickness and make adjustments in the gap (14-7B). Make sure you install the shims as shown in A or B, especially when working on the hinge side of the door. If you install the shims as shown in C of 14-7, you will cant the jamb, causing the door to bind on one side and preventing it from closing properly. There are times, however, especially toward the bottoms of the jambs, when you will need to insert additional shims (14-6) to achieve a proper doorframe installation.

14-6 *An overall view of shim positioning.*

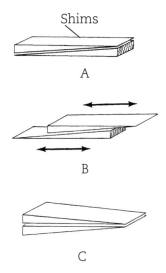

Shims

A

B

C

14-7 *A and B show correct use of shims; C is incorrect.*

Once the shims are in place, make sure you are satisfied with the gap. The gap should be uniform between the door and frame on all three sides—both jambs and the top of the doorframe. If the gap is not the same, either push shims in or pull them out in order to close or open the gap. Because the shims are tapered, you can gradually and accurately adjust the gap.

Once the shims are adjusted and you are satisfied that the gap is even, you can begin to nail the frame into the rough opening using 8d finish nails. Use two nails and spread them as far as possible without getting too close to the jamb edges. Make sure the finish nails go through the shims, and are long enough to pierce the framing member to hold the doorframe stable. Nail into the faces of the jambs, through the shims, and right on into the trimmers. It is not necessary to put nails in the top of the doorframe. Set the nails using a nail set, and cut the shims off by scoring them on the wall side with a utility knife and breaking them off with your hand. You might need to score the shim more than once. Be careful not to cut the side of the jamb with your utility knife if you are forced to cut from the door side.

Doors, windows, & base moldings   229

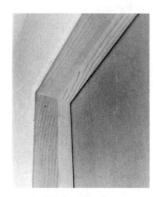

14-8 *Maintain the proper gap distance.*

The next step is to remove the top doorstop prior to reinstallation of the two jamb doorstops. It is important not to install the doorstop directly up against the door on the hinge side. Keep the stop back from the door at least ⅟₁₆" so the door will clear the doorstop. Also, you will need this clearance once the door has been painted or finished (14-8). Begin by attaching the doorstop on the hinge side using 3d finish nails, and set the nails.

Now you are ready to reinstall the top doorstop with two temporary nails, one at each end. It helps if a second person can hold the door closed and flush with the edge of the jamb. Once the door is in position, you can install the doorstop on the bore side of the door and, if necessary, make adjustments to the top doorstop.

In some situations, you won't be able to get the door flush with the edge of the jamb on the bore side of the door. If this happens, you have a couple of choices. You could try to move the bottom of the wall in or out; this is an unlikely but possible solution unless the walls have been finished. The best solution is to adjust the doorstop, in which case the door will not be flush. The next time you install a prehung door, try fitting it before the wallboard goes up. That way, you'll have access to the nails, and you'll be able to move the wall in or out for the adjustment. If you choose to do this, remember to remove the door and cover the frame to protect them both during the installation of wallboard and texturing.

Don't be surprised if you find, once the door is completely installed, that you have to cut off the bottom of the door to match the slope of the floor or to achieve the proper distance off the finish floor.

The best way to cut the door is to lay it across two sawhorses. Be sure to protect the door face from getting scratched or otherwise marred by the sawhorses. Mark your cutting line with a straightedge and score it with a utility knife. Apply masking tape to the cutting area on the face of the door, and use 12" masking paper to protect the portion of the door face where your circular saw will touch the door. Using a couple of spring clamps, fasten a straightedge across the face of the door so the circular saw will ride up against the waste side of the straightedge.

Adjust the straightedge so the saw blade will cut just to the waste side of the scored line. The score mark keeps the door from splintering while you make your cut, but you must take care not to cut into the score mark. Keep the blade slightly to the waste side of the mark. After the cut is made, use a hand block sander to sand the cut edge up to the score mark. When you are through, there should be a slight bevel on the bottom of the door face.

Now you are ready to install the casing (molding) around the door. Before installing the casing, check the wall around the frame of the door. If the wall is slightly higher than the frame, use a hammer to pound down the area (marked with Xs on 14-9) close to the frame. This will allow the nose of the casing to lie flat on the edges of the frame. Make sure when you pound the area marked with Xs that you don't go beyond the width of the casing!

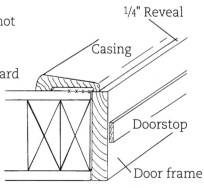

14-9 *Use care when you pound the area marked with Xs!*

If the wall extends out farther than the frame, attach wooden strips (frame extensions) to the edges of the frame flush to the wall (14-10). This situation occurs frequently where new wallboard is applied over existing walls. Hold back the extension about ¼" from the edge of the frame and then hold the casing back about ¼" from the edge of the extension.

If your doorframe installation does not require extensions, hold the casing back to create a ¼" reveal on the edge of the frame as shown in 14-9.

I find it is easiest to install the casing by starting with the jambs. There are a couple of ways to measure the casing. One way is to use a tape to measure from the floor up to the bottom edge of the top of the doorframe and then add ¼" for the top reveal. The other way is to stand the casing up against the jamb and mark it at the bottom edge. When you cut the casing off, add an extra ¼" for the top reveal. After carefully measuring, cut the tops of the side casings at a 45° angle using an electric or hand miter box. If the frame of the door has been set in properly with 90° angles on the inside top corners of the frame, then casings cut

14-10 *Treat exposed jamb extension as a finish trim piece.*

at 45° angles should fit and properly trim the door. In some cases, though, you might have to cut the casing a degree more or less than the 45°.

Temporarily nail the casings in place using 3d nails on the thin (inside) part of the casing and 5d or 6d on the thick (outside) part of the casing (14-11). By measuring from outside edge to outside edge on the jamb casings, you will obtain the measurement needed for the top casing. It's a good idea to add a good 1/16" to the measurement. It's better to be a little long than to be short so you can fit the top casing to the side casing if the frame is out of square. Then cut the top casing and fit it into place between the two jamb casings.

14-11
Temporarily set nails until you trial fit next piece of casing.

If you are working in a dormer area, be prepared for the unusual. You might have to trim the moldings to fit the ceiling (14-12).

14-12
Moldings might have to be trimmed.

When you are satisfied with the fit of the joints, complete the nailing and set the nails. If the casings are prefinished, use a matching putty stick to camouflage the nail holes and wipe off any excess putty with a white rag and some solvent; otherwise, use a sandable filler for the nail holes that will accept stain or paint. Installation of the door handle is covered in chapter 16.

Windows are normally installed at the beginning of the project during the framing stage. However, it is OK to install windows at this point in the project as long as you plan for it.

Basically, wooden windows are installed like a door. Sometimes you have to shim the bottom (sill) of an outside corner of the window frame (vertical) in order to square a window in a rough opening that is out of square. The only real difference between door and window installation is that before the inside casing is installed, you will need to stuff insulation all around the window frame between the frame and the rough opening. The insulation prevents outside air from entering your home. In most cases, exterior trim will come with the window. If it doesn't match the existing trim on your house, purchase and install matching trim. Wooden windows can be custom-made to fit an existing rough opening.

Metal windows are great to work with and they too can be custom-made to fit frames of existing windows. Figure 14-13

Windows

14-13
Partial frame will be used as stop for custom-made window unit.

Doors, windows, & base moldings   233

shows an exterior opening where the window was removed but the trim and part of the window frame were left intact. Because the window is solidly anchored in the brick walls, the partial frame will be used as a stop for a custom-made window unit. Keep in mind that not all aluminum frames are manufactured the same, so it is important to pay close attention to the construction details of your frame in order to determine how much of the frame you might need to remove. If you need to cut the frame of the existing window, stay on the interior side of the nailing fin so you don't cut the frame apart. What is nice about this type of installation is that you don't have to disturb the exterior siding, especially if it is brick. If your bathroom project is in the basement, you won't have to face the difficulties of installing a window in the foundation (14-14).

14-14
Have window custom-made to fit existing frame.

Manufacturers can produce windows with or without a nailing fin. The trick is knowing when you will need a fin, and there are several measurements that will influence your decision.

What is the distance from the interior face of the existing frame to the interior surface of the finish wall? This measurement will help determine whether or not the new window has to be installed by the nailing fin or by the face of the exterior frame. Keep the new window back about 1½" from the finish wall to allow sufficient room for the window to be framed and cased out.

What is the total width from the edge of the interior face of the existing window to the trimmer, including the gap between the window frame and trimmer? To get this measurement, remove all the interior trim around the window—wood or wallboard—in order to expose the complete window frame and the rough opening. This will help determine if there is enough available space—framing plus gap—to be used as a stop to accept the new window. It will also give a clean overview of the situation to determine how much of the window frame it might be necessary to cut away.

How wide is the face on the exterior side of the new window? This measurement will help to determine if there is enough width (at least ¾") on the new window for a proper installation up against the face frame of the existing window if you choose to install by the face frame instead of the nailing fin.

One measurement that is important when you order a custom-made window is the *perimeter measurement* around the exterior nailing fin. Do not confuse this exterior frame with the nailing fin. The nailing fin protrudes beyond the four sides of the exterior frame, and the exterior and interior frames protrude outward perpendicular to the nailing fin (14-15). Depending on the situation, the exterior frame of the new window could be installed to fit up against the backside of the existing window frame or it could actually protrude beyond the existing frame as the nailing fin fits against that backside.

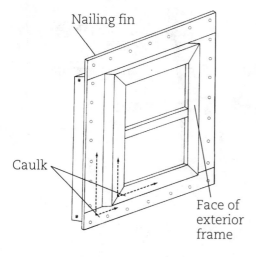

14-15
Areas where caulk should be applied for two types of installations.

When placing your window order, make your intentions clear to the window manufacturer as to how you plan to install this window so that it can be manufactured to meet your measurements. Keep in mind that custom windows are not returnable. If you find yourself in a situation where the perimeter measurement of the face frame will fit the existing window frame but the nailing fin stops you from getting past the existing framing (rough opening), then go ahead and trim the nailing fin with a hacksaw or tin snips to a measurement that will allow you to fit the window into the rough opening.

Whether you install a window with or without a nailing fin, a good exterior caulk is required for the installation (14-15). In the first case, caulk is applied to the exterior side of the nailing fin. For a finless window, caulk is installed on the interior side of the existing exterior frame. In both cases, the windows are installed from the interior of the home with the caulk in place, and pushed into the existing frame toward the exterior. Figures 14-16A and B show side views of proper caulk and insulation placement, the former with a nailing fin, the latter without one.

Aluminum window with nailing fin

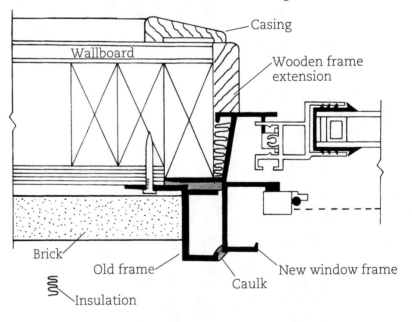

14-16A
Casing out a window in wood.

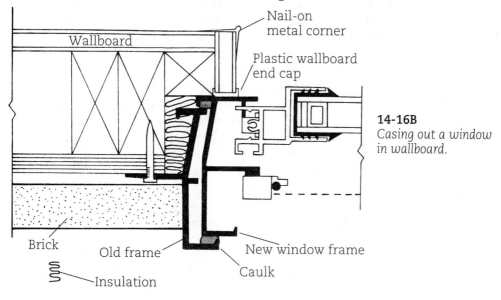

Aluminum window without nailing fin

Wallboard

Nail-on metal corner

Plastic wallboard end cap

Brick

Old frame

Insulation

Caulk

New window frame

14-16B
Casing out a window in wallboard.

Once the window is in place, wipe the excess caulk from the exterior frame. At this point, I generally nail a couple of temporary blocks to the trimmers up against the new window frame to hold the new window in place until the caulk sets up. Don't forget to remove these blocks when you are ready to trim out the window. On the interior, trim out the window either using wallboard, wallboard plus a stool (wooden sill) and apron, or by installing a wooden frame extension and casing (14-16A and B).

Trimming a window is the same as trimming a door. If you installed a window into either a 2×4 or 2×6 rough opening, you'll notice the frame of the window does not extend out to be flush with the finish wall. Just as a doorframe that doesn't meet the wall requires frame extensions, a window may also need frame extensions.

Before making any extensions, check to see if the window is sitting level in the rough opening. If the window has been installed closer to one trimmer than to the other or closer to the header than to the sill, attach furring strips to the framing

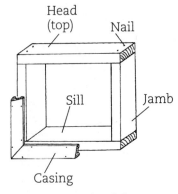

Head (top)

Nail

Sill

Jamb

Casing

14-17 *A completed frame extension unit.*

material of the rough opening. What you are doing is building up the rough opening to create a uniform measurement around the face frame of the window. You are squaring the rough opening to the window frame. That way, when you do install frame extensions, they will look balanced on the window.

For windows, it is best to install the top (head) and bottom (sill) extensions first followed by the jamb extensions. You can also assemble the pieces in the same order to build a complete box and put the casings on the box to make a complete (frame) unit (14-17). Trial fit all your pieces before assembly. If you make the box too large, it will not fit in the rough opening.

Do you remember the plants lined up on Grandma's windowsill? What about the nice trimming details that used to surround that window? If you wish, you can recreate these trims in your own home. By extending the sill out about 1½" from the finish wall and the length of that sill beyond both sides of the window, you create a *stool*. The extensions of the sill beyond the window are called *ear extensions* (14-18). This area provides a platform for the casings. Your extensions can be up to 1" beyond the wallboard jamb extensions (without casings), or beyond the casings, or remain even with the outside edges of the casings (14-18 and 14-19). If you choose to install a stool, you will need to add an apron, and you can use different types of finish moldings to create your own apron style (14-20).

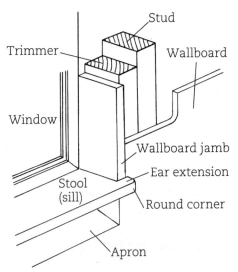

Stud

Trimmer

Wallboard

Window

Wallboard jamb

Ear extension

Stool (sill)

Round corner

Apron

14-18 *Parts of finished window (not including casing).*

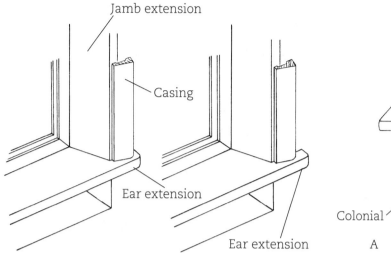

14-19 *Casing in relation to two ear extension applications.*

14-20 *Side views of three moldings.*

Wooden base molding can enhance a bathroom and give it a rich look (14-21). I recommend that you prefinish your molding before installation, and apply matching stain to your freshly cut miters. It also helps to nail the molding to the studs (use a stud finder). After you have set the nails, use a matching putty stick to conceal the nail holes. Excess putty can be removed with a white rag and a solvent that will not hurt the clear finish. Be sure to read the solvent label to make sure it is safe for use over

Wooden base molding

14-21
Overall view of moldings in a half-bathroom.

Doors, windows, & base moldings 239

clear finishes. If it is at all possible, purchase moldings long enough to be installed along an entire wall length. Try to avoid seams. If you do have to make a seam, do not make a butt joint; miter joints are less noticeable.

Rubber base molding

Installing rubber base molding, also known as *cove base*, is not as easy as it looks. Just as installing the prehung door required a few tricks, the same is true of rubber base molding.

When working on outside corners, it is important that you notch the cove base. Bend the base backward and use a utility knife to cut a notch on the backside. Be careful not to cut too much out (14-22). Apply contact cement to the wall for about 2" on either side of the corner. Then apply contact cement to the corresponding area on the back of the cove base and spread cove adhesive over the remaining area (14-23). Allow sufficient time—check the manufacturer's instructions—for the contact cement to dry.

14-22 *Backside of cove base cut for outside corner.*

14-23 *Allow time for contact cement to dry.*

Normally when applying cove adhesive, you would spread it lengthwise on the piece. Figure 14-23, however, shows the adhesive applied vertically, and that's OK since the piece was small and it was easier to apply the adhesive in the direction as shown. What is important is that you keep the adhesive back about ⅜" from the top edge and about ¼" from the ends to prevent any adhesive from oozing up on the wall or onto an adjoining piece at a butt joint (seam). Once the contact cement has dried, mount the cove as shown in 14-24A, pushing down on the cove at the same time you apply it to the wall (14-24B). Use your other hand to prevent the molding from flopping onto the finished floor—this saves you from a messy glue cleanup!

Inside corners are simple. You only have to make 45° angle cuts on one of the two pieces: the toe of the cove and the backside (14-25A) so it can ride on the adjacent piece without raising out of position (14-25B). Experiment with a scrap piece to get a feel for cutting the material. Cove base comes in rolls or 4' lengths; most likely you will be using 4' pieces. When fitting an area over this length, be sure to cut the second piece up to ⅛" longer than the measurement of the remaining wall. You will have to pop this piece into place, but it will tighten up the other joints

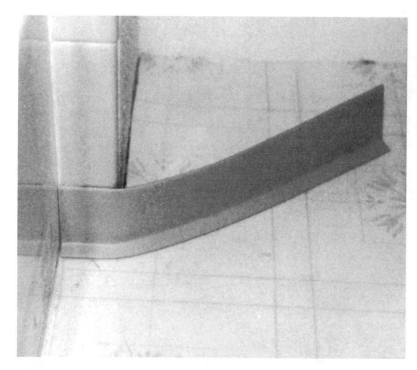

14-24A & B
Press cove base into contact cement on wall.

14-25A & B
Experiment with a scrap piece and get a feel for cutting cove base before you cut the real thing.

and create a snug fit. Temperature changes can cause the base to shrink and open joints; cutting it a little longer prevents this.

When installing cove base up against tile, it is best to cut the toe of the cove to match the curve of the tiles (14-26).

14-26
*The professional look you
want to achieve.*

Now that the door, the window, and the base moldings are installed, you can move on to the next step: installing the electrical and plumbing fixtures and trim. What are you waiting for?

Electrical & plumbing fixtures & trims

I⊤'S ALL DOWNHILL FROM HERE. Installation of finish electrical and plumbing fixtures is also my favorite part of the job because each piece I install brings me closer to the final picture. Just like putting a puzzle together, the final results can be incredible!

Before installing any fixture, be sure to read the installation instructions supplied by the manufacturers. These instructions list the specific tools and materials required for each job.

Before you begin any electrical work, check to make sure the power is turned off. If necessary, check with a receptacle circuit tester.

The best place to start is to install the light fixtures, including any trim for lights and grills for exhaust fans. Figure 15-1 shows the installation of a bar light above a medicine cabinet. When choosing bulbs for this type of fixture, keep in mind that they come in different sizes and shapes. Be sure to use the wattage recommended by the manufacturer. Figure 15-2 shows the installation of a recessed light can and a fan housing. Make sure that the wire hooks are in place before pushing in the finish trim pieces. The lighting will help you to see as you install the remaining fixtures and trim pieces.

When hooking up receptacles, there are a few tips that can help you in the final installation. Figure 15-3's explanation on side wiring and quick connection will help when working with switches and GFCI receptacles. Depending on the switches or receptacles you purchased, you might be able to go one way or

Electrical fixtures

15-1 *Bar light above medicine cabinet.*

Electrical & plumbing fixtures & trims   243

15-2
Make sure wire hooks are in place before pushing in finish trim pieces.

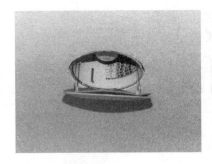

Side wiring
Loop wire around terminal screw. Screw head locks wire against terminal. For copper or copperclad aluminum conductors.

Quickwire connection
Insert wire into wire well. Wire is automatically clamped by spring action—rensuring good electrical connection. For copper conductors only.

Quickwire and screw
Option of (1) side wiring or (2) Quickwire connection. Note: For continuous wiring, both sets of terminals (screw and Quickwire) can be used together.

Two-circuit conversion
Of duplex receptacles to power each outlet is done separately by simply breaking off the fin between the two terminals.

Back & side wiring
Option of (1) side wiring—or (2) back wiring; insert wire into well. Tighten screw—thus clamping wire against terminal. Back wiring for copper conductors only.

15-3 *Wiring connections.* Leviton Manufacturing Co., Inc.

the other, or even both, when connecting the wires to the terminals. I find the quick connection to be both the easiest and the fastest.

When all the receptacles and switches have been installed, consider next the type of wall plates you plan to use. Wall plates come in different styles, shapes, and sizes (15-4). You can also have them custom made to match your decorating scheme. If you have a wall-mounted hair dryer, built-in ironing center, or a heated towel bar, install them following the manufacturers' instructions.

As mentioned in chapter 9, there are different types of heaters from which to choose; take this time to complete the installation of the unit you selected, following the manufacturers' directions. Figures 15-5A through D show the complete installation of a wall heater. There are, however, a few things to remember:

15-4 *Consider porcelain wall plates.* The Broadway Collection

- Make sure you use a strain relief connector or a junction box wire connector (blue) on the power source and connect it to the housing (wall can).

- Connect the ground wire to the grounding pigtail or green screw provided in the housing, and be sure to use the proper size wire connector when connecting wires.

- Check to make sure the wires are not caught behind the motor when you insert the heater assembly into its housing.

15-5A *Rough opening for a wall heater.*

15-5B *The wall can.*

15-5C *Installing the unit.*

15-5D *The grill. If your model has a built-in thermostat, slide the thermostat knob onto its shaft.*

Plumbing fixtures

When it comes to the installation of plumbing fixtures, I find it best to start with the simple items such as the shower head, valve, and spout (15-6 and 15-7). (Be sure to remove the valve template before installing the trim piece.) Again, follow the manufacturers' installation instructions, and I suggest you keep in mind the following tips as well:

- Be very careful when handling these items. They are the finish pieces and you will see them every day once they are installed. Use the proper tools and take care not to mar or scratch the finish.

- Be sure to install the finish flanges—the trim pieces that go over the pipe and up against the finished wall around the shower neck (15-6) and the shutoff valves for the toilet and sink.

- For items that have threads, be sure to use pipe joint compound or wrap white sealing tape with Teflon around the threads before installation to achieve a good seal.

- Be careful not to overtighten screws on any fixture or trim piece.

15-6
Typical shower head installation.

15-7
Typical tub and shower valve and spout.

It is possible, especially if you live in an older home, that you have galvanized pipes that require threaded shutoff valves. Alternatively, you might have copper pipes, in which case your plumbing might have been set up with either threaded shutoff valves or compression fittings, which are not threaded. Since using threaded shutoff valves is straightforward, I will discuss the proper installation of compression fittings here (15-8).

Shutoff valves

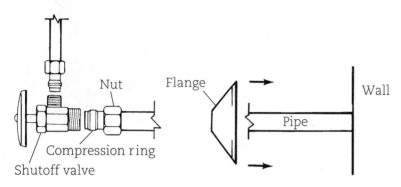

15-8
Diagram of basic compression shutoff valve.

Before installing the compression fittings, be sure to clean any debris or foreign material such as wallboard, adhesive, or paint from any water lines that extend out from the wall or possibly from the floor. Once these lines are clean, install your compression fitting following these steps:

1. Cut your copper piping to length (2" for wash basins, 1½" for toilets).
2. Slide the flange over the pipe.
3. Slide the nut onto the pipe, including the compression ring. Do not push the compression ring and nut up against the flange.
4. Fit the shutoff valve onto the pipe. Applying constant pressure to the valve, slide the compression ring and flange nut up to the threads on the valve and tighten the nut. Be sure to keep pressure against the fitting. The tightening action pulls the parts together, forming the compression.

Wash basins

It is best to attach the drain, stopper assembly, and faucet to the wash basin before setting it into the vanity. The manufacturers of your units provide directions. There are different methods of attaching the faucet to the sink; 15-9 merely shows one way of doing it.

There are many styles of wash basins, but there are only four basic types of installation:

- Mounted under the countertop (15-10).
- Set into the countertop (15-11).
- Wall-hung, which includes some pedestal-style wash basins (15-12).
- Preformed vanity top and bowl (15-13).

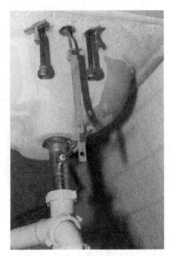

15-9 *Underside of wash basin showing faucet installation.*

15-10 *Undercounter installation.* The Swan Corporation

15-11 *Drop-in installation.* The Swan Corporation

15-12 *Wall-hung installation.* American Standard Inc.

If you are mounting your wash basin under the countertop, make sure you provide sufficient support under the basin (as shown in 15-14). Apply latex caulk both to the top of the sink rim and to the underside of the countertop edges, or use the hardware that comes with the bowl (15-15). When it is completely installed, caulk around the perimeter with latex caulk where the counter meets the wash basin. The caulk serves a dual purpose: it helps to hold the wash basin in place and it prevents water from getting under the countertop.

Two types of wash basins can be set into the countertop: self-rimmers and wash basins with hold-down clips (15-16). These basins also come with or without a chrome rim that provides a neat transition between the countertop and the wash basin.

Using the template supplied with the wash basin, make the cutout in the countertop. First trace the template, then drill a hole larger than a jigsaw blade just inside your traced line. Finally, use a jigsaw to cut the hole, but before you cut, mask the bottom side of the shoe of the jigsaw to protect the

The Swan Corporation

15-13 *Preformed vanity top and bowl.*

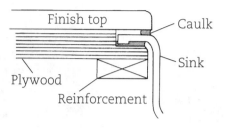

Finish top — Caulk

Plywood — Sink

Reinforcement

15-14 *Support for undercounter basin installation.*

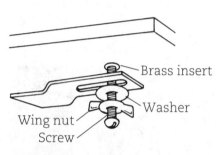

Brass insert

Washer

Wing nut

Screw

15-15 *Undermount bowl clip system.* The Swan Corporation

15-16 *Hold-down clip is on left.*

laminate countertop. Use a blade that's not too coarse and take your time to cut carefully. If you don't have an extra pair of hands when making the cutout, then cut the section out in two pieces to prevent damage to the finished laminate top. For wash basins with hold-down clips, use plumber's putty between the basin and the counter. Apply caulk for a self-rimming basin—it might even be supplied by the manufacturer. Once the wash basin has been installed, run a bead of latex caulk around the perimeter where it meets the countertop. Once the caulk has been applied, trace over it with your index finger, following the perimeter where the basin meets the countertop and wiping your finger on a white rag (15-17). Follow that with a clean wet white rag or a small wet sponge.

15-17
A finished drop-in sink installation with caulk.

Wall-hung wash basins require the mounting of a wall bracket about 33" off the finish floor or at a height that is comfortable for you. Make sure this bracket is level (15-18A). Use lag screws and center the bracket over the drainpipe. Mount the wash basin on the bracket (15-18B) and apply latex caulk to the place where the sink meets the wall. If you wish, you can install tile on the wall for a back splash (chapter 13).

15-18A *Use lag screws and center the bracket.*

15-18B
Tile back splash nicely finishes wall-hung installation.

A popular item in many bathrooms today is a countertop with a wash basin molded right in to create a single unit. Some of them come with a molded back splash and some have a separate back splash, which gives you the option either to use it or to install tile. Trial fit the unit first. If it doesn't fit properly on the cabinet, you might have to sand out any imperfections on the backside.

250   Bathroom Remodeling

Once you are satisfied with the fit, apply clear silicone caulk to the cabinet frame and corner braces. Apply enough caulk around the perimeter of the cabinet and an ample amount on the corner blocks to ensure a secure bond to the cabinet. Place the counter and basin unit down over the cabinet, and check the overhangs on each side of the cabinet to make sure they are even *before* you firmly press the unit down into the caulk (15-19). Again using a latex product, caulk the area where the unit meets the wall.

15-19
Firmly press basin onto cabinet; keep adjustments to a bare minimum.

Don't be alarmed if you discover when hooking the P-trap up to the tailpiece of the wash basin assembly that the tailpiece is 1¼" in diameter. You can use a P-trap that is either 1¼" or 1½". If you use a 1¼" P-trap, use a reducing slip-joint washer at the trap connection at the wall. If you use a 1½" P-trap, the reducing washer will be at the tailpiece of the wash basin. Finally, hook up the drain and connect the shutoff valves to the faucet (15-20 and 15-21).

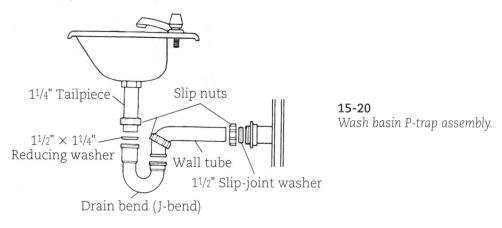

1¼" Tailpiece   Slip nuts

1½" × 1¼"
Reducing washer   Wall tube

1½" Slip-joint washer

Drain bend (J-bend)

15-20
Wash basin P-trap assembly.

Electrical & plumbing fixtures & trims   251

15-21
Wash basin supply installation.

Toilet You are now at the stage where you are ready to install the toilet flange. Before you set the flange in place you might have to enlarge the hole around the soil pipe to accept the flange (15-22). Use a reciprocating saw (see chapter 4, 4-1) and cut only enough for the flange to slide over the soil pipe and rest on the finish floor. If you cut out too much, the screws that hold the flange to the floor will have nothing to bite into, so trial fit the flange carefully.

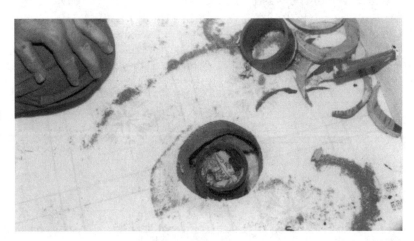

15-22
Cutout for toilet flange.

Now cut the soil pipe an ample ¾" below the finish floor using an inside pipe cutter or an abrasive cutting disc for a below-the-floor cut. Place the saw blade on the inside of the pipe and make the cut from inside to outside. Before installing the flange, make sure the holes for the closet bolts are parallel to the wall (15-23) so the toilet tank will sit parallel to the wall. Mark and remove the flange. If ABS pipe is being used, spread ABS solvent cement on the inside of the flange and around the outside of the pipe and install. Whatever type of solvent cement you use—ABS or PVC—make sure it is approved for use in your area. Twist the flange slightly and press it to the floor over the soil pipe (to the area as previously marked) all in one motion; once it is in place, don't play with it. Then screw the flange to the floor and install the closet bolts into the flange. You might want to pack some putty around the bolts in order to keep them in place. Now you can install the wax bowl ring. Take the time to make sure the ring is seated properly and the wax is sealed to the flange. If necessary, use your hands to work and press the wax to the flange. Even though manufacturers recommend placing the wax bowl ring on the toilet, I find it easier to fit the ring to the toilet flange and then put the toilet down on top of it.

15-23
Pull all the screws into toilet flange; you don't want any vacant screw holes.

Before installing the toilet, decide whether or not you want to attach the tank to the bowl first. Remember that the toilet does get heavy with the tank attached.

When you are ready to install the toilet, you might want to turn the bowl on its side to check the location of the opening that will fit into the wax ring. Then straddle the bowl with your knees, place both of your hands back of the bowl where the toilet seat attaches, pick up the toilet, and place it over the closet bolts and wax bowl ring. Once in place, twist it slightly and press down so the toilet is sitting on the floor parallel to the wall (15-24A). Apply constant pressure to the toilet until it compresses the wax bowl ring and the toilet is firmly seated on the floor.

15-24A
Placing the toilet.

Once you feel comfortable with the placement of the toilet, install the washer and nut to the closet bolt and tighten. *Do not overtighten.* Overtightening the closet bolts can crack your toilet. Then carefully cut the excess bolts off with a mini hacksaw (15-24B) and install the finish caps that were provided with the toilet (15-24C). Vacuum up the metal filings promptly. Now you can hook up the toilet valve (15-25).

15-24B *Work carefully so you don't scratch toilet.*

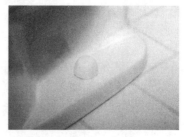

15-24C *Toilet bowl caps neatly conceal closet bolts.*

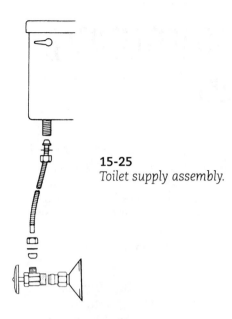

15-25
Toilet supply assembly.

If you have a laundry room in the bathroom and you've installed a new washing machine outlet box, break out the factory plug to the drain—but do not use a hammer. Instead, insert a long heavy-duty screwdriver into the factory seam and pry off the plug. Then install the trim piece.

You are at the stage now where your bathroom is almost complete, but there are still a few more items to be installed. Chapter 16 will detail those final items that will bring you to the end of your bathroom remodeling project!

Laundry room

CHAPTER 16

Caulking, trimming, & touch-up

THE FINAL STAGE! In this chapter, you'll learn professional tips on installing door handles and stops, towel and grab bars, caulk, trims, and miscellaneous items. This chapter is very important because these touches can make or break the final appearance of your bathroom. Special care has to be taken in *detailing*, which is essential for achieving the highest quality bathroom. With that in mind, let's start by installing the door handles.

Door hardware

16-1A *Prebored holes for a door handle and latch bolt.*

16-1B *Prerouted and prebored hole for a strike.*

If you installed a prehung door, you can see that the door was prebored for the handle and the jamb was mortised for the strike (16-1A and B). When you purchase a door, check the edge of the bore side (stile) to see how the door was prepped for a latch bolt. Some manufacturers will bore a hole for a "drive-in" latch, or they will mortise an area for a latch plate. Knowing this could make a difference when it's time to purchase the handle. Latch bolts come in either style, and some contain an optional plate that can convert a drive-in latch to a latch plate, so it is a good idea to check the lockset before purchasing.

To bore for a handle in a door blank installed in an existing frame, close the door and lightly mark the door's face even with the center of the strike plate, usually 44" down from the top. Transfer the mark to the center of the stile, then mark the face of the door at 2⅜" or 2¾" in from the edge (stile), depending upon the backset of your latch bold (16-2).

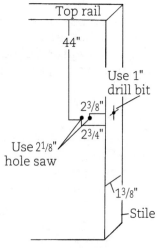

16-2 *Proper location for the door handle and latch bolt.*

When drilling for the latch bolt, use a 1" Forstner-style wood bit. For the handle, drill a 2⅛" hole using a hole saw. When using the hole saw, drill through on one side until the pilot bit appears on the other side of the door. Stop there and drill from the other side where the hole appeared from the pilot bit. This procedure prevents the door skin from splintering.

If you have to mortise for the latch plate, turn the latch bolt around backwards and insert it into the 1" hole. This will bring the latch plate flat against the stile. Trace around the latch plate, but first make certain you have an equal distance from the edge of the latch plate to the edge of the door on both sides. Use a chisel about ¾" wide. Be careful when using the chisel because you'll be mortising an area 1" or 1⅛" by 2¼" in either a 1⅜" or 1¾" door and there really isn't room for a mistake. Don't forget to mark, drill, and mortise for the strike on the corresponding jamb. When you purchase a new handle, it will come with a set of instructions and a template that you can use when marking for the handle, backset for the latch bolt, and strike.

There are a few points you might want to consider when installing a lockset. Always predrill the holes for the strike and latch bolt to prevent the jamb and stile from splitting. Figure 16-3 shows how the pieces of the lockset go together. Install the latch so the curve on the latch bolt faces the direction the door closes. Then press in the latch bolt and push the spindles and stems of the interior assembly through the latch. Finally, install the exterior assembly and screws.

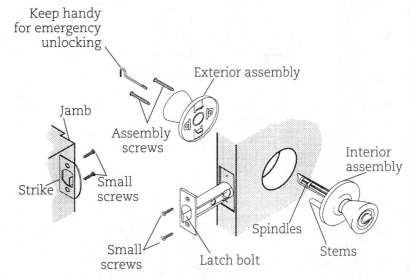

16-3 *Lockset assembly.* Kwikset Corporation

Tighten the two screws to the point that you can still move the handle. Grab both knobs and gently slide the unit up and down until you find the center point of the 2 ⅛" hole. Once you are satisfied, tighten—but don't overtighten—the screws. Now install the strike and do a trial run. If the door will not latch, reinstall the strike closer to the door. If the door is loose after it is closed, then you might need to bend the tongue on the strike toward the doorstop. At this point, your door should operate properly!

Doorstop

You will want to install a doorstop to protect the wall from damage by the door handle when the door opens. Before installing the doorstop, I recommend using a self-drilling, one-piece anchor first if there is no backer (16-4). In fact, this type of anchor can come in handy as you install other items mentioned throughout this chapter. An anchor is specifically designed for use in wallboard when you are not able to mount into a stud; one was used when installing the doorstop shown in 16-5.

 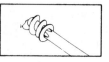  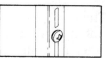

1. Place #2 Phillips screwdriver or cordless screwdriver into recess of E-Z Ancor.

2. Press into drywall, while turning the anchor clockwise until it is seated flush with the wall.

1. Place fixture in position over in-stalled E-Z Ancor. Insert screw with screwdriver.

2. Tighten fixture in place. Do not overtighten.

*Not recommended for ceiling applications.

16-4 *E-Z Ancor.* ITW Buildex

16-5
E-Z Ancor was inserted for secure installation of doorstop assembly.

When installing towel bars and other related fixtures, it is a good idea to use a level. Hold the fixture up against the wall and place a level on it. Once you are satisfied with the fixture's placement, use an awl to mark the wall. Push the awl through the screw hole and on into the wallboard. If you don't hit a stud, then use anchors for a solid installation. Figure 16-6 shows the sequence to follow when installing a toothbrush holder: the holder is leveled, then the location for the plastic anchors is marked. If you are mounting a mirror, follow the manufacturer's recommended installation instructions.

Accessories

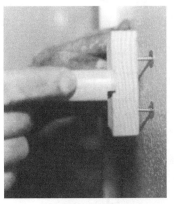

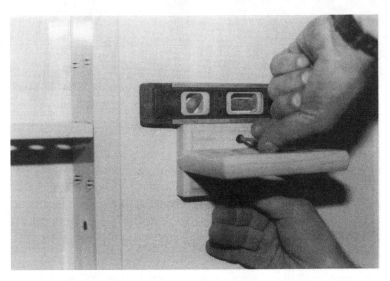

Use the same procedure to install a towel bar, soap dish, and tissue holder. As corny as this sounds, the best way to install a tissue holder is to sit on the toilet seat and position the holder so it feels comfortable. When you are satisfied that you have found the correct location, mark the wall and install it. Also, make sure you do not install towel bars over wall heaters or electrical outlets.

16-6 *Level toothbrush holder, insert plastic anchors, and glue on finish screw hole plug.*

During the framing stage, do you remember installing backers—blocks to facilitate the installation of grab bars? Follow the manufacturer's recommendations when installing these items and use a masonry drill bit if you are working with tile. Also, for grab bars in a shower area, caulk might be required around the screws that hold the bars in place; again, follow the manufacturer's specifications. Figures 16-7A and B show only two of a multitude of possible grab bar applications.

Grab bars

16-7A *Grab bar and folding seat.* Häfele America Co.

16-7B *Another grab bar application.* Häfele America Co.

Caulking

This stage of the job is critical. Caulk serves two purposes: it seals areas from moisture and it provides an aesthetically pleasing finish around fixtures. The caulk you choose could make or break the final appearance of your bathroom. Some caulks come in colors and you might want to check them out. Colored caulks can blend a corner together, as well as joining a self-rimming sink to the countertop.

Caulks come two ways: a type you can use by hand (tube), and a cartridge which has to be inserted into a caulking gun. They also come in three basic formulas: latex, acrylic latex with silicone, and 100 percent silicone. I recommend that silicone (rubber) caulk be used with a gun and latex caulk be applied by hand. There are some places where a specific caulk is required. It is important that 100 percent silicone not be used on any surface that might need paint later, because it does not accept paint well.

Silicone (rubber) is best used in wet areas—where tiles come together in corners and around the shower door frame and track. Clear silicone works well inside the shower track where it meets the frame at the wall. This spot is also a critical area for leaks, so take your time in this area and seal it well. Silicone (rubber) also works well where tile meets the countertop (16-8) and where the floor meets the tub, shower, and toilet.

16-8
Caulk gives your countertop a finished look and blends it into the back splash.

The plumbing code requires the joint between any fixture, e.g., a toilet, and the wall or floor be made watertight. The easiest way to do this is to apply caulk. With silicone (rubber) you have to work fast—you cannot play with it. I recommend doing the two side walls of the shower or tub surround first, and then the back wall the next day so you get neat, clean intersections in the corners. When you cut the nozzle on the caulk tube, cut it as small as you can. The smaller the bead of caulk you can apply, the easier it will be to work with. Apply the caulk in one direction. Wipe off the excess using your index finger, and wipe your finger on a white rag or paper towel as you go along.

If you prefer, you can use a caulk finisher instead of your finger. It scoops away excess caulk and leaves a professionally finished joint (16-9A and B). The caulk finisher works well on smooth surfaces. It works with all types of caulk and silicone sealers, and can be trimmed to a specific bead size for a variety of caulking jobs, inside or out.

Working with latex or latex-with-silicone caulk is easy. Just apply a bead of caulk from the tube; then wipe the excess with your finger, and wipe the area clean with a wet sponge (16-10). The trick is to make sure your sponge is clean after each wipe. This helps to eliminate a film on fixtures or surfaces after

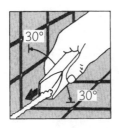

1. Apply caulk.

2. Hold tool up and away from surfaces and push forward.

3. Can be trimmed for a larger bead.

16-9B *Caulk finisher in use.*

16-9A *How to use caulk finisher.* Homax Corporation

16-10
Using latex or latex-with-silicone caulk products.

wiping, especially on chrome plumbing fixtures and trims. As I mentioned before, silicone works well on the floor where it meets the tub or shower, but you are limited in colors. You might want to use a colored acrylic latex caulk with silicone as shown in 16-11.

Remember when working with any caulking product, apply as little as possible to an area you can handle comfortably, work quickly, and don't play with it. Once you are satisfied with the results—and this is going to be hard—I recommend you not use any items (such as the shower) where caulk has been applied or where water is going to be for at least 72 hours.

16-11 *Color-coordinated caulk products can make that final seal look invisible.*
Kampel Enterprises, Inc.

Take this time now to check to be sure that everything in your new bathroom works correctly: heat, light, and faucets. Check all water connections, fixtures, and tub/shower doors for leaks; and look for places where touch-ups might be required, especially around areas where there is tile and where grout was applied. You might have to bring out your paintbrush again, although sometimes just a cotton swab will work.

I hope your remodeling project turned out as well as the dream bathroom pictured in 16-12. Take a moment to pat yourself on the back for a job well done. Enjoy your new bathroom!

16-12
A finished bathroom.
Florida Tile Industries, Inc.

Contributing organizations & companies

Bathroom Remodeling would not have been possible without the information, photos, and drawings provided by the organizations and companies listed here. I am grateful for their cooperation and assistance.

Accessories

Clairson International
Corporation
720 S.W. 17th Street
Ocala, FL 32674

IronAWay, Inc.
220 W. Jackson
Morton, IL 61550

Associations

American Plywood
Association
7011 South 19th Street
Tacoma, WA 98411

Eastern Paralyzed Veterans
Association
75-20 Astoria Boulevard
Jackson Heights, NY 11370-
1177

Gypsum Association
810 First Street, N.E.
Suite 510
Washington, DC 20002

Resilient Floor Covering
Institute
966 Hungerford Drive,
Suite 12-B
Rockville, MD 20850

Tile Council of America, Inc.
P.O. Box 326
Princeton, NJ 08542-0326

KraftMaid Cabinetry, Inc.
1422 Euclid Avenue, Suite 239
Cleveland, OH 44115

Cabinets

Kampel Enterprises, Inc.
8930 Carlisle Road
Wellsville, PA 17365

Caulk

Alvin & Co., Inc.
P.O. Box 188
Windsor, CT 06095

Drafting

Leviton Manufacturing Co.,
Inc.
59-25 Little Neck Parkway
Little Neck, NY 11362-2591

RACO INC
P.O. Box 4002
South Bend, IL 46634

Electrical

BROAN MFG. CO., INC.
P.O. Box 140
Hartford, WI 53027

FANTECH, INC.
1712 Northgate Boulevard,
Suite B
Sarasota, FL 34234

Fans

Armstrong World Industries, Inc.
P.O. Box 3001
Lancaster, PA 17604

Floor covering

Häfele America Co.
3901 Cheyenne Drive
Archdale, NC 27263-4000

Kwikset Corporation
516 E. Santa Ana
Anaheim, CA 92803

Hardware

ITW Brand Merchandising
226 Gerry Drive
Wood Dale, IL 60191

ENERJEE LTD.
32 S. Lafayette Avenue
Morrisville, PA 19067

Gyp-Crete Corporation
920 Hamel Road
Hamel, MN 55340

Heating

Plumbing

American Standard Inc.
P.O. Box 6820
Piscataway, NJ 08855-6820

BathEase, Inc.
2537 Frisco Drive
Clearwater, FL 34621

The Broadway Collection
1010 W. Santa Fe
Olathe, KS 66061-3116

International Cushioned
Products Inc.
8360 Bridgeport Road #202
Richmond, BC CANADA V6X 3C7

Lyons Industries, Inc.
P.O. Box 88
Dowagiac, MI 49047

NIBCO INC.
500 Simpson Avenue
Elkhart, IN 46515

Oatey Co.
6600 Smith Avenue
Newark, CA 94560

RE-BATH CORPORATION
1055 S. Country Club Drive,
Building 2
Mesa, AZ 85210-4613

Sunrise Specialty Company
5540 Doyle Street
Emeryville, CA 94608

The Swan Corporation
One City Centre
St. Louis, MO 63101

WARMATOWEL/MR. STEAM
43-20 34th Street
Long Island City, NY 11101

Skylights & windows

VELUX-AMERICA INC.
450 Old Brickyard Road
Greenwood, SC 29648

Tile

American Olean Tile Company
1000 Cannon Avenue
Lansdale, PA 19446-0271

Florida Tile Industries, Inc.
P.O. Box 447
Lakeland, FL 33802

Tools

CooperTools
P.O. Box 728
Apex, NC 27502

DeWalt Industrial Tool Co.
P.O. Box 158
626 Hanover Pike
Hampstead, MD 21074

Hart Tools Co.
P.O. Box 862
Fullerton, CA 92632

Hitachi Power Tools U.S.A. Ltd.
3950 Steve Reynolds Boulevard
Norcross, GA 30093

Homax Corporation
P.O. Box 5643
Bellingham, WA 98227

Hyde Tools
54 Eastford Road
Southbridge, MA 01550-1875

Malco Products, Inc.
Highway 55 & County Road 136
Annandale, MN 55302-9135

Milwaukee Electric Tool
Corporation
13135 West Lisbon Road
Brookfield, WI 53005

Robert Bosch Power Tool
Corporation
One Hundred Bosch Boulevard
New Bern, NC 28562-4097

Ryobi America Corp.
P.O. Box 1207
Anderson, SC 29622-1207

Skil Corporation
4300 West Peterson Avenue
Chicago, IL 60646

Stanley Tools
600 Myrtle Street
New Britain, CT 06050

Takagi Tools Inc.
337 A Figueroa Street
Wilmington, CA 90744

United States Gypsum Company
125 South Franklin Street
P.O. Box 806278
Chicago, IL 60606-4678

Wallboard

INDEX

A

ABS pipes(*see* PVC pipes)
accessibility (*see* barrier-free design)
Accessible Building Design, 10
American Plywood Association (APA), 37, 175
Americans with Disabilities Act (*see* barrier-free design)
Americans with Disabilities Act Resource Catalog, 9
analyzing the job, 1-5
  building code requirements, 3
  floor finish, 4
  interior wall finish, 4
  outdated appearance, 2-3
  plumbing removal/replacement, 4
  size considerations, 4
  toilet removal/replacement, 4
  tub removal/replacement, 4
  updating the bathroom, 3
  water damage, 1-2, **2**
  worn appearance, 2-3
asbestos removal/disposal, 47
attic crawl space used to enlarge existing bath, **8**

B

Barrier-Free Design: Selected Federal Laws..., 10
barrier-free designs, 9-15, **10, 11, 12, 13, 14, 15,** 186, **187**
  fixture selection, 79-80, **80, 81**
  sinks, 84, **84**
base molding, 239-242, **239, 240, 241, 242**
  rubber, **239,** 240, **241, 242**
  wooden, 239-240, **239, 240, 241, 242**
boring tool, 35, **35**
building codes, xiii
  Building Official and Code Administrator (BOCA), xiii
  electrical wiring, 128
  Southern Building Code Official (SBC), xiii
  Uniform Building code (UBC), xiii
  updating bathrooms and meeting codes, 3
Building Official and Code Administrator (BOCA), xiii

C

cabinets, 185-193, **185**
  barrier-free designs, 186, **187**
  bracing wall cabinets during installation, 190, **191**
  countertop installation (*see* countertops)
  dimensions, 186
  filler strips, 186, **187**

finish panels for exposed ends, 186
framing, 76
installation, 190-193, **191, 192, 193**
laundry room, 188, **188**
lower cabinet installation, 191-192, **191, 192, 193**
moisture and finishes, 188
organizers for cabinets, **188**
preparing cabinets before installation, 189
preparing walls and floors before installation, 189-190, **190**
secure attachment with screws/nails, 191
tools required, 188-189
wall cabinets, 186
wash basin installation, 248-252, **248, 249, 250, 251, 252**
carpeting, 39, 171
caulking, 110, 260-263, **261, 262, 263**
ceilings
  framing, 65-66, **65, 66**
  lowering high ceilings, 65-66
  skylights, 67-70, **67, 68, 69, 70**
cementitious backer units (cement board), 38, 183, 143-144, **144**
change orders, contracts, 30
contractors, 21-30, 41
  bids, cost vs. quality work, 26
  Change Orders, 30
  choosing a contractor, guidelines, 24-27
  complete remodel from start to finish, **21, 22**
  contents of project, 29
  contracts
    Change Orders, 30
    contents of project, 29
    contractor-provided contract forms, 30
    date of work, 29
    date, name, address, 29
    Extra Work Orders, 30
    general conditions found in most contracts, 27-29
    generic forms, 30
    payment schedule, 29-30
    signature and date, 30
  cost estimating, 41
  cost vs. quality work, 26
  dates of work, 29
  do-it-yourself vs. contractors
    financing, 23
    professionalism, 23
    skill requirements, 23
    time requirements, 23-24
    tool requirements, 23
  electricians, 24

estimates, 43
Extra Work Orders, 30
gypsum wallboard installers, 24
itemizing bid items, 42-43
payment schedule, 29-30
plumbers, 24
references, 26-27
specialty contractors, 41-42
subcontractors, 41
contracts (*see* contractors)
copper water supply pipes, 103-111
  clamps, 104, **106, 107**
  fittings, 104, **105, 106, 107**
  I.D. and O.D. requirements, 103
  inspections, 110
  reducers, 104, **105, 106, 107**
  repairing dented pipes, 109, **109**
  separation of hot and cold lines, 103
  soldering, 104, 107-109, **108, 109**
cost estimating, 40-43
  contractors, 41
    specialty contractors, 41-42
  disposal costs, 40
  estimates, estimate forms, 43
  inspections, 40
  itemizing costs, 42-43
  materials, 40
  permits, 40
  researching costs, 40
  tools, 40
cost vs. quality work, contractors, 26
countertops, 38-39, 194-203, **194, 195, 196, 197, 198, 199, 200, 201, 202, 203**
  edging, hardwood edging, 195, **195,** 196
  height adjustments, 194, **194**
  laminate installation, 196-202, **196, 197, 198, 199, 200, 201, 202**
  level line and cleat placement, 194, **194**
  overhang, 195-196
  particleboard base for countertops, 194, **195**
  sanding base countertops before laminate installation, 196
  tile countertops, 202-203, **203**
  wash basin installation, 248-252, **248, 249, 250, 251, 252**
CPVC pipes (*see* PVC pipes)

D

dates of work for contractors, 29
demolition work, 44-51, **50, 51**
  asbestos materials, 47
  base molding removal, 45
  floors
    asbestos products, 47
    covering material removal, 47-49, **48**
    underlayment, 47-49, **48**

gutting room completely, 49-51, **50**, **51**
nails, 45, **45**
plumbing trim piece removal, 45
safety precautions, 44
shower rod or door removal, 45
studs, removal/addition of studs, 46
tiling tub/shower area, step-by-step ,
  44-46
toilet removal, 47
tub/shower installation, 49
wallboard/gypsum wallboard wall
  removal, 45-46, **46**
window casing removal, 45
design and layout, 16-20
disposal of demolition materials
asbestos, 47
cost estimating, 40
do-it-yourself vs. professionals (*see*
  contractors)
doors, 226-233
alignment of studs, 57, **58**
barrier-free design, 15, **15**
casing (molding) installation, 231-233,
  231, **232**, **233**
cripple studs, 57, **58**
cutting door to size, 230-231
cutting opening for new door, 55, **55**
dimensions of standard doors, 16
doorstop installation, 230, **230**
electrical wiring, new door openings, 58
floor covering beneath door, 226-227, **227**
framing, 53-59, **56**, **57**, **58**
hardware installation, 256-258, **256**, **257**
leveling and plumbing opening for
  door, 227, **227**
nailing door frame into rough opening,
  229-230
plumbing, new door openings, 58
rough opening for door, **226**
shimming door, 228-229, **228**, **229**
shower doors, 222-225, **223**, **224**
stop, doorstop installation, 258, **258**
swing of door, 226
tools, 227
trimmers and plates, 56-57, **56**, **57**
drains (*see* plumbing; PVC pipes)
drills, 32, 33, **33**
bits, 35, **35**
countersinks, 35, **35**
Hole Hawg right-angle drill, 112, **112**
ductwork, 59-62, **59**, **60**, **61**
framing for dryer-vent ductwork, 59-
  62, **59**, **60**, **61**
tools required, 35
Durgo Air Vents, 103
DWV pipes (*see* plumbing; PVC pipes)

E

Eastern Paralyzed Veterans Association,
  9
electrical wiring, 114-140
240- vs. 120-amp circuits, 128
bar light above medicine cabinet, **243**
boxes, 119-120, **119**, **121**, 128
building code requirements for
  updates, 3, 128
circuit breaker box, 124
color codes for wiring, 123
connectors, wire connectors, 120, **120**,
  128-129, **129**
disconnecting circuit before work, 114
exhaust fans, 115-116, **115**, **116**
extension bars for lighting fixtures,
  129, **130**
fixtures, 243-245, **243**
ground fault circuit interruptor (GFCI),
  3,3, 3
ground fault circuit interruptors
  (GFCI), 3, **3**, 124-125, **125**, 128, 132,
  132, 243
grounding, 120, **120**, 131
gypsum wallboard, cutting openings
  for outlets/fixtures, 150-151
heaters, 116-118, **117**, **118**, 245, **245**
hot tubs, 128
inspections before concealment, 77
laundry rooms, 128
light fixture selection, 115-116, **115**, **116**
new circuits, adding circuits to panel
  box, 124
new products, 114-115, **115**
openings for doors and windows, 58
outlets, 125-126
appliance outlets, 131, **131**
"fishing" walls for outlets, 131
switch/outlet combination, 133-135,
  137, **138**, **139**, **140**
wall plates, 245, **245**
panel box, 124
placement of outlets/switches, 128
quick connections, 243, **244**, 245
recessed lighting, 243, **244**
Romex wire, 123
safety guidelines, 114
side wiring, 243, **244**
stapling wires to framing, 128, **129**
studs, drilling studs to accept wiring,
  129
switches, 126-127, **126**, **127**
dimmer switches, 127
fan speed control switches, 127
four-way, 127, 133, **137**
illuminated rocker, 126, **126**
outlet/switch combination, 133-135,
  137, **138**, **139**, **140**
passive infrared occupancy sensor, 127
pilot light rocker, 127
single-pole, 127, 132, **133**, **134**
three-way, 127, 132-133, **135**, **136**
wall plates, 245, 245, 245
symbols used, 118, **119**
testing new installation, 130, **130**
tools required, 36
updating wiring, 3
wall plates, 245, **245**
whirlpool baths, 128
wire nuts, 128-129, **129**
wire size and capacity, 121-122
wire specifications, 123
wiring diagrams, 131-140,
electricians, 24
estimates (*see* cost estimating)
extra work orders, contracts, 30

F

fans, 3, 115-116, **115**, **116**
faucets, 246-247
Federal Register, Title III of ADA, 9
felt paper, 38
fiberglass tub/shower enclosures, 205-
  207, **205**, **207**
financing, 23
fittings, plumbing, tees and Ys, **89**
fixture selection, Victorian, modern,
  etc., 78-81, **78**, **79**, **80**, **81**
floor plans, 6-20
attic crawl space used to enlarge
  existing bath, **8**
barrier-free design, 9-15, **10**, **11**, **12**,
  13, **14**, **15**
before and after view of master bath,
  52, **52**, **53**
design and layout, 16-20
dimensions
doors, toilet, tubs, and vanity, 16, **16**
electrical wiring symbols, 118, **119**
laundry room/bathroom, **17**
master bathroom design, **17**, **18**
recreational bathroom with
  sauna/hot tub, **17**
scale drawings, 19
size of bathroom, increasing usable
  size, 6-9, **7**, **8**
templates, 20, **20**
three-piece layout
small space & standard, **17**
upper-, lower-floor bathrooms, **19**
whirlpool, **18**
floors, 4, 168-184
asbestos floor materials, disposal, 47
cabinet installation preparations,
  189-190, **190**
carpeting, 39, 171
cementitious backer units (cement
  board), 183
cross-section of typical floor
  members, **50**
exposed joists of floor, **50**
framing, 62-65, **62**, **63**, **64**, **65**
hot tubs, weight considerations, 72
increasing strength, 63-64
insulation, 62, **62**
moisture barrier, 62
plumbing, joist drilling to accept
  pipes, 99-100
removal/replacement, 47-49, **48**
resilient flooring, 168-170, **170**
resilient flooring, sheet-goods
  installation, 178-182, **178**, **179**, **180**,
  181, **182**
rim joist, **60**
tile installation, 182-183, **183**, 184

floors (cont.)
 tools required, 36, **36**
 underlayment removal/replacement, 47-49, **48**
 underlayment, 62-65, **62, 63, 64, 65, 62,** 172-177
  felt paper, 38
  over concrete, 173-174
  over existing flooring, 172-173
  plywood as underlayment, 37, 175-177, **176, 177**
 warranties for flooring materials, 171-172
 whirlpool baths, weight considerations, 72
 wood floors, 39, 171
flux, soldering copper pipe, 108, **108**
framing, 52-77
 cabinets, 76
 ceilings, 65-66, **65, 66**
 corners, 71, **71, 72**
 doors, 53-59, **56, 57, 58,** 227, **227**
 dryer-vent ductwork, 59-62, **59, 60, 61**
 floors, rim joist, **60**
 heaters, 76-77
 hot tubs, 72-76, **73, 74, 75, 76**
 inspections of wiring/plumbing before concealment, 77
 master bath, before and after view, 52, **52, 53**
 medicine cabinets, 76
 partition walls, 71, **71, 72**
 skylights, 67-70, **67, 68, 69, 70**
 tub-support framing, 64-65, **64, 65**
 underlayment, 62-65, **62, 63, 64, 65**
 walls, 145-146, **145, 146**
 whirlpool baths, 72-76, **73, 74, 75, 76**
 windows, 53-59, **54, 55**

G
grab bar installation, 259, **259, 260**
ground fault circuit interrupter (GFCI), 3, **3,** 124-125, **125,** 128, 132, **132,** 243
Gypsum Association, 141
Gypsum Construction Handbook, 141
gypsum wallboard, 141-142, **141**
 adhesives, 147-148, **147, 148**
 bathtub installation, typical, **145**
 ceilings, 150
 compound, joint compound application, 155-162, **155, 156, 157, 158, 159, 160, 161**
 corners
  compound, 156-157, **157,** 158, **158**
  corner bead, 152, **152**
 cutting openings for outlets/switches/plumbing fixtures, 150-151
 embedding tape in compound, 156, **156**
 finish coat, 160-162, **161**
 floating vertical corners and ceiling, 150
 installation, 146-162
 nail head coverage, 157, **157**
 nailing schedule, 148-150, **149**

 screw placement, 149
 screws vs. nails, 147, **147**
 smooth wall finish, 162
 stress-relief (*see* floating vertical corners and ceiling)
 taping joints, 153
 textured wall finishes, 162-166, **163, 164, 165, 166**
 tools required, 36, **36** 154-155, **154**
 topping coat, 158-160, **159, 160**
 water-resistant, 142-143
gypsum wallboard installers, 24

H
hairdryer, wall-mounted, 115
hammer drill, 33
hammers, 35, **36**
handicapped (*see* barrier-free designs)
heaters, 116-118, **117, 118**
 building code requirements for updates, 3
 framing, 76-77
 in-floor heating, 116-118, **118**
 updating heating systems, 3
 wall-mounted heater, 116-118, **117,** 116, 245, **245**
Helping Hands Guide to Hiring a Remodeling Contractor, 30
Hole Hawg right-angle drill, 112, **112**
hot tubs, **17,** 72-76, **73, 74, 75, 76**
 electrical wiring, 128
 floor strength considerations, 72
 framing requirements, 72-76, **73, 74, 75, 76**
 sunken installation, 74-75, **74, 75**
How to Install and Maintain Ceramic Tile, 212

I
inspections, xiii-xiv
 building codes: BOCA, SBC, UBC, xiii
 cost estimating, 40
 framing, inspection before concealment, 77
 plumbing, 110
 water supply pipes, 110
insulation, floors, 62, **62**

L
laminate, 196-202, **196, 197, 198, 199, 200, 201, 202**
 tools required, 37
 trimmer tool, 32, **32**
laundry room/bathroom, **17**
 cabinets, 188, **188**
 electrical wiring, 128
 ironing center, 115
lavatories (*see* wash basins)
lighting (*see also* electrical wiring), 115-116, **115, 116**
 building code requirements for updates, 3
 fixtures, 243-245, **243**
 updating lighting, 3
linoleum (*see* resilient flooring)

M
manufacturers and suppliers, 264-267
materials, 37-39
 carpeting, 39
 cementitious backer units (cement board), 38, 143-144, **144,** 183
 cost estimating, 40
 countertop materials, 38-39
 felt paper, 38
 gypsum wallboard, 38, 141-142, 144
  water-resistant, 38, 142-143, 144
 plywood, 37
 seasoning or curing materials before installation, 39
 tile, & wood flooring, 39
medicine cabinets, framing, 76
moisture barrier, floors, 62

N
nails
 gypsum wallboard, 147, **147**
 removing nails, 45, **45**

P
painting, 167
 tools required, 37
payment schedule for contractors, 29-30
permits, cost estimating, 40
physically impaired (*see* barrier-free designs)
pipes (*see* plumbing)
plans (*see* floor plans)
plastic laminate countertops (*see* laminate)
plumbers, 24
plumbing (*see also* tub/shower), **51,** 78-113
 ABS pipes (*see* PVC pipes)
 access panels, 4
 barrier-free design fixtures, 79-80, **80, 81**
 building code requirements for updates, 3
 cast iron pipe, 95-96, **97**
 cleanouts, 96-97, **97**
 CPVC pipes (*see* PVC pipes)
 DWV (drain/waste/vent)
  ABS and PVC pipes (*see* PVC pipes)
  cast iron, 95-96, **97**
  components, 89-91
  fittings, key to NIBCO fittings, **90**
  fittings, tees and Ys, **89**
  PVC pipes, 91-99
 faucets, 246-247
 fixture selection, 78-81, **78, 79, 80, 81,** 246-255
 floors, joist drilling to accept pipes, 99-100
 gutting room, complete plumbing redesign, 49
 gypsum wallboard, cutting openings for fixtures, 150-151, **150, 151, 152**

hole cutting for plumbing, 112-113, **112**, **113**
inspections before concealment, 77, 110
lead-pipe hazards, 3
obstacles to straight-run pipes, 101, **101**
openings for doors and windows, 58
overflow drains, tub/shower, 110, **110**
poor plumbing practices, 100-101, **100**
PVC pipes (*see* PVC pipes)
radon problem areas, 110
reciprocating saw in use, 113, **113**
removal/replacement, 4
right-angle drill in use, 112, **112**
rough-in layout, 81-82, **82**
sealing and caulking, 110
shower heads, 246-247, **246**
shower, self-sealing drain installation, 110-111, **111**
shutoff valves, 247, **247**
slope of horizontal drains, 100-101, **100**
supports, pipe supports, 100
toilets, 99, **99**, 252-255, **252**, **253**, **254**, **255**
  dimensions, 83
tools required, 35, 111-113, **112**, **113**
trim piece removal, 45
updating fixtures, 3
vent pipes, 84-88, **85**, **86**, **87**, **96**, 101-103, **102**, **103**
walls, stud drilling to accept pipes, 99-100
wash basins, 83-84, **84**, 98, **98**, 248-252, **248**, **249**, **250**, **251**, **252**
washing machines, 84, 98-99, **99**
wastepipe layout, 97-98, **98**
water supply (*see* copper water supply pipes)
plywood, 37
  grades of plywood, 175
  underlayment, 175-177, **176**, **177**
professionals (*see* contractors)
PVC pipes, 88-89
  bead of cement, 92
  components, 89-91
  cutting PVC, 91
  excess cement, 92
  fit and position pipe, 92
  fittings, **93**, **94**, **95**
    key to NIBCO fittings, **90**
    tees and Ys, **89**
  installation of DWV piping, 91-99
  primer, 91-92
  smoothing ends, 91
  solvent cement, 92
  test fits, 91

R
radon problem areas, sealing and caulking around plumbing, 110
Re-Bath, 44
references for contractors, 26-27
resilient flooring, 168-170, **170**
  backing, 170
  cut-and-fit installation, 178

cutting sheet flooring, 179-181, **179**, **180**, **181**
  "grout line" pattern alignment, 178, **178**
  inlaid-color floors, 169
  installation, 178-182, **178**, **179**, **180**, **181**, **182**
  mastic application, 181, **181**, **182**
  no-wax floors, 169-170
  pattern making before cutting, 178-179
  printed patterns (rotovinyl), 169
  rolling smooth, 182, **182**
  seam sealing, 169
  sheet vinyl, 168
  tiles, 168
  wear layer or clear coat, 169
roofs
  skylights, 67-70, **67**, **68**, **69**, **70**
  vent pipe exit, 101-103, **102**, **103**
router, 32

S
safety equipment, 31
sanders
  belt sander, 33, **34**
  orbital (finish) sander, 34
  palm sander, 34, **34**
sauna, **17**
saws
  circular saw, 32
  hand saws, 35, **35**
  jigsaws, 32
  miter saw, 31
  reciprocating saws, 32, **32**, 113, **113**
  table saw, 32
scale drawings, 19
screwdrivers, 33
sewers (*see* plumbing; PVC pipes)
sheetrock (*see* gypsum wallboard)
shutoff valves, 247, **247**
sinks (*see* wash basins)
size of bathroom, 4
  increasing usable size, 6-9, **7**, **8**
skill requirements, 23
skylights, 67-70, **67**, **68**, **69**, **70**
soldering copper pipe, 104, 107-109, **108**, **109**
  cleaning pipe, 108, **108**
  flux, 108, **108**
  heating joints, 108, **109**
  supporting pipes during soldering, 108, **108**
  wetting the pipe, 107
Southern Building Code Official (SBC), xiii
squares and levels, 35, **35**
subcontractors (*see* contractors)
subflooring (*see* underlayment)
Swanstone tub/shower enclosures, 204-205
SwanTile tub/shower enclosures, 204, **204**

T
Telephone lines in bathroom, 114
templates for floor plans, 20, **20**
Therma-Floor Easy-Mix flooring, **117**

tile, 39, 182-183, **183**, 184, 208-222
  bullnose tile to finish, 218-219, **218**, **219**
  categories of tile, 209
  caulking, 260-263, **261**, **262**, **263**
  cementitious backer units (cement board), 38, 143-144, **144**, 183
  clean-up, 220-221, **221**
  color, 208-209, 209
  countertops, 202-203, **203**
  cutting tile, **215**, 216-219, **216**, **217**, **218**, **219**
  decorative designs, **208**
  glazed tile, 209
  grout, 210-211, **211**, 219-221, **219-221**
  installation, 182-183, **183**, **184**
  layout, 212-213, **213**
  mastic application, 214
  pregrouted tile, 211
  repairs, 221, **221**
  setting tile, 214-216, **214**, **215**
  shapes, special shapes, 209, **210**
  sizes for tiles, 209, **210**
  tile combined with other materials, 221, **222**
  tools required, 36, **36**, 211-212
  tub/shower area, 44-46
  unglazed tile, 209
Tile Council of America, 184, 209
time requirements, 23-24
toilets, 252-255, **252**, **253**, **254**, **255**
  barrier-free designs, 10, **10**, **11**, 12, **12**
  dimensions of standard toilet, 16, **16**, 83
  installation steps, 252-255, **252**, **253**, **254**, **255**
  plumbing, 99, **99**
  removal/replacement, 4, 47
tools, 23, 31-37
  boring tools, 35, **35**
  cabinets , 188-189
  clean-up tools, 34-35
  cost estimating, 40
  doors installation, 227
  drills, 32,33, **33**, 35, **35**
  electrical work tools, 36
  finish-work tools, 35
  flooring tools, 36, **36**
  gypsum wallboard tools, 36, **36**, 154-155, **154**
  hammer drill, 33
  hammers, 35, **36**
  hand tools, 35-37
  laminate tools, 37
  laminate trimmer, 32, **32**
  nail cutter, 45, **45**
  paint and finish tools, 37
  plumbing tools, 35, 111-113, **112**, **113**
  power tools, 31-34
  rough-work tools, 35
  router, 32
  safety equipment, 31
  sanders
    belt sander, 33, **34**
    orbital (finish), 34

tools (*cont.*)
palm, 34, **34**
saws
circular saw, 32
hand saws, 35, **35**
jigsaw, 32
miter saw, 31
reciprocating saw,32, **32**, 113, **113**
table saw, 32
screwdrivers, 33
squares and levels, 35, **35**
tiling tools, 36, **36**, 211-212
vents/ducts tools, 35
wallpapering tools, 37
tub/shower, 204-225
barrier-free designs, 13, **13**, 14, **14**
dimensions of standard bathtub, 16, 82-83
fiberglass enclosures, 205-207, **205**, **207**
floor strength, 63-64
installation, 49
liner for existing tub, Re-Bath, 44
overflow drains, 110, **110**
removal/replacement, 4
self-sealing shower drain, 110-111, **111**
shower doors, 222-225, **223**, **224**
shower heads, 246-247, **246**
shower rods, 222
Shower Tower installation, 207, **207**
Swanstone enclosures, 204-205
SwanTile enclosures, 204, **204**
tile enclosures, 208-222
bullnose tile to finish, 218-219, **218**, **219**
categories of tile, 209
clean-up, 220-221, **221**
color, 208-209, 209
cutting tile, **215**, 216-219, **216**, **217**, **218**, **219**
decorative design, **208**
glazed vs. unglazed, 209
grout, 211, 210, **211**, 219-221, **219**, **220**, **221**
height of tiled area, 213
layout, 212-213, **213**
mastic application, 214
pregrouted tile, 211
repairs, 221, **221**
setting tile, 214-216, **214**, **215**
shapes, special shapes, 209, **210**
size of tile, 209, **210**
tile combined with other materials, 221, **222**
tools, 211-212
tub support framing, 64-65, **64**, **65**
wall installation, typical, **145**

U
U.S. Department of Justice, ADA *Resource Catalog*, 9

underlayment, 62-65, **62**, **63**, **64**, **65**, 172-177
felt paper, 38
over concrete, 173-174
over existing flooring, 172-173
plywood as underlayment, 37, 175-177, **176**, **177**
Uniform Building Code (UBC), xiii

V
vanity, dimensions of standard vanity, 16
vent pipes, 84-88, **85**, **86**, **87**, **96**, 101-103, **102**, **103**
roof exit, 101-103, **102**, **103**
ventilation (*see also* fans), 3
building code requirements for updates, 3
updating fans and ventilation, 3

W
wallboard (*see* gypsum wallboard)
wallpaper, 166-167
tools required, 37
walls, 141-167
base molding removal, 45
bathtub installation, typical, **145**
cabinet installation preparations, 189-190, **190**
cementitious backer units (cement board), 38, 143-144, **144**
corner framing, 71, **71**, **72**
framing and lath exposed, **51**
framing trouble areas, 145-146, **145**, **146**
gypsum wallboard (drywall), 141-142, 144
adhesives, 147-148, **147**, **148**
ceilings, 150
compound application, 155-162, **155**, **156**, **157**, **158**, **159**, **160**, **161**
corners, compound, 156-157, **157**, 158, **158**
corners, corner bead, 152, **152**
cutting openings for outlets/switches/plumbing, 150-151, **150**
embedding tape in compound, 156, **156**
finish coat, 160-162, **161**
floating vertical corners and ceiling, 150
nail head coverage, 157, **157**
nailing schedule, 148-150, **149**
removal, 45-46, **46**
screw placement, 149
screw vs. nail, 147, **147**
smooth finish walls, 162
taping joints, 153
textured wall finishes, 162-166, **163**, **164**, **165**, **166**
tools required, 154-155, **154**
topping coat, 158-160, **159**, **160**

water-resistant, 38, 142-143, 144
materials, 141
painting, 167
partition wall framing, 71, **71**, **72**
plumbing, stud drilling to accept pipes, 99-100
smooth finish walls, 162
studs
addition of studs for tub/shower area, 46
drilling studs to accept wiring, 129
textured wall finishes, 162-166, **163**, **164**, **165**, **166**
trouble areas, 145-146, **145**, **146**
wallpapering, 166-167
warranties for flooring materials, 171-172
wash basins, 248-252, **248**, **249**, **250**, **251**, **252**
dimensions of standard wash basin, 16, 83-84, **84**, 186
plumbing, 98, **98**
washing machines, plumbing, 84, 98-99, **99**
water damage, 1-2, **2**
water supply (*see* copper water supply pipes)
wheelchair accessibility (*see* barrier-free design)
whirlpool baths, **18**, 72-76, **73**, **74**, **75**, **76**
electrical wiring, 128
floor strength considerations, 72
framing requirements, 72-76, **73**, **74**, **75**, **76**
sunken installation, 74-75, **74**, **75**
windows, 233-240
apron, 238
caulking areas, 235-236, **235**
dimensions of window, 234-235
ear extensions, 238
exterior framing, finishing, 58-59
fiberglass tub/shower enclosures, 206-207, **207**
frame extension units, 238, **238**
framing, 53-59, **54**, **55**
leveling and plumbing rough opening, 237-238
metal windows, 54, **54**, 233-234, **233**, **234**
perimeter measurement, 235
removal, framing-in, 55, **55**
shimming, 233
sill, 238
skylights, 67-70, **67**, **68**, **69**, **70**
stool, 238
trimming exterior, 233-234, **233**, **234**
trimming interior, 238, **238**, **239**
wood caing for windows, **236**, 237, **237**
wood flooring, 39, 171
worn appearance, 2-3

TO ORDER FORMS:

Special offer

	Product	Price (Ea.)	Quantity	Amount
Extra Work and/or Change Order Sheets	1EWCO	1.75	_____	_____
Contract/Agreement Sheets	2CA	1.75	_____	_____
Itemized Bid Sheets (3-Page Set)	3IBS	3.50	_____	_____
Itemized Bid Sheets (4-Page Set)	4IBS	4.75	_____	_____
Complete Contractors Helping Hands™ Packet	5CHHP	10.00	_____	_____
Shipping & Handling (Orders Up to 6)				3.50
		SUBTOTAL		_____

TO ORDER BOOK:

	Product	Price (Ea.)	Quantity	Amount
The Helping Hands™ Guide To Hiring A Remodeling Contractor	HHG	14.00	_____	_____
Shipping & Handling (Orders Up to 2)				2.25
		SUBTOTAL		_____
		WA (Only) 8% Tax		_____
		TOTAL		_____

Make Check or Money Order Payable To: C.R.S., Inc.
P.O. Box 4567
Spokane, WA 99202-0567
Phone: (509) 926-1724

Name _____

Address _____

City _____ State _____ Zip _____

Phone _____

C.R.S., Inc.

About the author

Leon A. Frechette has more than 20 years' experience in construction, remodeling, and related fields. He has appeared on many TV and radio talk shows, fielding a wide range of questions from the public; provided expert testimony in court cases; filmed demonstration and training videotapes; and designed and patented a toy collection. He demonstrates tool usage and techniques at trade shows around the country.

Leon authored and published *The Helping Hands™ Guide to Hiring A Remodeling Contractor*, which featured his simplified business forms. He's the author of *The Pre-Development Handbook* for the City of Spokane and the Spokane Housing Authority, a user-friendly guide for builders and developers to the many agencies overseeing construction and rehabilitation within the city. Other book projects are currently in development.

nd testing
has tested
uction-
or in-
ade
nonthly in
ors.